TWO DIARIES OF
THE LONG PARLIAMENT

TWO DIARIES OF
THE LONG PARLIAMENT

Maija Jansson

Yale Center for Parliamentary History

ALAN SUTTON · Gloucester

ST. MARTIN'S PRESS · New York
1984

First published in Great Britain in 1984
Alan Sutton Publishing Limited
Brunswick Road
Gloucester

British Library Cataloguing in Publication Data

Two diaries of the Long Parliament.
  1.   England and Wales. *Parliament. House of Commons*—History—Sources
  2.   Great Britain— Politics and government—1642–1649—Sources
  I.   Jansson, Maija   328.42′072   JN673

ISBN 0-86299-082-3

First published in the United States of America in 1984
St. Martin's Press, Inc.
175 Fifth Avenue
New York, NY 10010

Library of Congress Cataloging Publication Data

Jansson, Maija.
  Two diaries of the Long Parliament.

  Bibliography: p.
  Includes index.
  1.   Great Britain. Parliament—History—17th century—Sources.
  2.   Great Britain—Politics and government—1625–1649—Sources.
  I.   Title.
  JN534 1641   328.41′09   84–15132

ISBN 0-312-82681-8

Typesetting and origination by
Alan Sutton Publishing Limited.
Photoset 10/11.5 Goudy
Printed in Great Britain

CONTENTS

To
M.C.J. and O.E.J.

ACKNOWLEDGEMENTS

I am grateful to the Library of University College London for permission to print William Drake's Notebook, and to the Beinecke Rare Book and Manuscript Library, Yale University, for permission to print the Anonymous Diary.

I can never adequately thank J.H. Hexter for teaching me how to do parliamentary history.

Helen Barber Gray and Glenn Gray's bequest of their papers and research materials to the Yale Center for Parliamentary History arrived after most of my work was finished but in time to check my notes against their transcripts, which certainly facilitated my labours.

Mary Frear Keeler kindly read my rough notes and transcripts and offered a number of helpful ideas for the editing of these manuscripts. Vernon Snow also made positive comments and William Bidwell provided encouragement, particularly with regard to the Anonymous Diary. I am especially indebted to Kathleen Sommers who assisted me with a final check of speeches and page numbers and made a number of perceptive suggestions regarding the annotation. My daughter, Lisa, was an invaluable help in reading proof. Carolyn Nelson shared with me her references to Diurnal Occurrences and James P. Reilly, Jr., as he has done before, again helped with the Latin. I would like to thank David S. Berkowitz for his inspiring comments, and to include a particular note of gratitude to Elizabeth Foster and Conrad Russell for carefully reading and commenting on the finished manuscript. Conrad made detailed notes of helpful suggestions and additions for which I am most grateful, but the errors and omissions in the book remain my own.

Maija Jansson

INTRODUCTORY NOTES

The proceedings during the first year of what later came to be known as the Long Parliament were critical to the establishment of the claim of supremacy on which parliament would justify its actions through the decade leading to the trial and execution of Charles I. Following the premature dissolution of the Short Parliament by the King the previous May, the members of the Long Parliament met together at Westminster on 3 November 1640 determined to deal immediately and effectively with what they conceived to be the growing grievances of the kingdom.

Many of these grievances were tied to individuals near the King. By the middle of 1641 the House of Commons had charged nine servants of the Crown on counts close to treason. Within the first seven months of the parliament Sir John Finch was accused of having subverted the laws of England while holding the offices of Lord Chief Justice of the Common Pleas and Lord Keeper of the Great Seal; Thomas Wentworth, Earl of Strafford, was impeached, tried, and beheaded by act of attainder for his counsels to Charles and his actions in Ireland; William Laud, Archbishop of Canterbury, was impeached and imprisoned in the Tower for his Erastian views delineated in the New Canons, and the six judges who had entertained extrajudicial opinions in the Ship Money Case of 1637 were explicitly charged by the House of Commons with having engaged in treasonous activities.

Besides proceedings against individuals who personified political, religious, and economic grievances the members of the Long Parliament were caught up at the outset in ecclesiastical polemics concerning the structure and function of the church. The momentous question of episcopacy in England, which was inextricably bound to the matter of England's relationship with Scotland, was debated at length in the session of 8 February 1641 in connection with sending to committee the London petition calling for the abolition of episcopacy. It was this debate which Samuel R. Gardiner believed marked the beginning of political parties in England.[1] Gardiner saw here for the first time in the history of English

ix

parliaments the formation of two groups within the House of Commons firmly opposing one another on the same issue, the question of whether to abolish episcopacy "root and branch" or simply to restrain the function of the bishops.

The various accounts of the proceedings during this critical year have not yet been fully gathered together and edited. Materials containing records of the activities of the Long Parliament in 1641 include the official printed Journals of both Houses, the unofficial manuscript journal accounts of business in the Lower House recorded by two of its members, Sir Simonds D'Ewes and John Moore; private diaries of other members; and also the manuscript and printed Diurnal Occurrences. There are more unofficial journals and diaries for the first five years of the Long Parliament than for the last five, and more for 1641 than for any of the subsequent years.

Parts of the journals of D'Ewes and Moore, the longest and most complete accounts of the proceedings in the Lower House in the early years of the parliament, have been printed.[2] Wallace Notestein edited the D'Ewes journal for 3 November 1640 through 20 March 1641 supplemented with annotation from Moore and several private diarists. Following the same format employed by Notestein, using D'Ewes as the base text annotated with entries from other diaries, Willson Coates edited the D'Ewes journal from 12 October 1641 through 10 January 1642.[3] The journals of D'Ewes and Moore covering the period between the end of the Notestein volume and the beginning of the Coates volume (22 March to 12 October 1641) have not yet been printed. The two diaries in the present volume provide some elucidation of the proceedings in parliament during part of that period. They are valuable as personal accounts of the business of the Long Parliament from January through June 1641. William Drake's notes include many of the debates that occurred both in select committees and in grand committees and consequently were not recorded in the *Journals of the House of Commons*. Drake also includes notes from the conferences between the Upper and Lower House and records the Strafford trial which was managed by the Commons and presided over by the Lords. The Anonymous diary contains more of the routine business of the Lower House than does Drake, including notices of readings of bills and petitions. These two diaries neatly complement each other, the anonymous diarist narrating business proceedings in the House and William Drake primarily recording activities in committee. (For a complete description of these diaries, see below.)

Besides the two printed in this volume there are six other diaries extant which contain proceedings in the House of Commons during the first six or eight months of 1641, and one that contains an account of business in the House of Lords for the same period: Framlingham Gawdy (Add. MS. 14, 828, British Library), recorded proceedings from 22 February–2 July 1641;[4] Sir John Holland (MS. Rawl. D. 1099, Bodleian Library), from 22 May through 8 August 1641; Sir Thomas Peyton (Minnesota University Library), from 3 November 1640–19 March 1642; an anonymous diarist (Harl. MS. 1601, British Library), from 1 March–10 April 1641; a second anonymous diarist, possibly William Strode (Harl. 5047, British Library), from 17 May–9 September 1641; and Geoffry Palmer (MS. KK. vi 38, Cambridge University Library) covered the first four days of January 1641. The diary of John Warner, Bishop of Rochester (Harl. MS. 6424, British Library), is an excellent source for proceedings in the Upper House, 13 January 1641 through 4 January 1642.

In editing the Drake notes and the Anonymous Diary I have quoted frequently and extensively in the footnotes from hitherto unprinted materials in the unofficial journals of D'Ewes and Moore as well as from the diaries of Peyton, Harl. 1601, and Warner. Although this policy increases the quantity of annotation at the same time it introduces and makes available to the reader as much manuscript material as possible.

Aside from the journals and diaries which record parliamentary proceedings during 1641 there are also many printed separate speeches as well as numerous Diurnal Occurrences (November 1640–June 1641), printed and unprinted, which record the activities of parliament.[5] However-er, the diurnals, daily reports compiled after the fact, as a whole tend to be briefer and often somewhat less accurate accounts than the diaries and journals, although they were apparently devised for wider circulation.

NOTES

1. Gardiner, *Hist. of Eng.*, IX, 281. On the matter of episcopacy see also Anthony Fletcher, "Concern for Renewal in the Root and Branch Debates of 1641", *Studies in Church History*, XIV, 279–286.

2. The parliamentary journal of Sir Simonds D'Ewes covers proceedings in the House of Commons from 1640 to 1645; John Moore's journal covers from 1640 through Feb. 1642 but is not continuous for the whole period. For complete bibliographic information concerning the journals, see Robert C. Johnson, "Parliamentary Diaries of the Early Stuart Period", *Bulletin of the Inst. of Historical Research*, XLIV (Nov. 1971), 293–300.

3. *The Journal of Sir Simonds D'Ewes from the beginning of the Long Parliament to the opening of the trial of the Earl of Strafford*, ed. by Wallace Notestein, New Haven, 1923. *The Journal of Sir Simonds D'Ewes from the first recess of the Long Parliament to the withdrawal of King Charles from London*, ed. by W.H. Coates, New Haven, 1942.

4. Where the diaries are comprised of several parts separately numbered I have included here references only to those parts that contain entries for 1641. For complete bibliographic information see Robert C. Johnson's article described above, n. 2. Notestein incorporated the notes of Gawdy, Holland, Peyton, Harl. 1601, and Palmer into his annotation.

5. A list of some of the less familiar manuscript diurnals which cover or partially cover the period from Jan. through June 1641:

> Beinecke Rare Book and Manuscript Library, Yale University: Osborn Collection, Tracts I, 2, no. 45h.
>
> British Library: Add. MSS. 6521; 33,468; 34,485; 36,828; 36,829; Sloan MSS. 1430, 1467; Stowe MSS. 361; Harl. 5074.
>
> Cambridge University Library: Add. MS. 89, 90.
>
> Houghton Library, Harvard University: MSS. Eng. 983, 984 and 1024.
>
> Inner Temple Library: Petyt MS. 538/20.
>
> Lincoln Cathedral Chapter Library: MS. 268.
>
> National Library of Scotland: MS. 2687–8; Phillipps MS. 2393, II.
>
> Public Record Office, London: S.P. 16:485/29; 16:485/66; Powis Collection 30/53.
>
> n the Historical Manuscripts Commission *Reports* Diurnals are listed as part of the)llowing collections: Hatton, Stanford, Harvey Cowper, Prescott, Stonyhurst, Chol-.nondelay, Molyneux, and Mainwaring.

> Printed diurnals will be listed in the forthcoming volume, *British Periodicals, 1641–1700: A Short-Title Catalogue*, edited by Carolyn Nelson and Matthew Seccombe. See *The Library Association Rare Books Groups Newsletter*, no. 21, May 1983, pp. 7–10.

> I should like to express my thanks to Carolyn Nelson for her help in the compilation of this list of Diurnals.

DESCRIPTION OF THE DIARIES

William Drake's parliamentary notebook (Ogden MS. 7, no. 51, University College London) is a small parchment-bound book (6" × 4") containing folios 1–95 written in ink by Drake himself. The positive identification of the notebook is possible through Drake's inclusion of his own name in his entry of the Protestation taken by members of the House of Commons on 3 May (see below, Ogden MS. 7, no. 51, 3 May and n. 184).[1]

The parliamentary notebook is number fifty-one in a series of fifty-four manuscript commonplace books that comprise what is inaccurately titled the "Bacon-Tottel" collection.[2] The name derives from the discovery of the books in the Tottel family home, when it was assumed that they were connected with William Tottel, Clerk of Chancery, who was believed to have been Sir Francis Bacon's Steward. That theory has now been disproved. In the early 1940s the books were found by Mr. Alan Keen at Shardeloes, near Amersham, Buckinghamshire, the home inherited by William Drake from his grandfather, William Tottel, in 1626. Between 1943 and 1945 Mr. Keen sold the commonplace books, then advertised as Bacon-Tottel manuscripts, to C.K. Ogden who later bequeathed them to University College London. It was not until the 1970s that the collection as a whole was reexamined with an eye to documenting Mr. Keen's contention that the books were compiled by Tottel at Bacon's direction. After a thorough study and comparison of the commonplace books with each other and with similar books known to have been written by Bacon, Dr. Stuart Clark established with certainty that they were not compiled for Bacon but rather were written primarily by and for William Drake. The books themselves provide overwhelming evidence for Clark's conclusion that "despite Keen's confident ascription they have little to do with Tottel and nothing at all to do with Bacon". Thirty-seven of them, in fact, could not have been written by Tottel as they date from the period after his death in 1626. Furthermore, no less than fifteen of the notebooks, including the parliamentary volume printed below, are in Drake's own hand.

William Drake was the eldest son of Francis Drake of Esher and William
Tottel's eldest daughter, Joan. He inherited Shardeloes in 1626 at the
time of Tottel's death and, seven years later, on his own father's death,
became owner of Esher, in Surrey.[3] Drake later sold Esher but further
augmented his Buckinghamshire property in 1637 with the purchase of the
manor of Amersham from the Earl of Bedford.[4] At about the same time
that Drake was expanding and consolidating his landholdings he
embarked on a professional career with the purchase of the reversion for a
position in the Fine Office in the Court of Common Pleas from Sir David
Cunningham.[5] Three years later, in April 1640, he began his parliamentary career sitting for Amersham in the Short Parliament. He was
subsequently returned to the Long Parliament and kept the seat until
secluded by Pride in 1648. He was elevated to knighthood in 1641 and
received a baronetcy in July of the same year. Drake's notebooks to a
certain extent chronicle his growing social and political interests; they
include estate accounts for a range of years as well as records relating to his
professional and parliamentary responsibilities.[6]

Drake was also a serious bibliophile, patron of the arts, and scholar of
sorts. He was formally educated at the Inns of Court, entering the Middle
Temple in 1626 (where he came to know Sir Simonds D'Ewes) and later
transferring to Gray's Inn. Although he never experienced the broad
curriculum of the university his notebooks reflect the eclectic nature of his
academic interests and attest to his ongoing desire to learn. The didactic
quality of the collection is clear from the jottings, such as the following,
found on the inside front and back covers of the volumes:[7]

> Get all projects and matters of trade and study them. Labor to understand fully the
> passages of the times and to dive into the practices of the world. . . .[8]

> Get my Lord Coke's abridgement to be translated; as many reports of the Star Chamber as
> I can get; the two Journals of 18° King James and 3tio Charles. . . . Get as many choice
> things concerning business and employments in the general as you may, and study them.
> Mr. Cotton for Journals of Parliament and Sir Simonds D'Ewes.[9]

> To the end to inform myself thoroughly in the state of this kingdom and proceedings
> thereof I think fit to read and meditate upon the histories of this kingdom . . . . [10]

> Learn every day something for business, and converse.[11]

By the end of his life Drake's reputation as a patron of learning was well
established. His epitaph in the Amersham church describes him as having
a scholarly nature, as being a "promotor and patron of letters". It states
that, "he collected from every quarter the best editions, he sought
especially Latin writers who taught true wisdom and pure common
sense."[12]

Drake's precise motive for keeping a notebook of the proceedings in the first part of the Long Parliament is not clear, although his fascination with and interest in parliamentary politics can be traced back almost ten years to 1632 when he compiled a commonplace book of speeches from the parliaments of James I and the early sessions of King Charles, some of which he may have heard about first-hand from a member of his family who was a regular parliament man.[13] William's father, Francis, of Esher, Surrey, had been returned to every parliament from 1621 to 1628, although in the latter his election for Bridport was voided in the House less than a month after the session began because the committee of privileges determined that insufficient warning had been given to the commonalty regarding the election.[14] The 1632 book, unmistakably in William Drake's hand, includes the name Francis. Possibly in this early period of Drake's collecting (born in 1606, he was twenty-six in 1632) Francis provided the liaison between his son and the Cotton family from whom William borrowed the original speeches from the early parliaments of Charles from which he made copies for his own books. Ogden MS. 7, no. 51, though, was not copied but written while Drake was sitting in the House. It bears all the marks of spontaneity—eratic pagination, an irregular hand, few dates, and virtually no punctuation. After the 1641 session Drake rewrote in fair copy some of the conference proceedings he recorded at the time of the meetings (see Appendix B, Ogden MS. 7, no. 52); however, the commonplace books indicate no master plan to rewrite all of the notes and, in effect, to leave for posterity a comprehensible record of the session.[15] The motive seems more personal. Perhaps as a relatively new member (he had first taken his seat in the Short Parliament) he wanted to study the procedures used in the House (an explanation compatible with his desire to learn about law and politics), or, more likely, he simply conceived of the notes as a memory device for his own day to day reference to earlier speeches and debate. Whatever his purpose in recording the business of the House, however, it is interesting to note that Drake himself was not very active in the first months of the session. Between the period of the opening of the parliament and the last entry in Drake's book (3 November 1640–3 June 1641) recorded evidence indicates that he spoke infrequently (although his later speech of 10 November 1641 is printed) and sat on only two committees: the committee for privileges and the committee for an act to disable clergy to exercise any temporal or lay office or commission.[16] Drake's diary corroborates a theory of negative correlation between activity and note keeping in the early Stuart parliaments. It was not unusual for the parliamentarians most actively involved in the business of the House to have little time for note taking, and vice-versa. Certainly, for example, in the Petition of Right parliament of 1628 Coke, Selden, Littleton, Eliot, Phelips, and the other House leaders were not the diarists; and on the contrary Grosvenor, Newdegate, and Nicholas, who were not the prime movers of House business kept excellent records of the proceedings. But whatever Drake's motive, the sheer numbers of commonplace books he left behind indicate that it was his interest as well as his habit to keep records.

The notebook printed below is sprinkled with what I have described as "philosophical observations". One glance through almost any one of the commonplace books discloses Drake as an avid collector of maxims, proverbs, and remarks (see Ogden, MS. 7, n. 9, below). In the parliamentary notes the observations are set off from the rest of the material on the folio by a space or short line. In the printed text, below, I have indicated these observations to the reader by footnoting them as such.

Drake used both ends of his notebook at one time, sometimes making entries in the front and back of the book on the same day, and usually turning it upside down when writing in the back; folios 1–50 are right side up, folios 51v–93v are upside down, and the final folio, 94–94v is again right side up. The last leaf, which is pasted against the back parchment cover, constitutes folio 95. Although most of the common-place books in the Bacon—Tottel collection follow the form described above of utilizing both ends of the book simultaneously there seems to be no rationale for this system of note keeping other than random choice. In the parliamentary notebook the committee notes, for example, are not all in the back of the book and the notes taken when the House was in session are not all in the front. Sometimes, however, several sequential folios contain speeches given in parliament on the same day, as on folios 4–5v (12 February) and folios 22v–24 (23 March).

Most of Drake's notes are fragmentary and undated. In editing them I found that business recorded in sessions of the House itself was not difficult to date using the Commons Journal, the Notestein volume of D'Ewes (see Introductory Notes, above), and the manuscript D'Ewes and Moore Journals for comparison. However, the dating of Drake's notes from committee sessions for which I could find no other extant records was problematical. It could not always with certainty be determined from the Commons Journal when committees that were postponed several times ultimately met. Therefore, in the cases of Drake's entries of committee meeting notes I have in each instance explained in the relevant footnote the reason for their assignment to a particular date.

The anonymous diary (Beinecke, MS. Vault Uncat. 226) is a small (6″

× 4″) leather-bound volume which was once hinged but whose hinges are now broken. The volume was part of Professor Wallace Notestein's collection of seventeenth century papers and at the time of his death it was presented to the Beinecke Rare Book and Manuscript Library, Yale University, by his widow, Ada Comstock Notestein. Containing ff. 1–134, written in pencil which has faded in many places, the notebook covers the period from 1 February through 1 July 1641. The contemporary foliation begins on the first note of the proceedings in parliament (1 February) and ends about a third of the way through the book on f. 30 (5 March). In the present text I have continued the foliation for the convenience of the reader. Preceding the first folio are seven unfoliated leaves. On the recto side of the first of the unfoliated leaves is the entry: *Put out John Smith, Gent. and put in E.F. Gloucestershire.* I am unable to determine what this means in relation to Gloucestershire. Following this note, upside down, is the entry: *Sir [illegible], Mr. Tomkins, [illegible], Sir Peter Heyman, Sir Miles Fleetwood* [Fleetwood's name has been crossed out]:[17] *Bi 6 June 1641.* (6 June was a Sunday; the House did not meet.) This is followed by another cryptic note which states that: *10 days after our Lady Day Mole/ 50 1. was promised to be paid in but it was not so. 21 April L. Northampton promised to take a speedy course about it. The 10 May I spoke with this Lord again and found that nothing was yet done by Mole, so he promised to take a speedy course in it.*

On the verso side of the second leaf is the end of a draft bill concerning benefices which begins on the third leaf. In the present volume the bill is placed in the Appendix following the diary. This draft and a few incomprehensible notes recorded on the inside back cover are the only parts of the diary written in ink rather than pencil.[18]

The fourth and fifth leaves are blank on both sides. On the sixth of the unfoliated leaves is the nineteenth century dedication of the volume to Charles Shoppee from George Sawtell, Esquire, December 1879. Leaf seven is blank.

At the end of the notebook the jottings on the verso of the last leaf are so faded as to be indecipherable.

The anonymous diarist included several passages regarding parliamentary procedure (27 February, 1 March, and 27 April) which may reflect his interest in the management of the House. He also included several notes of speeches at the back of his book (printed below on 10, 11, and 19 March and in the Appendix following the text), which suggest an interest in ecclesiastical matters.

There are a number of gaps in the diary entries. The first is the two week period ending around 5 April when the diarist's mother died. There are no entries, although the pages are dated, from 31 March until 12 April when he writes that he returned to the House. We can safely assume, I believe, that the author was not present in the Commons during that time and may have been outside of London in the country. In view of this gap the excused absences bear looking at.

Around the end of March and the beginning of April five men requested leave from the House. Two of them, Francis Godolphin and Alexander Rigby, can be dismissed as possible authors of the diary on the basis of their handwriting.[19] A third, William Cage, can probably be dismissed on the same grounds, although in the absence of a holograph the judgement must be made solely on the basis of his signature.[20] He was known to have been a note-taker in the 1629 session of parliament (although his notes are no longer extant); and on 20 April 1640 Cage's record was cited as evidence in the examination of the violation of the privilege of the House in 1629.[21] That passage, included in the *Commons Journal*, is similar in format and brevity to the entries in the Anonymous diary; furthermore, it reflects Cage's evident interest in procedure. However, the argument for Cage's authorship is weakened by the fact that the 1641 diarist includes a speech by William Cage on 10 March with no suggestion that he is recording his own voice.

A fourth recorded absentee was Henry Benson of Knaresborough, granted leave on 2 April, but he is certainly not the diarist. Benson left the House because of his father's death. Unlike the diarist, he apparently did not return to Westminster, did not take the Protestation, and in June was reported by a neighbor to have been in Yorkshire "for the past eight weeks".[22]

The last case is that of Hugh Potter who requested leave on 26 March. Potter, who sat for Plympton, Devon, and was secretary to the Earl of Northumberland, had been a commissioner of sewers in Sussex in 1630 and again in 1637, and through that service may have known Herbert Morley, M.P. for Lewes in 1641, who also had been a Sussex sewer commissioner in 1637. A relationship between the two would explain why on 28 June the diarist records a bet with "Mr. Morley" concerning the amount the poll money would bring in. Could this have been a gentleman's wager between old friends? On 20 March in a petition to the House the Earl of Strafford requested Potter (and others) to testify at the trial. The Commons did not prohibit them from so doing but encouraged them to act as they thought fit, "without offense to the House". I do not, however, find his name in the trial records. Going one step further toward determining authorship I looked for evidence to confirm the date of

Potter's mother's death but was unable to find burial records for Susan Potter, nee Osborn.[23]

On 6 April Sir Sydney Montagu and Robert Hunt were granted leaves of absence, as was Sir John Holland on 7 April.[24] In view of the fact that these men requested leave within the period of the gap but after the date of the mother's death (5 April), I discounted tham as possible authors. Furthermore, Sir John Holland kept his own diary from 8 May–8 August 1641 (Rawl. D. 1092). Hunt took the Protestation on 10 May, a day the anonymous diarist was present.

Brunton and Pennington, in their study of membership in the Long Parliament indicate that about 507 members were returned in November 1640.[25] Through examination of the *Commons Journal* and the other accounts of proceedings in the session it is possible to identify at least sixty-two members who were in the House during the period of the first gap. In fact there were many more present, but the nature of the record precludes the possibility of discovering who were the "divers others" so frequently mentioned in the accounts of the debates. There remains the eternal problem for the parliamentary historian of how to identify the present but non-speaking members.

After the diarist's return to the House on 12 April there are frequent omissions of entries (although, as in the earlier case, the pages are dated). No notes are recorded from 15 through 23 April; on 29 and 30 April; from 3 through 6 May; on 8 and 11 May; from 14 through 26 May; from 28 May through 5 June; from 15 through 17 June; from 21 through 23 June; on 26 and 30 June. During these later gaps it is more difficult to establish with certainty that the diarist was absent; it may be that he simply chose not to take notes on those days. However, on the days for which there are entries we know for a fact that he was present. With this in mind it is useful to examine the dates of the Protestation; although no definite conclusion can be reached the exercise offers a list of possible contenders for the authorship of the diary. Of the thirteen days on which there is a record of the Protestation's having been taken the diarist was present and took notes on only seven: 7, 10, 12, 13, 27 May, 8 and 18 June. From the *Commons Journal* we can identify forty-nine M.P.s who took the Protestation on one of those days. Was the author one of the forty-nine or did he not take the Protestation at all? (Members also subscribed on 3, 8, 11, 17, 18, and 19 May, days on which there are no diary entries.) Again, because the parliamentary records never give an accurate picture of who is bodily in the House at any given moment the conclusive proof of the author's identity will rest not on deductive evidence of presence or absence but on confirmation of his mother's death through burial records.

Following a different tack I attempted to discover the identity of the
mysterious Mole included in the notes at the beginning of this diary (see
above) and to discern how he was involved with Spencer Compton, Earl
of Northampton, and whether he were in any way connected with a 1641
M.P. The only Mole I could find was one Mr. Mole who was a wool
broker's agent from Shrewsbury questioned in the 1621 parliament
regarding business practices and questioned again in 1624 regarding the
staplers' patent.[26] In checking the Shrewsbury M.P.s for 1641 I found that
William Spurstow sat for the town but had resided in London since 1602
and was an active member of the Mercers' Company there.[27] Although I
could in no way link his name to that of Mole, knowing that he and Mole
had two points of common interest, Shrewsbury and the wool trade, I
decided to continue the investigation and try to determine Spurstow's
mother's death date. The fact that he resided in London rather than in the
country could explain his not requesting permission from the House to
leave town when his mother became ill. I checked Shrewsbury records for
five parishes and could find no evidence of a Spurstow burial in 1641.[28]
Then, assuming the mother may have moved up to London to be with her
son's family and died in the City, I attempted to examine the registers of
St. Stephan's Coleman Street where the Spurstows were known to have
been members, only to find that the records for this period have
disappeared.[29]

Clearly, as stated above, the critical fact in determining the authorship
of MS. Uncatalogued 226 is the date of the diarist's mother's death. Future
scholars with easy access to large libraries of parish records can exercise
their wits regarding the identity of the author (and his mother) who for
the immediate must remain anonymous.

NOTES

1. The identification of Ogden MS. 7, no. 51 as William Drake's notebook was made
   prior to Stuart Clark's definitive article on the manuscript collection of which the book
   is a part: "Wisdom Literature of the Seventeenth Century: A Guide to the Contents of
   the 'Bacon-Tottel' Commonplace Books", Pts. I and II, *Transactions of the Cambridge
   Bibliographical Society*, VI (1976) and VII (1977), Cambridge University Library, pp.
   291–305 and 46–73. (Hereafter cited as *Clark*.) A fifty-fifth commonplace book in
   William Drake's hand is in the House of Lords Record Office, see below, n. 13.
2. All of the information printed here regarding the provenance of the manuscripts is
   from *Clark*.
3. Keeler, *L.P.*, p. 159; *Clark*, Pt. I, p. 295.

4. Regarding Drake's purchase of Amersham see P.R.O., Ind. 9990, f. 357a. I am indebted to Professor Conrad Russell for this reference.
5. *Clark*, Pt. I, p. 295 and n. 27; Aylmer, *King's Servants*, p. 97 & 98.
6. See *Clark*, Pt. I, pp. 294–295 and Pt. II, pp. 47–56.
7. Printed below are examples of Drake's jottings culled from the volumes I was examining for parliamentary materials; I have not studied the entire collection.
8. Notes from the back of book no. 45.
9. Notes from the front of book no. 7.
10. Notes from the back of book no. 11. In calling for a translation of Coke Drake may be commenting on his own education. Stuart Clark believes Drake may have been a client of the great manuscript collectors and antiquarians. *Clark*, Pt. I, p. 297.
11. Notes from the front of book No. 11. Drake mentions in several places the need to converse. For example, in the back of book no. 4 is the note:

> Hearken who are the activest and of most general and universal acquaintance among solicitors and specially according to the diversity of persons to have conversation with, some one at least who is well intelligenced in each several ways. . . . Make acquaintance with the authors . . . and sharpen and enlarge my own invention and project by discoursing with them, such as Sandys that undertakes the waterworks.

Furthermore, in book no. 21 Drake includes many entries of conversation with "Mr. P.". The contents of the entries suggests that P. may stand for Pym.

12. Professor James P. Reilly of the Pontifical Institute of Mediaeval Studies kindly translated the Latin.
13. The Commonplace Book in the H.L.R.O. was purchased by Mr. Percy Millican in 1935 and later given to the Record Office. See M. Bond, *Guide to the Records of Parliament* (London, 1971), p. 267; W. Notestein, H. Relf and H. Simpson, eds., *Commons Debates 1621* (New Haven, 1935), VII, 15.
14. Robert C. Johnson, Maija Jansson Cole, *et al.*, *Commons Debates 1628* (New Haven, 1977), II, 427.
15. Some of the rough notes included in book no. 51 Drake rewrote in fair copy in book no. 52. Ogden MS. 7, no. 52 is a small notebook about the same width and having pages 1/2″ longer than those in no. 51. It is unfoliated and contains at the front copies of various speeches c. James I as well as neatly copied Long Parliament entries for 17, 18, 22, 23, and 25 March, and 28 May (these entries are printed below in Appendix B of Ogden MS. 7, no. 51). At the back of book no. 52, upside down, are notes on Machiavelli, copies of various Star Chamber speeches, terms from Cowell's *Interpreter*, etc. See *Clark*, Pt. II, for a detailed description of the entries.
16. *C.J.*, II, 21, 99. On Drake's membership on the committee of privileges see Keeler, *L.P.*, 160. For the printed speech see Wing, *S.T.C.*, no. 2138.
17. Fleetwood died on 8 March 1641. Keeler, *L.P.*
18. The notes look like: *20sh best [illegible] 8, brdg 8.*
19. For letters written in Godolphin's hand, see B.L. Add. 28,052, ff. 2, 5, 10, and 15. for Rigby, see S.P. 16/479:63.
20. For the signature, which has an open italic final *e* and taller, more relaxed *l*'s than those in the diary, see B.L. Add. 38,855, f. 56. I found no correspondence in the British Library or the Suffolk County Record Office, nor was I able to find the record of the burial of Cage's stepmother (his own mother died in 1597. M. Keeler).
21. Cage's notes are not mentioned in W. Notestein and F.H. Relf, *Commons Debates 1629* (Minneapolis, 1921).

22. Keeler, *L.P.*

23. Keeler, *L.P.* I was unable to find a sample of Potter's handwriting. He took the Protestation on 19 May, a day for which the diarist makes no entry.

24. *C.J.*, II, 116, 117.

25. D. Brunton and D.H. Pennington, *Members of the Long Parliament* (Cambridge, 1954), p. 2. Brunton and Pennington calculate another 45 members were returned in by-elections between November 1640 and August 1642.

26. Notestein, Relf and Simpson, *Commons Debates 1621*, II, 271, 544; IV, 65–66; V, 394 n. 4, 506–507; VI, 291, VII, 489, and see Sir Richard Grosvenor's diary 26 May 1624 (YCPH transcripts), p. 375.

27. Keeler, *L.P.*, and see T.C. Mendenhall, *The Shrewsbury Drapers and the Welsh Wool Trade in the XVI and XVII Centuries* (Oxford, 1953), 65, 92, 130n, 142, 143, 201, 207.

28. *Shropshire Parish Registers* (Privately printed for Shropshire Parish Record Society, 1916).

29. Keeler, *L.P.*, pp. 346–347 and "Churchwardens accounts of Parishes within the City of London", a handlist, Guildhall Library, p. 29. M. Keeler, however, suggests that Spurstow's mother may have been dead by 1634. *Visitation of London* (1633, 1634, 1635), II, 259.

EXPLANATION OF EDITORIAL PRACTICES

Spelling: Spelling in the text of both diaries and in the footnote citations that quote from manuscript sources has been modernized. For the spelling of names of persons I have followed first Notestein, *D'Ewes*, then Keeler, *L.P.*, and *Cal. S.P. Dom.*, with the exception of Anthony Ashley Cooper's name which, contrary to Notestein, has been kept as Cooper. The spelling of Irish names and peerages is from G.E. C[okayne]'s *Complete Peerage* and *Cal. S.P. Ireland.* For place names the *Oxford Dictionary of English Place Names* and Keeler, *L.P.* have been followed. Short forms and abbreviations of more than one letter have been extended without the use of brackets.

Capitalization: Within the text and footnotes the use of capitals has generally been limited to proper nouns. Following the conventions of editing parliamentary history capitals have been used for the names of speakers speaking in regular sessions of the House rather than in committee, in which case the names appear in lower case letters. Occasionally the capitalization is erratic in quotations from printed sources which appear in footnotes.

Dates: The dates as recorded by the diarists are old style. Where dates have been inserted into the text within brackets they follow the Gregorian or new style calendar, as do the dates in the notes.

Brackets: Words or letters which have been inserted into the text for clarification of a point or for grammatical considerations are within brackets. In the cases where a speaker's name has been inserted into the text in brackets I have not in each instance footnoted the source from which the name has been supplied. In those cases where the source is not identified in a footnote the speakers' names have been supplied from Notestein, *D'Ewes*, *Commons Journal*, Rushworth, *Hist. Collections*, or Cobbett, *Parl Hist.*, in that order.

Folio numbers and dates have been inserted into the text within brackets. In the text of the Drake diary the folio numbers are not in sequence, reflecting Drake's choice of random pages for his entries. The Drake diary contains two folios with the number "3" which I have kept as "3A" and "3B".

Where the diarists did not distinguish between the morning and afternoon sessions that distinction has been made by the insertion of the word *Afternoon* within brackets in the appropriate places in the texts.

In cases where the diarists' notes were indecipherable I have put *illegible* in brackets, preceded by as precise as possible an indication of how many words appear to be illegible. [*Illegible*] on its own indicates a single word is unreadable.

Annotation: As stated in the Introductory Notes, I have cited wherever possible to unprinted manuscript sources. The annotation to secondary sources has been kept to a minimum and occurs only when manuscript notes fail to elucidate the point in question.

ABBREVIATIONS AND SHORT TITLES

Anon. diary (Yale Uncat. 226).   An Anonymous Diary of Proceedings in the House of Commons, 1 Feb–1 July 1641. MS. Uncat. 226. Beinecke Rare Book and Manuscript Library, Yale University, New Haven, Conn. Printed in this volume.

Ashton, *City and Court*.   Ashton, Robert, *The City and the Court 1603–1643*. Cambridge, 1979.

Ashton, *Crown and Money Market*.   Ashton, Robert, *The Crown and the Money Market 1603–1640*. Oxford, 1960.

Aylmer, *King's Servants*.   Aylmer, G.E. *The King's Servants, The Civil Service of Charles I 1625–1642*. London, 1961.

Brook, *Lives of the Puritans*.   Brook, Benjamin, *The Lives of the Puritans*. 3 vols., London, 1813.

Brunton and Pennington, *Members of the Long Parliament*.   Brunton, D., D.H. Pennington, *Members of the Long Parliament*. Archon Books, 1968.

C.J.   *Journals of the House of Commons*. London, 1742.

Cal. S.P. Dom.   *Calendar of State Papers: Domestic Series*. London, 1857.

Cal. S.P. Ireland.   *Calendar of State Papers: Ireland*. London, 1912.

Cobbett, *Parl. Hist.*   Cobbett, William, *The Parliamentary History of England. From the Norman Conquest, in 1066, to the year, 1803*. 36 vols., London, 1806–1820.

Commons Debates 1628.   *Commons Debates 1628*, ed. by Robert C. Johnson, Mary Frear Keeler, Maija J. Cole, William Bidwell. 4 vols., New Haven, 1977–1978.

D'Ewes (Harl. 163, 164).   Sir Simonds D'Ewes's Journal of Proceedings in the House of Commons, 1641. Harleian MSS. 163, 164. British Library.

D.N.B.   *The Dictionary of National Biography Founded in 1882 by George Smith*, ed. by Sir Leslie Stephen and Sir Sidney Lee. New York, 1885 1904.

Drake. William Drake's Parliamentary Notebook, 23 Jan.–24 June 1641. Ogden MS. 7, no. 51, University College London. Printed in this volume.

Gardiner, Hist. of Eng. Gardiner, S.R., History of England from the Accession of James I to the Outbreak of the Civil War 1603–1642. 10 vols., London, 1886.

Hamilton, Northcote. Note Book of Sir John Northcote, Sometime M.P. for Ashburton, and Afterwards for the County of Devon, ed. by A.H.A. Hamilton. London, 1877.

Hatsell, Precedents. Hatsell, John, Precedents of Proceedings in the House of Commons. 4 vols., London, 1818 ed.

Howell, S.T. A Complete Collection of State Trials and Proceedings for High Treason . . . Compiled by T.B. Howell. 21 vols., London, 1816.

Keeler, L.P. Keeler, Mary Frear. The Long Parliament, 1640–1641. Philadelphia, 1954.

Larking, Proceedings in the County of Kent. Larking, Rev. Lambert B., Proceedings Principally in the County of Kent, in Connection with the Parliaments Called in 1640. . . . Camden Society, 1862.

L.J. Journals of the House of Lords. London, 1767.

Moore (Harl. 476, 477, 478). John Moore's Journal of Proceedings in the House of Commons 23 Feb. 1641–28 Feb. 1642. Harleian MSS. 476–480, British Library.

Notestein, D'Ewes. The Journal of Sir Simonds D'Ewes from the Beginning of the Long Parliament to the Opening of the Trial of the Earl of Strafford, ed. by Wallace Notestein. New Haven, 1923.

Oldfield, Hist. of the Boroughs. Oldfield, Thomas, H.B., An Entire and Complete History, Political and Personal, of the Boroughs of Great Britain. . . . 3 vols., London, 1792.

O.R. Return of the Name of Every Member of the Lower House of Parliament. 2 vols., Accounts and Papers, Session of 1878 [London], 1878. The Official Return.

Peyton. The Parliamentary Diary of Sir Thomas Peyton, 3 Nov. 1640–19 March 1642. Minnesota University Library (Microfilm at the Yale Center for Parliamentary History).

Rushworth, Hist. Collections. Rushworth, John, Historical Collections of Private Passages of State, Weighty Matters in Law, Remarkable Proceedings in Five Parliaments. London, 1659.

Russell. Russell, Conrad, Parliaments and English Politics 1621–1629. Oxford, 1979.

Scobell, Memorials. Scobell, Henry, Memorials of the Method and Manner of Proceedings in Parliament in Passing Bills. . . . London, 1660.

Verney. Verney Papers, *Notes of Proceedings in the Long Parliament, temp. Chas. I*, ed. by John Bruce. Camden Society, 1845.

Warner. The Parliamentary Journal of John Warner, Bishop of Rochester, of Proceedings in the House of Lords, 13 Jan. 1641–4 Jan. 1642. Harleian MS. 6424, British Library.

Whitelocke, *Memorials*. Whitelocke, Sir Bulstrode, *Memorials of the English Affairs*. . . . London, 1709.

I

William Drake's Parliamentary Notebook

Ogden MS. 7, no. 51, University College London.

[23 January 1641 – Afternoon]

King's speech.[1] Lords and gentlemen, a principal cause of my coming here because I foresee the inconveniences of the slow proceedings of this parliament.

Two armies in a great charge lying upon the land. I shall not commend the treaty and the delay.

I shall concur with you [MS. *torn*] to reform the abuses in the commonwealth. I will not say but bishops may have overstretched their power which I am willing to have regulated.

There is another rock, the bill in parliament.

No increase nor improvement of his revenue within these last 7 years; cast up and aground upon that.[2]

[25 January 1641]

[f. 2] The charging of freehold by taxing 4d. upon every house where/[3]

[27 January 1641]

[f. 92v] Had I not been pre-engaged/[4]

The first law against priests and Jesuits was vizt. [2]7timo Queen Elizabeth.

Response: Primer King James, *cap.* 4, no. 5 part. The constant opinion of the state in parliament is against them.

[1 February 1641 – Afternoon]

[f. 91v] Powder Committee.

The sole making of powder is engrossed into one hand and must be brought into the Tower as the magazine, whereby the price is enhanced. Men discouraged to keep powder in their houses. The danger to the

1

commonwealth in having all the powder of the kingdom in one hand; your enemies were skillful marksmen before powder became so dear.[5]

Question: How long has powder been in one man's hands? 2ly, whether the price was lower when there is a free liberty to make it who would.

What ground had you to inhibit the importation or, if you know not, if you know who was the means of the inhibition by proclamation or who procured the same. The proclamation came out February 1636, whereupon the price was presently enhanced though the old powder was far better. [f. 92] This powder was sold. [f. 91] The merchants and retailers paid 10l. and sometimes 8l. for a license and they were fain as they said to bribe the Earl of Newport's servants besides. One paid at least 30l. for licenses to my Lord of Newport's secretary, one Barman. As also 40 at times to Mr. Meautys's man, one Mathews. Meautys likewise received 12s. of another.[6]

The Earl procured a restraint of selling without license and terrified men with the Star Chamber.

[8 February 1641]

[f. 1v] [SIR BENJAMIN RUDYARD.][7] They have not [sic] suffered in the disease; let them not suffer in the remedy.

The LORD DIGBY. All the prudence, all the forecast, will be all little enough meet with the inconvenience as unbiased by popular opinion as by court expectation.

All the hand/

I find myself inflamed with indignation, and to cry rightly with the loudest of the 15,000, 'Down with them, Down with them'. It is natural with the multitude to fly into extremes.

I cannot give vote till I know[8] it flows from the nature and I see what frame they would introduce, and when that model be practical and not a mere idea which in the appearance having [no] hindrance but in the practice would prove extremely inconvenient.

Instead of putting down a bishop in every diocese we shall set up a pope in every parish. [f. 2] The King cannot give way to the total abolishing, but he ought give way to the presiding/

Let's lay aside all thought of abolishing episcopacy. That there may be a committee of both Houses to take into consideration the government [of the church] with some great/

LORD OF FALKLAND. Speaking of the clergy, they are like that hen that laid an egg every day upon such a proportion of barley and the mistress of that hen doubled the proportion thinking to have doubled the number of her eggs. She made her hen so fat as she laid no eggs at all.[9]

Religio peperit divitias et filia devoravit matrem [6 words illegible].[10]

MR. FIENNES.[11] If we refuse this petition will it not seem an act [of] will–and may this not produce an act of will in the multitude which is considerable because a multitude? [f. 2v] Fire, as long as it keeps in the chimney, is of excellent use but if it breathe out into the house it is dangerous. Likened to the clergy meddling out of their function.

PLEYDELL.[12] They that were against episcopacy urged extremely for the commitment to draw it into such hand as might be for their purpose, who by their opinion would give a great step unto their design. Those of another opinion were against the commitment.

TREASURER VANE. We have all one end—reformation. We differ in the way to it; some stick at the root and branch. The Londoners propound the considerations in the way of it.

[f. 3] There was a great deal of art and skill to frame the question so as may serve their own design.

MR. PYM[13] moved that some consid[eration] might be taken of the present state of the King's expense and to settle things in that way. He moved that could in [illegible] be disposed to the most necessary and material uses in the first place.

[9 February 1641]

SIR JOHN STRANGWAYS. Preparations to the business of episcopacy; that he should be unwilling to allay one devil and to raise twenty in the room of it.

He spoke much of parity and said that if a party were once raised in ecclesiastical matters were a question whether they would rest there, but they would ask a parity in matters civil.[14]

MR. PALMER's[15] question that the committee should touch upon episcopacy. If that be resolved we shall go better and not shackle upon our [f. 3v] selves that we shall not be able to touch upon any of the corollaries of episcopacy but will be said that we touch upon episcopacy.

[10 February 1641]

[f. 76v] Mr. Holles petitioned against Sir Anthony Cooper.[16] It appeared Holles had a suit in Court of Wards against Sir Anthony and he labored fearing delays in the suit.

Upon his privilege to keep out Sir Anthony. Upon suggestion of minority, for he preferred it to be whole bus[iness] of the kingdom, *mala cui/*

[f. 93v] For the King's army.[17]

TREASURER. There is a vast charge lies upon the kingdom. We are to consider how we may comply with it. If you agree that there shall such a proportion go out of the 4 subsidies, there is so much laid quiet and settled, we may go on to the next consideration propounded by Vane to move the House: the disbanding of both armies. The charge whereof stands the kingdom in 37, 5 thousand pound[s][18] a month; [for] the army, with the payment of the garrisons, comes to 50 thousand pounds, the subsidies comes to 12 thousand.[19] That being the stock you are to go upon we are to consider of the saving words.

Another point they took into consideration was of great weight and consequence [f. 93] as the giving the soldiers somewhat more and above the pay, otherwise they would be ready to possess the country.[20]

Agreed that 50 thousand pound of the City's money shall go to the payment of the King's army and garrisons.

Ordered that my Lord General be moved that the country's way be paid out of the 50 thousand pound according to the proportion for a month's billet for the soldiers' arrears, and that which is first due to be first paid.

The next point, agree that the next 25,000*l.* to be raised after this 50 thousand shall be disposed of to the supply of the northern parts.[21]

What men cannot carry it is wisdom to secure for and to promote it.[22]

[11 February 1641]

[f. 3v] [SIR WALTER EARLE.] Report concerning the Irish army. 7,000 papists of 8,000 foot and possessing themselves watch of the strong places both maritime and inland, castles and forts; and if by salvation to land in Wales or England/[23]

[MR. REYNOLDS.][24] Letters to Earls of Worcester, Bridgewater and others for the transmitting power to the Earl of Worcester.

A man's stock discreetly managed may yield him above 8 per cent.[25]

MR. PYM moved for the speedy dispatch of the procuring of the money of the City.

Moved that as the money came in the House might be sealed up, which would prevent a double telling.[26]

[12 February 1641 – Afternoon]

[f. 4] At the committee for vintners.

Wilson[27] being called in, Mr. Pym began:[28]

You are a tradesman and therefore should not be an actor in those things that burden, and it was a great fault and folly in you.

They charged Wilson with selling wines 40s. a tun, done before he entered into covenant with the King; he denying it was. Told him he should be wary what he denied, for it were fatal to double the committee which would proceed to judgment.

Wilson has 4 or 5 taverns and selling by retail makes 4l. a tun. Wilson denying it, Mr. Herbert propound[ed] that he should be required to give in a perfect note what he has reported since 1 of January 1637, since the project first began, and how you have disposed them. [f. 4v] He haunts and stocks young men with wine, putting them in houses for this purpose. A [*illegible*] in a quart comes to 4l. a tun.

He was asked whether [what] he sold vented to the young men at the same rates as he would have sold to another man.

Sir John Culpepper said that it let them put their contract into as many shapes as they please. Let them be asked if their young men placed in taverns drew not their wine as tapsters do in inns, at a dearer rate than it was paid in at.

1 of January '37 the contract began in. 40s. a tun began in June '38. French wines at 6d. a quart by the [*illegible*] and claimed it 7d. Canary wines at 13 and sell at 14. 19l. a pipe for canary wine. You must allow in your w/

[f. 5] Culpepper. You must allow in your wines your leakage, small cask and leaks and long keeping.

40s. a tun the vintners were to pay by their contract to the King, and they raised the price upon the subject to 4l. a tun; 2 a quart makes 5 a tun. Mr. Kilvert was the setter and driver of this project.

Mr. Hales said that though wines are sold at 14d. the quart yet vintners gained not more than they did, for before the project they paid 5d. the 40s. a tun, which being defalcated. We are to consider the just pro[portion] of the importation and how it has been issued and vented.

[f. 5v] [Anonymous] We shall make a quicker progress in the business if we settle the projects upon which we shall treat.

Mr. Coventry would not have us prejudice offenses for that will show as though we sought offenders than reformation. The business lies in straight, narrow room. We/

The beaver makers project was to give the King 12l. a hat and restrain the felt makers from making covers.

The King sets out a proclamation and prohibits the importation upon pain of 9s. and 4d. a hat. This project as was proposed contrary to the Commons. Effect of monopolies, hats fell from 5s. to 3s.

The Earl of Sterling had a lease of this 1*d.* imposed upon every hat. Sir James Cornmichall was a passee with Lawrence Whitaker and others.

[16 February 1641]

[f. 94] There is none of so mean a heart but is delighted with joy at this day's gracious as[sent]; and therefore moved for solemn thanks to the King.[29]

But the House inclined to go[30] rather a parliamentary way and to quit all complaints and to express themselves rather in deeds than words.[31]

SIR BENJAMIN RUDYARD. Things were now put in such a state that we could not well receive hurt but from ourselves.

The Lords sent down a message for the joining with us in public thanks to/

MR. WALLER moved that the whole House might present their thanks, for he said public actions *sunt ad favorem* [illegible] and this was of that nature that the knowledge is necessary to all posterity and the rather that they might pay their subsidies with the more alacrity.

[Afternoon]

[f. 92] Lord Keeper,[32] he is to give his Majesty humble thanks in the name of ourselves and whole kingdom, which is of singular comfort and security. We shall not come to the end of our journey unless we go step by step.

[17 February 1641]

[f. 6] At the committee for the King's army and the northern relief. Mr. Hyde in the chair.

[Sir John Hotham.] 16 of February '40, due to the Scotch army by the agreement of the northern counties: fifty-two thousand pounds.

After a great silence some called upon the others of the Chequer and Court of Wards to lend.[33]

They themselves desired that they who it more merely concerned might furnish it—the northern counties.

[Illegible] propounded the customers, and it was no expiation but a molification only; and if it were a matter of convenience only he should not think it fit, but because of necessity he saw not why we might not go the way.

Mr. Pym said the securing—for the manner of it—would be considered.

There will be due over and above the subsidies, one hundred and 12 thousand pounds.

It has come in proposition to have it from the customs officers. It will be considerable. How we may match [ink spot] our credit to that pitch as we may make it probable to men that they are secured for the money they lend, which I see not yet.

[f. 6v] It was propounded by some for a committee to treat with the pertinent persons for the furnishing of money.

Some motioned to greater clergy.

Then they fell upon the point of the navy.

Treasurer said that the setting out 20 ships could come to 40 thousand pound. Had we made timely provisions we should have made them in November. Now we shall do at far greater charge.

The great customs come to 1,000l. a day, which he moved might be applied to the Navy.

Whatever part of my revenue is grievous to the public shall lay down and rest until affections of my subjects. Treasurer: His Majesty said it.

We are not like to do business like good husbands unless [we] have money beforehand.

Treasurer. There are two things considerable in the business: the raising credit; the getting money on that credit. If you find a way to pass over the first difficulty, I shall show you the means to get the money.

[f. 7] Mr. Whistler said the country will not be fed with painted grapes. We talk of disbanding [the] Irish army, of taking of the ship money, but we have not done anything to perfection.

Mr. Johns [sic]³⁴ was extremely disliked for speaking of a legislative power but he qualified that, it so apt to speak for strangers was silent for him.

Mr./   ———

1. It was moved that a committee should treat with the City.

It was objected the dignity of the House would suffer in it.

Falkland said that we are to consult with our dignity but, indeed, not only so but with our safety and interests; how to reconcile these. We are to consider we have/

I shall propound this: that a committee shall appoint what persons they think fit.

[22 February 1641]

[f. 89v] Monday, February the 22, 1640, in the case of Earl of Strafford.[35]

Mr. Maynard said that for matter in law, as if a question rises how much such a fact weighs in law, there courses may be assigned for matter of fact whether done or not done. No counsel is to be allowed; for let us consider what the duty of a counselor is: he is to press that which may advantage his client and to concede that which may hurt him. Now every man by his oath ought to discover treason, which cannot stand with him, I confess, for he cannot do his duty without breach of his oath.

[23 February 1641]

[f. 92] A committee for the Bishop of Llandaff, Bishop[s] Maynwaring and Montagu.[36]

[f. 88v] 23 February[37]

Deputy Lieutenants.

A petition against the Earl of Bridgewater.

The substance of the complaint was that the Earl, upon a pretended affront to the muster master's office by countenancing a presentment of an jury, and presented it as a grievance by Sir John Corbet.

The said Earl procured a commitment from the Lords of the said Sir John to the Fleet. The counsel on the Lord's side said that Sir John, to improve his cause, has laid it to our charge as though we were enemies to the Petition of Right.

A presentment was presented. A warrant was made for John, June '35. Copies of letter were accounted no evidence, not being authentic.

[f. 88] Mr. Palmer. It is apparent that Sir John Corbet had deserved very well of his country and has been very well requited. For the twenty letters, it is a bare relation, no intendment or provocation.

For my Lord of Bridgewater, I see not how he can stand single in this business or that it falls personally upon my Lord of Bridgewater, but might fall upon the other Lords of the Council; and therefore moves to have the question put that my Lord of Bridgewater, together with the other Lords, had of the Council ought to give damages to Sir John Corbet.

It was Cicero's counsel to Catiline where he would have brought in Caesar into his faction, brings in woe more than you can well grapple with.

A man that sees one post would wonder how that should uphold the balcony, but many joined together would easily uphold the structure.

[24 *February* 1641]

[f. 87v] Lord of Canterbury's report.

[MR. PYM.] My Lord of Strafford has made his ultimate end in overthrow[ing], it was to invade liberty. My Lord of Canterbury has crept on to his end in a cunning undermining way. My Lord of Strafford has been a club in the Archbishop's hand.

[25 *February* 1641]

[f. 87] They have tried me all manner of ways: sometimes they butter me, sometimes they pepper me, sometimes they sweeten me.

Lord of Canterbury loved to stand behind the curtain and act by others. He wrote such to a commissary: do what you can of yourself, if you meet with [*illegible*], I'll strike in and help you.[38]

MR. WALLER gave [2 *illegible words*]. There was a mutiny started and then that it came in question [10 *illegible words*] that drew them would be put to death and that he that blew the trumpet only saved; but it was resolved that all that drew their swords should be saved and the trumpeter only executed because he mewed up [the soldiers].

I conceive that [what] was done applied to the business of the voting the Council order for sending the man to the castle; which he would have only laid on Canterbury, and the rest of the Lords freed.

[f. 87v] VANE. It very well becomes this House to be tender of the liberty of the subject. You know what steps this business had [had] it been on the High Commission. You know whose setting on it was and laid it upon Canterbury but to hinder the Council's order from being voted as a grievance at present. He said that it could not appear whether all that were present gave their votes and therefore said whether they will go presently to voting before you know who involved in the order, I leave it to you.[39]

[*Afternoon*]

[f. 86v] Earl of Strafford. Answer read in the House.[40]

1. He said he has been a means of making many wholesome laws in Ireland.

He has opposed projects invented for private gain. His Majesty's revenue is increased by his means from 80 thousand pound[s] to 10,000*l.* per annum. The charge of the Navy is much lessened. Portland made a/

The Earl of [*Blank*], proposition to him to take the customs of Ireland,

and said that he was offered 13,000*l.* per annum. The Earl [of Strafford] advised with some that understood the business of that nature; he got 16,000*l.* per annum and 8,000 five/

The Earl of Portland bid him conclude the bargain with them that offered, for if they had time to consider and understand the business they would not give those rates.

[f. 87] Earl of Strafford's speech that the King's little finger should be heavier than the loins of the law. That Ireland is a conquered kingdom and might be governed as the King pleases. He told Mountnorris that not so much as a hair of his head should fall by that sentence. That/

[f. 86] The Earl of Portland told him that if he would be a party in the farming of the customs, he should have liberty to advance the book of rates. It was so conceived that the King must be an adviser to alter the book of the said Earl to take the said bargains.

He prohibited the transporting of pipe staves and then got great sums for licenses. He got the monopoly of tobacco and then extremely enhanced the price when he had got the sole sale into his own hands. Likewise he got the monopoly of starch, iron pots, and other things of regular use.

He sowed flax upon his own lands in great proportion and then got the sole selling the same. He got his flax seed in the Low Countries.

He said that his Majesty liked the Irish army so well that he might make it a pattern for his 3 kingdoms.

[f. 85v] He confesses he advised the raising of two hundred thousand pounds by loan until a parliament could be assembled.

He let fall some speeches that might make them think that he meant to land his Irish force in England the more to distract the Earl of Argyle; and that he might let fall some such speech to Sir George Ratcliffe that he might report it to the King that having tried the affections of the subjects, and they hav[ing] failed, he was dissolved of all rules of his government, he/

That Secretary Vane said that he thought the Commons would not give a penny, whereupon voted a breach.

[f. 85] He confessed that he said at Council Board that it were good to match against the city of London; they were put to their fine and ransom which he said was only to quicken their remissions.

The French King used to send troops of horse into the country and took customs. That this was a point was of his Lordship's consideration.

The Cardinal of France sends commissioners out into Paris and other cities. And they view every man's shop, books, and value them according to their estates, and the subjects have seen the balance of their estates. It is by a letter from Earl of Leicester, Ambassador to the Council, these appeared.

[f. 84] [Anonymous.] There he procured so many subsidies of that nation. This was in March 1639. He said in his answer that the little finger of the law was heavier than the King's loins. That will cast such a damp upon the business, will extremely disadvantage.

[f. 84v][41] He speaks of parties in his projects but one of them was his own servant and the other [i]s Sir George Ratcliffe, as Sir John Clotworthy informed us.

[f. 84v] [Anonymous.][42] Unless to contrary, it will become you by some noble action to get yourself from the weight of ill tongues. The number of the Scot's army is said not to be very great, which still lays the weight heavier upon you.

[f. 83v] At the committee for the customers.[43]

Collector of the customs, Sir Thomas Dawes [2 *words illegible*].

Order from the committee:

1. Read the names then thereafter what be desired directions.

Mr. Green[44] said that we have to deal with wise men and potent men. It were fit to proceed warily and first to consider which will be best: to send for them only that are now customers or else to begin with those who were the customers the first year of the King. It will be first fit to consider upon what heads to proceed, and in what order.

1 head will be to take their accounts. The difficulty of every business is most in the beginning – *dimidium facti bene coepit* [*illegible*].

Question to be asked – what they have received in such a year, what in such a year. And if we are not satisfied upon their answer then we may send for their books. First let them bring their patent in.

Mr. Treasurer Vane said the first thing you are to go upon is to send for the parties themselves before you send for Toomes,[45] otherwise it will give them ground [f. 83] to say that you seek not offenses but offenders. I speak it not to prejudice your business but to advantage it. If when they come you shall find they double or prevaricate with you, then you may send for Toomes or any whom you think fit, and in the meantime you shall do well to take all the information you can and consider what questions you will ask them: what receipts, what payments, what defalcations. Mr. Toomes, surveyor general of all his Majesty's customs and impositions upon trade.

Sir James Bagg, Sir Dudley Digges, Sir John Hosen were sharers in the customs.

[*27 February 1641*]

[f. 7v] MAYNARD. Our *esse* is to be taken into our consideration before our *bene esse*.

At the committee upon consideration they resolved not to treat with any obnoxious or likely to be. They applied themselves to the most popular men who expressed a great deal of forwardness and alacrity, but they met with this difficulty and obstruction: they found a distaste in many to the Scotch commissioners for men's papers lately set forth, said HYDE.

These papers had a different operation like they find, MR. HAMPDEN claims.

So then was it [*2 words illegible*] when they lend and some worthless [*4 words illegible*].

MR. TREASURER. We are met for the public and therefore let us not fall upon particular animosities, one upon another, or divert us. It becomes wise men to apply themselves to their end and as much as in them lies to avoid all matters in their way; how all end we may differ in the way to them.

There was much heat about the Scotch paper matter.

[f. 8] HAMPDEN said that the part that was set for our debate we have receded from and fall upon a paper,[46] a paper that we know not from whom it comes or who will avow it, and if it be avowed and there be just cooperation in it, it will most properly come to us from the commissioners. That we have referred the treaty to them and we cannot take cognisance of it; but coming in this way if either the Scotch commissioners will avow the paper or not; if they do, it must come by the lord commissioners.

SIR G. GERRARD.[47] Wise men have ever to do with the time present and the time to come. [*9 words illegible*] It is reformation in me to/

Hampden told Hyde when he asked him about episcopacy that we are all of a mind in desiring what is best.[48]

[f. 8v] SIR BENJAMIN RUDYARD.[49] I care not how long the Scots stay. I should only to make a thorough light to see where they are and where we are. Exception was taken at the lords' papers for putting them in the Upper House. The wiser sort inclined would have it taken as not, comes from the head but as a slip of the sense.

Great dispute about committing the Scots' paper.

MR. HAMPDEN said that our sense were consistent, that we all desired all expedition to be used, that there was nothing but in what words to put this sense of ours, and this only we may refer to a committee.

HAMPDEN said cause was conceived, there was no difference in substance. The substance might be voted and leave the putting it into a form to a committee.

[1 March 1641 ∽ Afternoon][50]

[f. 82v] Queries to the customers:

1. Asked Sir Job Harby[51] whether he were one of the farmers or collectors. He said he came in '38 into the great and petty farm for 3 years.

[2.] What is the great and petty farms? The great farm is the subsidy.

[3.] What is the petty farm? Ans.: The petty farm is only for wine and currants. That is the 3l. upon the tun of French wine and upon currants.

Partners with him: L. Goring, Sir Abraham Dawes, Sir John Jacob, Sir Nicholas Crispe and Sir John Nulls.[52]

[4.] What constant rent did you pay? We agreed to pay for/

[f. 81] Let us propound some method in our proceedings. The first thing to be taken into consideration will be the matter of fact, the next the abuses.

Monday, March 1, 1640

1. Required by Sir Job Harby an abstract of the whole last year's receipt from Dec. '38 to Dec. '39.

The subsidy of London inwards, 90 thousand one hundred pound. The subsidy/

Sir Job Harby said that the advance out of his own stock 20,000l., and was engaged for the King two hundred thousand pound.

Particulars of the present state of the farms advanced to the King's use so much. So might/

Sir Jo/

Sir Paul Pindar told us that they gave the King at one time 10,000l.; to L. Treasurer Weston, 1632, 3,000l.

For wines given to several persons at Christmas 1,000l. and or part.

[f. 80v] Sir John Suckling, Sir William Cooker, Sir Ralph Freeman, Sir William Acton.[53]

The matter lies in a/

For rewards given away at Christmas 62,000l.

[Illegible] petition against Mr. Lad.[54]

[f. 82] The great farm 165 thousand. For the petty farm 65 thousand. Upon an offer of 15,000 made by Sir Paul Pindar and Sir John Harrison[55] they agreed to the same increase of rent, 7,500 upon the old.

And then you are so careful that you keep book of all your receipts.

Required to bring an account of their particular receipts; therefore bring a total of all your receipts. Have you not any abstract or breviat of your rate book? You do not act your business at random, I conceive. What impositions are there (1) upon the pretermitted customs, the pretermitted customs in London? Sir John Jacob's revenues.[56] There is an impost upon lead and some other thing which Sir John Wolstenholme[57] receives. Upon silks inward, Mr. Edward Abbot[58] has. Lord Goring[59] has the impost of tobacco.

[f. 81v] What was the profit you made above your rent? You are so provident that you kept an exact account.

Sir Paul Pindar said that he has been a farmer under several grants, his first grant being the first year of the King, 1625.[60] He held it by a verbal contract for a year. Afterwards had a grant under the Great Seal; he took that farm for 8 years. He further said that Sir Abraham Dawes and one [illegible][61] raised the book of rates.

[Illegible.][62] Whether you or any to your knowledge made any representation to the King that some commodities would bear a higher rate than others.[63]

[Committee for Irish petitions.]
[f. 77] Londonderry business.[64]

It appeared there was a decree in Star Chamber for the taking away of 5,600[l.] per annum, which the City had improved from nothing to that value, upon pretense of breach of trust and covenants, as not planting.

Londonderry. It lies in the north part of Ireland; it seems to have been a desolate barren place. The City were importuned and pressed to it. There were these inducements to persuade them to it. That they should have granted to them the whole county of Coleraine, should be granted unto them [sic]. It was told that there was but 2,000l. expected of them; after, 13,000l. more. This was after passed by parliament upon a particular. They devided this country into 12 proportions according to/
They built two towns, Coleraine and Derry.
[f. 76v] They built, they planted, they fortified, they settled preachers.

[4 March 1641 — Afternoon]

[f. 89v] At the committee for lieutenants.
Sir William Russell's business was agitated, where I observed much [illegible].[65] The complaint against him was for being a reputed papist and adhering to the Roman party. The petition likewise charged, under pretence of pressing 600 men there were mustered 3,000 and the rest discharged for bribes to his servants and dependents.

[f. 89] For the first charge the committee acquitted him and conceived it rather a certainence to make his other charges have a sweet passage.

Dutton, that was for him, desired it might be asked whether there were not two that petitioned [that were] papists themselves. It was likewise moved for his advantage that all that had not been present at every day's debate might not give their voices.

Divers witnesses were read to show that he had not been at church, at his parish church, but it was alleged that every witness in the affirmative was worth twenty in the negative. Another said that for his charity it might possibly with some render him more suspected, but being directed and applied to ministers of the Protestant religion it was conceived it might free him of all suspicion. There was much skill used to frame the question so as to make it a common case with other deputy lieutenants thereby to engage them for him.

[5 March 1641]

[f. 79v] Turkish Pirates.

It was much urged that the King should for the setting out 6 men of war for the taking Turkish pirates which, being called for the question, that which was considerably said and objected against was by MR. SELDEN, who said that we could not move the King in it without control and limitation; for how will it appear that are pirates without legal conviction? It is as with felons' goods by land. Then how do we know how the league stands between this kingdom and the Grand Seignor, which would be first known. This business stirred from a letter from L. Admiral importing the infesting the western coasts by Turkish pirates.

PYE.[66] Secretary Coke['s] course was to consult with his own experience and reason together with the masters of the Trinity House; whether with the masters of the Trinity House in business of the navy.

[5 March 1641 – Afternoon]

[f. 10] Fen Business.[67]

78 thousand acres in Lincolnshire. 5s. an acre imposed on the owners, afterward 13s. 4.

A letter from the King to pay this tax. If they did not pay it then the land was to be assessed by the undertakers. The pretence was the public good and to meliorate these lands.

11th of the King the Earl of Lindsey is the sole undertaker. They have engaged great men in their business and made them parties. They had got letters and orders of the Privy Council. They have made commissioners those which were sharers.

[6 March 1641]

[f. 9] Committee for the Earl of Strafford.[68] MR. WHITELOCKE made the report.

They think fit not to put in any replication in writing but to finish the proofs *una voce* and to manage them by members of their own; and desires a conference concerning some propositions and circumstances tending to the business. Therefore HAMPDEN moved that some few might prepare the materials and heads and particulars of this conference, which were voted should be that there might be convenient place appointed for the members to be at the trial, [and] witnesses. Some contemplate to exclude strangers; they are not so much engaged and interested in the good of posterity so much as other men are. They are not acquainted with the/

TREASURER. We cannot apprehend suddenly the consequences and prejudice of a specious proposition.

[8 March 1641]

[f. 78v] It was moved to go speedily to a conference with the Lords concerning the Scots' last army. Some[69] would have the proposition for to disband the Irish army to go along with it.

MR. TREASURER said that while we sought to grasp both we should lose both. I think both do crave necessity; but whether you will do it presently, I shall leave it to your consideration.

CONTROLLER.[70] I conceive the matter in doubt whether the message that was ordered for this morning should go single or not. If it goes up single it will give this occasion to see clearly whether or when the Scots will disband while there is an army within our bowels, whether it will be so.

Having my pressing; the disbanding of the Irish army I'll leave to you. I believe if a business can be put off there is a great advantage gotten by them that are against it.

[Afternoon]

[f. 11] At the committee for gunpowder.[71]

The statute of purveyance gives 10d. a mile. When the commission was touched upon Mr. Treasurer said he would have no blast laid upon the commission till the King's counsel were heard.

Let us not loosen all at once. A warrant by Secretaries Vane and Windebank for the commitment of this Mr. Vincent expresses no cause and is against Magna Carta and the Petition of Right.[72]

The lords of the Council have no power to lay tax or charge upon any man.

Mr. Coke moved that it is against the order of the committee for any man that is concerned should be present at committee. And I conceive Mr. Secretary Vane should withdraw.[73]

He[74] answers that truly Mr. Coke has moved that which I myself would have moved. Here is only a complement, and not so fully moved as I conceive may give just satisfaction. I am a member of the House. It may be my case today, it may be gone tomorrow; but I shall withdraw.

When the committee were going [f. 11v] to show their opinion for reparation upon the lords of the Council for the ten pound cost against him,[75] Mr. Bridgeman desired the order of the House might be read, which it seemed it gave not powers large enough.

Mr. Bridgeman, after the order was read: Truly this order is very large but I conceive it touches not the lords of the Council; by which he got off Secretary Vane.

Bridgeman. There are some cases when the lords of the Council may commit, but it does not appear whether they did it as councillors or commissioners. If they did it as commissioners it is, I suppose, not justifiable.

Sir John Heydon,[76] being asked why foreign gunpowder was prohibited, he answered, because that the powder should not be adulterated.

Why should men be restrained from having as much as they would? He answered: because there were warrents from [f. 12] the lords that there should not issue out powder without a warrant out of the King's magazine; for is there no danger in the lying of so much powder in one place?

Sir John Heydon said that the Tower was conceived the fittest place because of the walls and strength of the place. It was once advised to send a good quantity to Portsmouth because of the fortifications there and garrison, and so not so subject to any practice that might be attempted by an enemy.

Charged upon Sir John Heydon that he should say that he had brought all the gunpowder of the kingdom into the King's magazine, not to be issued, so, he hoped, to get the arms of the kingdom into the King's hand. Confessed by one of his servants.

[f. 12v] That the pike makers should bring in 1,500 arms a month for foot, so many for horse, and so many muskets into the Tower.

[9 *March 1641 – Afternoon*]

[f. 80] Sir Henry Herbert and Serjeant Wilde's business. [77]

SPEAKER said: The business lies in a narrow room, being matter of fact. Did you strike the serjeant or not? Clear that point first, whether there was a committee sitting or not.

One witness being examined was asked him upon what occasion he came thither. What condition are you of? Speak your whole knowledge of the matter and the circumstances.

[9 – 10 *March 1641*]

[f. 78] [MR. CREW.] Report from committee. [78]

Heads: 1. Legislative and judicial power in parliament; judicial power in Star Chamber.

2. The commission. The sole power in ecclesiastical things in matters of sole ordination.

[3.] The work of the great reverence of deans and chapters, and the little use of them.

Habits are attained by frequent repetition of the like activities.

[10 *March*]

MR. BRIDGEMAN moved that some might be heard of the other side.

GLYNNE. The point now in agitation is secular employment, and therefore let us apply ourselves to that.

Aiming at drawing things in length they moved in the 2d place for to have the House turned into a grand committee. [79]

[MR. BAGSHAW.] Abbots had anciently voices in parliament as well as bishops. It is inconvenient for the commonwealth, it is inconsistent with their spiritual function.

[MR. WHITELOCKE.] The 3 estates is the King, the Lords, and Commons. Whether the legislative power/

HAMPDEN. Convenient that the word "inconvenient" had too much alloy in it. That for inconvenience to make so great a mutation in the state and therefore disliked that word, prejudicial to the commonwealth.

[f. 13] [ANONYMOUS.][80] They have not that to be engaged in the good; they have not that provocation to be interested in the good of posterity or others by reason they are but tenants for life. Then it is again, they understand not the commonwealth in relation to foreign states so well as others that have seen and travelled in foreign parts. But above all things if we do any and weigh the ground of all our present dissensions they flow chiefly from the fountain of life.

I must confess it is better to prevent the blow than after we have received it to cover our bodies. And I think it is heard we had frequent parliaments, we should have prevented things before they had come to this pass.

[f. 13v] It was the Bishop of Ross that in the late Queen['s] time by his counsel brought the French into Scotland. It was the counsel of a bishop that brought the Turk into Hungary, the event which counsel was dismal, for in one battle the King and most of the nobility and gentry were slain and the whole kingdom lost. These examples together with our own experience is sufficient to exclude forever from being counsel in this kingdom.

The objection that I find sticks with many is the/[81]

It may in the/

MR. JOHN/

[f. 77v] March the 10, 1640, Ash Wednesday.

Resolved on the question that the legislative and judicial power of bishops in the House of peers in parliament is a hindrance to the discharge of the spiritual function, prejudicial to the commonwealth, and fit to be taken away by a bill; and that a bill be drawn to that purpose.

Time and place are servants to occasion.

[15 March 1641]

[f. 14v] Mr. Speaker,[82] that Sir, which you heard in debate the last day we met in this place consisted of two parts; the one was the disbanding of the new Irish papist army of papists; the other was the increase and enforcement of the old army. For the first, if it be fully settled I shall not speak in it; but as I remember there was an objection made that it was not fit presently to disband this new army till we saw the full issue of the treaty between us and the Scots. Truly, Sir, if our brethren of Scotland should give us occasion to alter that style, I am of opinion, Sir, pardon me if I am in an error, that we cannot put a stronger weapon into the Scots' hand than to put arms into papists' whether English or Irish. For consider, Sir, what zealousness and animosity there are between [f. 15] the two religions. They cannot serve together without distracting and dissettling affairs. Instead of being a strength and advantage are both to/

For do we not all remember the last summer, what distractions and distastes it bred? Did we not hear of evil and execrable murder committed from our bowels?

I am sure we had part of a town fired by papists, and if you examine the occasions you will find the disorders arising most frequently from that ground.

Now truly, Sir, I must tell you my opinion clearly. I am one of those that apprehend a great deal of danger in the disbanding of this Irish army if it be not done with a great deal of care and caution. Therefore, I am for the reinforcing the old army in such a proportion as this wisdom of the House shall think fit, together with that I shall humbly propound somewhat further: that order be taken that all muster rolls of that country be carefully perused and that there be a supply of defects of men and munition. Thus if the sounder part [f. 15v] of the country be joined in a key dependency with the army it will be a double advantage, for it will be a means to secure against any foreign force as also to secure upon any sudden accident that may arise from domestic practice. Let us not, I beseech you, Sir, rest longer in generals, particularity must bring things to speedy execution. Therefore, I beseech you, Sir, let's have a free conference with the Lords that so things without long delay be put in execution.

[f. 16v] A message from the Lords that the House of peers did desire a conference concerning Earl of Strafford's trial and some circumstances concerning that business, presently if/[83]

JEF. PALMER said that was not only the statute 1mo of the Queen that the High Commission/[84]

But they grounded their proceedings upon the King's prerogative [illegible] pretending the same power to be in the King which the Pope usurped. Therefore desired that a committee might consider of this vast and uncertain power and to have it limited to a certainty.

I am one of the meanest of them that offered to engage myself for 1,000[l.],[85] mine was upon condition that the London m[ayor] and aldermen would to give in themselves.

Mr./

[f. 16] Business about removing Queen's servants.

When SIR JOHN HOTHAM would have that head of the conference with the Lords concerning the papists about the Queen's person, and that we should take it up at another time, HAMPDEN said: Truly I agree with that noble and worthy gentleman that last spoke that to incline to moderation and that certainty is the best way to crave our purpose, but under his favor I must crave leave at this time and in the way to crave to differ from him. For we are now in parliament and here are to consider what [are] the laws of the kingdom. We sit here to see the laws observed, not broken.

DIGBY. Sometimes the timing of things are as prudential as the things themselves. Let us consider whether we are in a state to war with France in case they should quarrel with the articles. I am not against the doing it, only whether you will do it at this instant or rather go up with the other heads.[86]

[f. 16v] [MS. torn] Let's not lay the burden upon the freest horse.

[16 March 1641]

[f. 17] About the Queen's servants.

The timing of things might be governed by occasion.

For a past foundation to go upon, MR. HOLLES propounded the statute to be read concerning the Articles of the treaty upon the marriage.[87]

MR. PALMER moved the thing might be declined till the point of law be cleared.

Great debate whether statute or Articles[88] should be tendered.

SIR FRANCIS GERARD[89] would have the statute first as covering, that would give us most light to conduct us.

TREASURER VANE. We shall but lose our wind unless we know the paper be an authentic copy.

HAMPDEN introduced a copy out of the record of the Lords House signed by the Clerk's hand.[90]

[17 March 1641]

[f. 17v] The business of the navy.

TREASURER said it was a business of great consequence to the whole kingdom and therefore moved for the turning the House in[to] a grand committee that by freeness of debate we might grow to some ripeness of resolution.

[Committee of the Whole House]

Vane.[91] I am glad to see so general an inclination and sense in this House to speed this business. There is ne'er a prince in Europe that these last twenty years has not increased in shipping.

1. This to be taken into consideration would be: what proportion of ships would be fit for a guard, then how to raise the money.

Last year there was 20 ships for the summer guard and 5 for the winter. Lord Admiral has intelligence that the French will set out 80 ships. 20 ships for 8 months will come to 80 and five thousand pounds. Propositions made to have ships of divers sizes and capacities, some are fit for commerce some for use. The lesser size was co/

[f. 18] Propositions made for 80 thousand pound for setting out 20 ships for 8 months. 8d. ob. per diem[92] a man was called a reasonable proportion. To speak with butchers, brewers, graziers, fishmongers and to find out the rates of things.

Treasurer Vane. Let this be one first step. Let that point be cleared what Sir William Russell[93] will advance for this service. The amount that the arrears was so hotly called upon for the last year's setting out that he could not, unless there might be such assignations made to him of such monies as came in as might be a foundation for his credit to go upon.

Sir Henry Vane went so manly to work as he brought his answer in writing and not by words. [2 words illegible] contra.

I should be glad to bring you home to the point. For Sir William Russell, I would not have [7 words illegible].

Moved for [the] committee to talk with Sir William Russell and others, as the men of the Trinity House. It appeared by that there was 120 thousand pound assigned for the King, his Queen, and children's daily maintenance.[94]

[f. 73v] 1640 March 17

Committee for to take into consideration the Scots' paper about the great straits and necessities of the kingdom.[95]

To comply with the necessity of the kingdom we have granted 6 subsidies. This stock is almost spent and the business of the conference would be to consider of a way and means to raise monies and to consult with their Lordships how to rid the kingdom of this vast charge that lies upon us, and that there may be no inconveniency fall upon the kingdom whilst the treaty lasts by either army.

There is 120 thousand pound left of the 6 subsidies. The House of Commons is very sensible and have used their best endeavors by granting subsidies, there has been no stone left unturned, [no] ways left untended that we could possibly think of for the raising monies, but could find none.

[f. 73] The urgency of the occasion. We desire their Lordships' counsel and advice in this great exigent for the safety of the kingdom.

[Afternoon]

[f. 75v] March 17, 1634 [sic]

Committee for monopolies.

One John Browne[96] complained of for having the sole making of iron pots, pans, contrary to the statute of monopolies, 21 *Jacobi:* [1], that he engrossed all the iron; 2ly, that there is an inhibition of import; 3ly, that the price is much raised, as appeared by enhancing the price suddenly upon the patent from 16s. to 23s. the ton.

Thick pots require more fire to heat them, more labor to carry them off and on than [one] thinks, which it appeared to be better [2 *words illegible*].

I was then told by one that had been a dealer in iron kettles that he observed in casting of iron pots the metal which grew thin was finer and lighter than those which were thick in the molds when cool.

[18 March 1641]

[*Committee of the Whole House*]

[f. 18v] [Sir Henry Vane, Jr.] Upon speaking with Russell, certain in committee met and it was expressed from Sir William Russell that he could not advance present money, but that he would give his credit as far as his credit would go.[97]

Treasurer Vane. Let's state the particulars whereupon we shall go by steps. 6,000*l.* is presently necessary, and whether Sir William Russell will presently supply this 6,000*l.*

I am glad we are come to so timely an issue of what is of great comment to the state. This way by Sir William's credit and Sir John Harrison's[98] advancement of twenty thousand pound[s] present money we shall provide for all and come to all our ends. You see a ground work for the speeding of this business. The greatest stop lies in preparation of victuals. The greatest question which will arise in this business will be whether you will go by the great by contracting with the victualer or make provision of yourselves.[99]

[f. 19] The *Triumph, St. Andrew,* [*illegible*], these are of the middle rank. The number of men that will man these ships are 1,500 and 5 men. The Trinity House masters called in to the committee for this.

Treasurer said 1,500 and 5 men you shall have, of which the rate of 8d. ob. a man, and you shall have half in hand and the other when your works at an end.

Treasurer. Upon proportion 3*l.* and a noble a ton a month, thus stands the state of our business. They are to set out 10 ships. They shall have 8,000*l.* in hand, the rest when these ships return.

Freeboaters are those that infest our coasts. They come with oars and small guns and set upon our ships on our Eastern and Western coasts.

Treasurer. Here is shortly the issue of the business. We can make no contract with you here. We can only prepare the contract and report it to the House. You see upon what disadvantage we are brought by not timing of things earlier.

[f. 19v] Hampden. Give the business all the advantage there the business will possibly bear. Your part is to see the victuals about which we expect in 5 weeks.

Sir John Heydon called in.[101] He was asked what number of ordnance would serve for these ships respectively. Then the names of the ten ships were read him and the names given.[102]

Let's consult a little with these Trinity men's experiences – how we may husband things to best advantage. Where their own interest is not concerned it is likely they will deal clearly with us.

The Lord of Northumberland represented to the committee that a number of forty ships would be necessary. He desired therefore that number might be perpetuated.

The result of all our debate rests upon these heads:
1. That 11 of the King's and ten of the merchants' [ships] shall presently set out. These to be set out by Monday come 6 weeks. [f. 20] The time of continuance, 6 months. To set this work a going you have had Sir William Russell['s] forwardness expressed upon the credit of the subsidy or the bill of tonnage and poundage.[103]

I am sure that when we have made so good a step into the business it should now fall into the grand/

[19 March 1641]

[f. 76v] MR. WALLER being against the bill of drawing down of usury said that no man's heart went more with the bill than his, but only for the time. That whether now it were fit to pass such a bill.[104]

Therefore moved that some merchants might be sent for and advised with whether it would not be as prejudicial to trade, which was the only way to choke and fail the business, they being most of them lenders.

[f. 75] Concerning the relief of the northern parts.

[SIR HENRY MILDMAY.] 1 step of our proceedings would be to consider what arrears there are. By the 16 of April we are out of purse more than 6 subsidies come to.

Mr. Treasurer[105] said we have a great work and a short time, it will behoove us therefore to husband our time.

Consider first how you stand with your money. You have passed 6 subsidies, the 4 you estimate at 40,040 thousand pounds. Let us consider how much of this money is gone. For the remainder you have the credit to go upon.

Treasurer said to time and method things will be fit. To think how we may comply with the charge and to keep all settled and quiet till the 16 of April and that after that we may see to the end and bottom of our charge.

[f. 74v] Therefore moved to have conference with the Lords and let them know upon what straits and necessities we are reduced for money and to desire their helping hands to get out of these difficulties.

[20 March 1641]

[f. 80] Lord of Strafford['s] petition debated;[106] whether to read not being he had not set his hand but being attested by Mr. Holles to be his hand. The desire was that he might have leave to have some members of the House to be examined as witnesses at his trial: Sir Thomas Jermyn, Sir Arthur Ingram, Sir William Pennyman.

I observed Treasurer Vane though fiercely against him was much for the reading it, meaning thereby to show his own moderation.

So I observed Sir Nathaniel Brent being examined upon what concerned the Archbishop's case, knowing there was weight enough upon him, he chose wise on the moderating himself and yet advantaged the bishop nothing thereby.

[f. 21] Monday, March 22, 1640[107]

[Trial of the Earl of Strafford]

At the coming first to the bar he kneeled, afterward stood above an hour till sat upon chair.[108]

Earl of Arundel began.[109] My Lord of Strafford, the Lords have called you this day to answer to the impeachment of the Commons of England whereby you are charged of High Treason. They are resolved to hear judicially and with indifference to your answer, and first you hear the articles against you.[110]

After the articles were read, his answer.

Then Arundel told him: I do not know whether with your Lordships [you] may speak, or how.

Lord of Arundel said that the House of/

[Afternoon]

[f. 73] Earl of Bristol at a conference with the Lords[111] told us that the Lords had commanded him to let us know how forward and willing they should be to any thing that might conduce to the settling of the great distempers of the kingdom; that they had taken special notice of the great case of the commonwealth by the House of Commons which no age could parallel in their lending monies and giving security by their own persons; that in this great exigent for money it was thought by their Lordships that it was not the granting of subsidies that would open credit by the settling of a firm peace, the doubts whereof [f. 72v] staggered men's minds and their fears of unquiet times made them keep their money in their purses.

[f. 72v] The Earl of Bristol told us further that their Lordships were agreed with the House of Commons concerning the disbanding the Irish army. The only difference was *sub modo*, they desiring to limit their joining with this condition: that the old army should be reinforced. That their Lordships were willing to join with us in anything that might remove those impediments that might give a stop to the loan of monies.

That they were resolved to see, as soon as possibly they could, the bottom of the Scotch demands and not to give them above a month, *non datum ultra*.

[23 March 1641]

[Trial of the Earl of Strafford]

[f. 22] [Mr. Pym.] We stand here to make good. We might sink under the weight of this great/

We have the sighs and tears and groans of the whole body of the people. We have the three kingdoms laboring to be deburdened of this mischief. There is no/

This Earl has/

It is the greatest basest of wickedness that it dares not be seen in its own colors. We have to take off the visors and masks and appearances of truth and goodness. [f. 22v] It was said in the proverbs of the woman, that she wiped her mouth and yet held her wickedness. For religion we shall say/

For habits are more perfect than acts because they are nearer to principle.

Deputy humbly desired to know why he might not take exceptions to the witnesses.[112] I do humbly conceive I [have] some occasion to except against him[113] for he was once sentenced in Star Chamber for a practice to take away his life.

Whether Sir/

One witness[114] being asked whether Sir George Ratcliffe entreated not once he put 500 horses upon him.

Deputy asked at what time this was done, and it appeared he was in England then.

[f. 23] Then the remonstrance being produced against him by the Irish parliament, which was read.[115]

[Strafford.] He said that things were claimed against him by faction. A conspiracy and practice and that all this storm rose upon him there since he was charged here of High Treason by the parliament in England.[116]

I desire justice against him, said Pym.

Mountnorris said he heard my Lord of Middlesex[117] tell Falkland when he was Deputy[118] that England had long enough nourished Ireland and that now they must live off their own milk.

[f. 23v] [Strafford.] My memory is exceeding weak and I am not versed in those proceedings.

To go in peace to my grave without any public employment whatsoever. I am in an unknown way and cannot answer suddenly but if you will give me leave to recollect myself.

Pym desired he might answer presently.[119]

[Strafford.] He answered that he desired he might not be surprised.[120] I shall never do otherwise than yield obedience to whatsoever.

The question is whether matter of truth or not truth in the preamble of his answer.

[f. 24] [Strafford.] He said he was against the increasing the book of rates. He said that he spoke it with all humility yet with all confidence. Then was 10,000*l.* debt owing from the crown, and when I came from Ireland there was 20,000 more left in the Exchequer which he had a care to lay out with all the advantage profits.

I will not dispute but obey perfectly in all things. The King's revenue was not able to bear the charge of the constant charge by at least 24,000*l.*

There is another thing which this noble gent[leman][121] has fixed upon, [it] is the misspending the King's money. He produced a letter of the King's own hand to show what the King on owing the loan of 4 thousand for [*illegible*][122]

[22 and 23 March 1641 – Afternoon]

[f. 71v] At a conference with the Lords Earl of Bristol told us that the Lords,[123] upon consideration, had resolved that [they] would join with us in giving security, but he made doubt whether that would do, for it was not the security the difficulty rested in, but the getting of the money. For the Lords, if money may be had, they are willing to join with us in giving particular security to such persons as shall advance monies and ourselves, for our indemnity, to countersecure ourselves by the security of the kingdom.

He told us that the Scots on Thursday would bring us their last demand and said there must be proportion of money to disband the King's army, a proportion of money for the Scotch army and a viaticum; and the Scots told him that when [f. 71] they were secured of what is promised, and when that was done, they should be ready to depart to their own homes at the day the parliament should prefix.

[24 March 1641]
[Trial of the Earl of Strafford]

[f. 24v] A drowning man will catch at any little narrow-hearted commissioner.[124]

That I have some heart, a little greater than to do any such thing. Unless I had the inspection of God it could not be laid to his charge.

The next thing was my cousin. The customs, he said, these were the same allowances or defalcations. Many men's mouths offend when their hearts do not.

You are in a court of honor which is a rule to itself.

[25 March 1641]
[Trial of the Earl of Strafford]

[f. 25] Robert Kennedy coming to be sworn. Strafford said that he had been sentenced for extortion.

Earl of Cork coming to be sworn.[125] He was very soon to speak what needs he must.

And it please you for my Lord of Cork, I conceive him no competent witness because there was an information exhibited in the Castle Chamber. He had it under his hand and seal. This appears by an information in *that he acknowledges*[126] that he is in the King's service and submitted himself.

Lord Digby s/

Lord of Cork said *made first a protestation* [that] when *he came over he had not the least thought* to accuse my Lord of Strafford, but after attested the words in the article.

Viscount Kilmallock[127] attested fully the words in the article.

My Lord of Strafford being then asked what he could say desires he might rest a little. [f. 25v] After study he said that he must stand *to what he has confessed in his answer*; as for other matters that come in *de novo*, it being not in *the charge*, I shall humbly offer *whether it be your pleasure I shall answer*.

He said that Earl of Falkland had as heavy complaints and was as much decried as any man except himself, yet afterwards cleared. Errors, I have had me. My heart has laid too near my tongue, I must confess. *I beseech you curl the case inward to yourselves, you will think it hard that every word should rise up in judgment against you and be cited.*

Lord Cork *to show for custom.* I should do very ill if I should do wrong to any of your noble progenitors; if I should think it otherwise.

[f. 26] *If you will take me in one piece* and *not take me all together,* which any man living may be convinced by his words; that therefore he desired he might be taken all together.

Deputy said that religion was increased [and] manufactories increased, to the great benefit of the town [of] Dublin since his coming over.

Glynne. You *shall find him like Jehu,* driving *on furiously* to an end. I will put *no sharp edge upon the business, then it will leave.*

When my Lord Ranelagh was brought to show that he had disposed lands by paper petition he[128] desired it might be asked by Lord Ranelagh whether he, being president of Connaught, may not practice the same in his government.

There can be no judgement construction of these words.

[Afternoon]

[f. 72] There was 3 things resolved after long debate with the Lords: the time, the persons, the sum. The time: Saturday in the afternoon. The persons: 8 of the Lords House, with such of the House of Commons as they should think fit.[129] The sum: 120 thousand pounds.

Bristol. That which would be first in our eyes and consideration would be, and that which we should apply our counsels and considerations to: to get a sum of money to facilitate. This he conceived, the removing of the obstacles and impediments, would be/

Secretary Vane said that in a consumption unless you cure the lungs it is no purpose to give all the physic in the world. We plant upon a rock, all will come to nothing.

Whitaker. He that makes himself a sheep, the wolf will devour him. Whether we go in a radical or legislative way.

[26 March 1641]

[Trial of the Earl of Strafford]

[f. 26v] Lord of Cork attested that upon an order at Council Board whereupon he was cited of possession, and witnesses punctually, what is charged in the 4 article.[130]

John Waldren proved the same words.

Whereupon Deputy desired to have him asked at what time these words were spoken and whether it was not upon question of church lands.

Upon his servants bringing him papers, counsel excepted.

Whereupon Deputy said, I hope these gentlemen will so *far compassionate me as not to press me* so fast on, but *that I may make* an humble and *modest defense.* I know how I have drawn his displeasure on me.

He desired that a letter might be read in nature of a certificate.

Maynard said it was a paper not directed to your Lordship but a *bare certificate* which we *know not* who will avow, *and if there* be any misdemeanor *in it* then is nobody *to be responsible.*[131]

[f. 27] A complaint of an order of parliament whereby all his trunks are sealed up, which he desired might be read; which was read.[132]

[Strafford.] I am a peer of this realm and here is as great a violation of peerage as ever was in the world.

He said the Council Board in Ireland was a Court of Record which does much difference it from England, and if I am guilty you must have a great herd of offenders.[133]

He produced a book of Baron Denham's to show the proceedings in former times.[134]

[Maynard.] A steward of a court is a judge in his divination, in his limits.

[Strafford.] If you grant me this as a ground, that church lands and plantation lands have been disposed constantly by the Council Board, I have fair weather with my Lords.

[f. 27v] Words have a limited type of question to be made treason by the 1 Ed. 6, ca. 12.[135] I shall not bring the words but truly I think I might speak the words and I trust the words have not so much sting and venom as to prejudice me. It were a heavy thing to punish a man for not being wiser than God has made him.

Mark, my Lords, L. of Cork, how *swift and quick and positive he is in witnessing the* formal *words of the article,* which shows how *prone he is to witness* against me. I'll say no more.

Earl of Strafford said that King James would say upon a reconciliation of parties that referred to him, when they would say they would [*illegible*] as far as honor and conscience would serve it, he would say that those things were always implied among persons of honor. He said that words may be saflier sworn to than ideas.

[f. 28] But I *pray note how my Lord* Kilmallock swears that my L[ord]— Sir George Ratcliffe, that he spoke of his echo, he that would set dear that truly for not [*illegible*] had it were [*illegible*] more, if your Lord had not pressed him.[136]

Waldren. I attribute so much to his testimony that I may urgently confess I might speak words tending this way.

Lord Audley being sworn at the Council Board and not at the bar gave his testimony in the place where he stood, that an act of state above the parliament, upon privilege as a Baron of England.

Maynard. *There is a fire which these words are but the smoke of, which is the malice of his heart.*

[March 27]

[Trial of the Earl of Strafford]

Lord Deputy made the King and Lords stay. My Lord Marshal said, my other Lord being late, Mr. Lieutenant, I pray be more careful hereafter to keep your hour hereafter.[137]

They began upon the 5th article concerning the Lord Mountnorris, his sentencing to death.[138]

[f. 28v] After the decree read Glynne, calling my Lord Mountnorris to witness, Earl of Strafford took exception, saying that he had a confession under his own hand to show him a great offender.
Glynne said that seeing/

December '35, Mountnorris said that Deputy summoned suddenly a Council of War by way of surprise and told L. Mountnorris [who] had no warning till overnight, he/

I think we must proceed against him as a mute.[139] Mountnorris desired he might have his charge in writing and that he might appeal by Council.
I told him I was misrepresented to his Majesty.

L. Deputy told him that he had rather lose his hand than he should lose his head, which was taken as a great scorn.

[f. 29] Deputy. I shall desire it may be asked him how long he was prisoner after the sentence.

When my Lord Dillon[140] was called as a witness Deputy said that my Lord Dillon was one upon whose integrity and honor he dared venture his life, but desires his testimony might be forborne lest he might prejudice himself.

L. of Strafford. Lord of Strafford said he would lose his right arm than Mountnorris should lose a hair on his head. He desired it might be asked L. Dillon whether he did not desire the Council of War not to look upon him no otherwise than as fellow councillor, and that he should not take the least offense at it.

Question: Did not my Lord Deputy after sentence thank him or not; whether did not deputy sit at the Board's end all the time.[141]

[f. 29v] L. Ranelagh attested that after he[142] had commanded Mountnorris to withdraw he told them he desired to be righted and that justice might be done him.[143]

Whether was it not delivered in a paper what they should say.

Deputy desired that Ranelagh might be asked whether I did deliver any opinion in the cause and whether I did not sit bare as a suitor, not as a judge.[144]

Thomas Denevill[145] executed by martial law. Witnesses to prove it were L. Dillon,[146] but he said only he saw a man hanged in the green on a tree.

Maynard. Desired to have it asked whether there was any cause expressed or not.

Maynard. Whether was not there some motion made to have him tried by law or not.

[f. 30] [Strafford.] I shall carefully apply myself to that counsel which was given me by the counsel at bar not to expatiate or make any excursion. That if I had been charged for felony this might possibly fall upon me. I desire my commission may be read.

After which he said that he exercised *his power with as much moderation as any governor preceding me* and *produced orders from my Lord Willmott,*[147] being general of the army.

He being called up said that they had martial always, since his memory. Willmott spoke with great respect to his judge, which was answered with very fine words on Strafford's part and he catched at words he let fall that Falkland and Grandison and Chichester once said my Lord had answered very nobly and done him a great *deal of right in saying that martial law is so necessary* in an army.

[f. 30v] That there had been orders made that there had been rebels executed it is not denied, but that there has been any executed in time of peace.

He would have had a book read of my Lord Falkland's, of proceedings, which they would not admit, being it appears not to be his hand nor a true copy.[148]

Maynard. Have you known any other executed by martial law than traitors and rebels?

Sir Robert Kinge said that he could not remember any since times of peace.

He produced a letter of the King's written by Sect. Coke.[149]

[Strafford.] You *must have discipline* or *something equivalent to it,* otherwise tis *impossible to govern* an army.

He produced a letter from himself and Council of War. He would not suffer his brother at the sentence of Mountnorris to give his voice, and sat bare himself all the while.

[f. 31] Deputy. I conceive, with all humility be it spoken, this sentence be given by *martial law.* I cannot *see how it can* be heightened to *High Treason or can have an complexion like it.*

He said that my Lord Mountnorris had so unsufficient a tongue as would provoke a saint. I speak the words in sobercy and truth.

He justified his hanging a man by martial law upon the practice of some general and said it was rather a diversion than a subvention of the law.

Who managed the business who sat there, but that was with his hat off, his style the more cunning and dangerous *for, mark it, that which would do my Lord Mountnorris any real advantage was kept from him. It could do him no good whether Lord Deputy sat with his hat on or off, but his presence* was the way to countenance the business.

[f. 31v] My Lord says he used a great deal of moderation, but why did he then surprise him? He was called overnight, he was put to answer in the morning.

[30 March 1641]

[f. 70v] At a conference with the Lords where the Lord Mayor and Aldermen came about loan of money.

Privy Seal told them that they had made entrance into a business at last meeting which he hoped we should now bring to a good conclusion[150] and said that the City had showed themselves ready in complying with the desires of the parliament with that alacrity and willingness as they could not but take notice of on their parts without singular comfort and assurance of the continuance of a good correspondency between the two [f. 70] Houses and the City.

Then Earl of Bristol said, seeing we have put our hands to the business let us now pull it up by the roots. If we can get them to take their security by the subsidies we will husband our own credits that we may have a stock we may be ready to give them upon a new occasion, but if they will insist upon it let us not break with them upon that point; and said that he would be as forward as any to be bound himself and desired the committee to signify to the House that they found an equal willingness in the Lords to join with them in giving their security.[151]

[1 April 1641]

[f. 71] [ANONYMOUS.] Mr. Speaker. The bill, Sir, that you have heard read unto you is a very good bill.[152] For if we look to the spring and wellshed of the present sad distempers this kingdom groans under they cannot, as conceived tis, be more properly be assigned to any one cause more than to some ambitious churchmen's busy meddling, or done of grievous men's own ends of who like them have their own function. Wisest counsel foresee things in their causes and present them before they break out further. For no man will deny, Sir, that it is *better to prevent the blow than after we have received the blow to cover our bodies and had we had frequent parliaments*, Sir, I am confident, [f. 70v] Sir, we shall long before this have prevented the prejudice that the commonwealth now suffers by from this cause; but better late than never. Therefore, I humbly desire, Sir, this bill may be committed where all things concerning it may be more maturely considered than sudden thoughts can suggest.

[5 April 1641]

[Trial of the Earl of Strafford]

Earl of Traquair,[153] being examined upon the 20th article, he said that Strafford said that the Scots' demands in parliament were a sufficient ground to put himself in a posture of war.[154]

Strafford said that the examination in writing where there was examination *viva voce*, the first was but preparatory.

Earl Morton's examination read.[155]

Strafford desired he must be cross-examined.

He then said Morton said that he was present at York the night before the meeting of the Great Council of the peers of England [f. 32] and heard the Earl of Strafford; that the Earl of Strafford said to the King that the unreasonable and exhorbitant demands were a sufficient ground to make a war, then caused the Scots' ships to be seized.

Sir Henry Vane examined what counsel you heard given by L[ord] of Strafford about the war.[156]

[Strafford.] *It is good to understand the question clearly before I make an answer.*

I desire it may be asked him whether he did not, about the 5th of May, hear my Lord of Strafford give/

[Sir Henry Vane.] He answered, whether it was upon the 5th of May or not, but then or shortly after, I remember a defensive war was proposed by myself but my Lord of Strafford was for an offensive war, and that is all I can say to that point.

[f. 32v] Earl of Northumberland[157] said presently, upon the breach of the last parliament he advised his Majesty to go on vigorously in an offensive and not in a defensive war against the Scots.

Strafford desired it might be asked whether there was not divers others of the same opinion as he was.[158]

Maynard desired it might be asked L. Traquair whether it was not more than once that Strafford gave that advice, at what times respectively.

Bishop of Armagh's testimony read:

He said that in a discourse between him, April 1640, and the said Earl, he told him that in case of eminent necessity he [the King][159] might make use of his prerogative, but in his opinion he was to try his parliament first.

[f. 33] Conway. I desired it may be asked him when the army was raised.

When he asked Strafford how they should do for money in case the parliament should not succeed, what course should be taken then.[160]

Conway desires to see what he had sworn.

Deputy opposed it.

Palmer said that it was not offered by us to have it done, but desired by [the] Lord[s]; otherwise it might be mischievous to my Lord, for he might suddenly fall into a snare of perjury and entangle himself.

Strafford told him that 12 subsidies would do much towards the war.

Vane, witnessed. That if the parliament did not succeed he would be ready to help his Majesty[161] in any other way.

Sir Robert Kinge examined. He said that Sir G. Ratcliffe told him that his Majesty had an army of 30 thousand men and his sword by his side. No man would pity him [f. 33v] if he wanted money.

You may condemn the impeachment of my L. Strafford by what has fallen from his credence.

Sir Thomas Barrington. Words of Sir George Wentworth[162] to him: That the kingdom was sick of peace and *that would not be well* till it *were conquered.*

Earl of Bristol examined on the word said, it is very true that about a year since that/[163]

I should not tell the word and the coherents and subsequents, he may do himself wrong and *the party be* witness against.

I remember after last parliament speaking of the distractions and distempers that were; at that time I conceived the best way would [*sic*] to quiet *the distempers* would be to *summon a new* parliament, *and told him* to engage *the people* in a war, without it the success would be *very hazarded* [f. 34] *because* the people, the *many pressures* upon them, and they grew hopeless upon the breach of the parliament. He *said that Strafford* told him that the King's disaffection and *frowardness* of some partial men *had given the King advantage to help himself* other ways.

Bristol, I observed, seemed to speak as much to my Lord's advantage as the words would leave, and *said truly* he must needs say that my Lord seemed to acknowledge the truth of what he had said.[164]

Treasurer Vane being asked what words he heard the Earl of Strafford use before our sitting or after the last parliament, he said he must desire to give his testimony returning the words to this effect:

[f. 34v] *After the last parliament* it was *controverted and debated* concerning an *offensive or an defensive war*; said some, being of an opinion *your Majesty for having tried* all ways *and being refused* in this case of extreme necessity, you *may employ* the Irish army *for reducing* this kingdom.[165]

Lord Steward desired it might be asked Treasurer before whom these words were spoken and at what time.[166]

Earl Clare would have Vane explain what kingdom he meant.

Maynard. To doubt of these words were [to] doubt whether the kingdom were this kingdom or no. His Majesty might use his power *candide et caste*.

[f. 35] Earl of Strafford[167] *said that* to do all that *a man* can for himself *is a very natural* motion. He said for the words spoken to Sir G. Ratcliffe, that he was not *conceived in them* for he never *knew a man* contest treason by *letter* of attorney or proxy.

If words were taken single a man could not speak any *words but might* be *made treason. If you take not the antecedents* and *consequents as, for example, if a man should* say I'll kill the King as soon as go to such a place is, this is as much to say I will not do it.

[f. 36v] If I had not spoken the words, I had been perjured toward God; and for speaking of them I must be accused of treason afore man, an extreme hard case. Opinion may make an heretic, but opinion cannot make a traitor. Yet in the first case it must be joined with pertinency, otherwise not. They have sought narrowly into my house sickbed bound. Earl of Bristol would I were fetched out of my sickbed.

Strafford. Do not think me so considerable as this thing that concerns me can concern true kingdoms. I stand not here to dispute your orders but to obey them perfectly in all things.

Boni judicis est amplificare jurisdictionis. Though the Lord be the [*blank*] as the arms in the body politic, yet it is the commands that are as the hands and fingers.

[f. 36] He desired to examine witnesses to the 15 [article, part] 2; 13.5. Let us take heed how we wake these sleeping lions.

Then, *coming to Sir Henry* Vane's testimony, he desired their Lordships to observe *that first he said that he would* deal *plainly and clearly with their Lords*, somewhat a *strange clause and expression* when he *comes afterwards and swears* to his *best remembrance.*

Earl of Holland said that he looked upon the army as clouds, or rather as meteors which, if they should meet, would fire the kingdom.

[f. 35v] He said I have troubled your Lordships longer than I would, but for the pledges of a saint in the garden, and then either wept or made show of doing it.

[*10 April 1641*]

[f. 68] Some things contained in the paper found by young Sir H. Vane in his father's cabinet, being a memorial of some notes taken at the Council Board 5° *Maii* 1640 and imported to Mr. John Pym:[168]

[*Ink stain*] offensive war with Scotland England will rest long quiet, and you (innuendo the King) will in the meantime languish as between Saul and David. Parliament hath forsaken you, loosened from all rules of government. The levies of ship money to be vigorously put in execution. The City to be called in to lend money which two ways will plentifully furnish monies.

Then was letters [of] Cott[ington].

The Lower House are weary of King and Church. 5 months in a war-like way will reduce the kingdom of Scotland. Subversion of the law is the taking of the legislative power out of the place where it ought to be, as the parliament, and placing it in a wrong place, as the King's person or in other person/

April 12, 1641

[f. 69v] A letter produced by Alderman Pennington from the L. Mayor, who received it from Amsterdam, which they would not suffer to be read because there was no name to it.

TREASURER VANE said it was grown to great heights and would be fit to receive a timely stop that these writings without names should be brought in in this manner. Moved therefore that the L. Mayor should be speedily required to discover from whom he received this letter which, he said, was for the honor of the House; to hunt to the bottom.

Mr. Cogan, Secretary to Treasurer Vane, interrogated:[169] 1, whether he knew how many studies there were; 2ly, whether he had the command of keeping of one of them; 3ly, whether there were not two cabinets or more in either of the studies.

[f. 69] In what manner did young Sir Henry Vane come to him? He heard that young Sir Henry Vane had told him he had ord[ered] that upon any letter from the Treasurer for the sons as having the keys delivered him.
Quaere: Did young Sir Henry Vane ask you whether he knew the keys or not?

MR. GOODWIN moved that the Treasurer would declare whom the other persons were.[170]

[TREASURER VANE.] He desired to be excused and that he might not be pressed to it, for he said his own hands being busy he desired he might first see the copy that was wrote out and then we should do what became an honest man.[171]

[f. 68v] MR. MAYNARD informed of those particulars from the committee of Earl of Strafford.[172] To desire a conference over/

There be a narrative made of the evidence that was to be given on Saturday last to which end they resorted to the bar. 2ly, that the House having taken consideration hereof touching/
3ly, that the counsels might be deeply looked into and searched to the bottom.

SIR BENJAMIN RUDYARD. I do think that the Earl of Strafford is as a flagitious, a facinerous, as dangerous a man be, is most *ingeniosissime nequar*.

Some moved to have the Treasurers[173] [*illegible*] by the House to declare themselves by the words of himself who [4 *words illegible*].

MR. TREASURER. You see upon what straits I am put for you to request me to declare upon a copy of a paper that was written out of a paper-bound for you to make any accus[ation] [of] a peer of the kingdom before I have taken time to consider and recollect myself. You may send me to the Tower, and presently, if you will, but you shall not make me go from this resolution.

[14 April 1641 – Afternoon]

[f. 36v] At the committee for the bill for the attainder of the Earl of Strafford.[174]

Waller. We must make a difference between a breach of the laws and the subversion of the laws; as in the laws of God there is the breach of the law and there is the subverting it. Every man is guilty of the breach, but an introducing of a new law, as Mohammed, is a subverter of the law.

Bridgeman. About subversion. One kind of proof sufficient to prove a crime and another to prove a treason. The subversion of the fundamental law is a subversion of all the fundamental law, but I conceive he has not overthrown all the fundamental laws.

The parliament or legislative power in Ireland is different from the state of England.

Rudyard. Let's take heed how we suffer shipwreck in the haven.

[f. 37] Lord of Falkland. When I would judge of the probability of doing a fault, I would consider the nature and disposition of the man, whether a "flagitious facinerous"[175] or base mean spirited man. Some will rather commit treason than pick a pocket; some will pick a pocket rather than commit a treason.

[1 May 1641]

[Committee for the Forests].[176]

[f. 66] Mr. Peard, upon the debate about the Forest of Dean, said that Sir John Winter had undertaken not to sell any timber after such a time.

Mr. Palmer answered that the committee had it in consideration, the great sum he paid and the rent resumed upon his patent. Therefore conceived fit not totally to restrain but to limit him only to the point of ship timber.

Mr. Matthew would have all timber excepted for there was no timber but might be fit.

[f. 65v] Ordered that there shall be an inhibition to restrain all selling of timber until it shall appear to the House what is ship timber and what not.

[3 May 1641]

[f. 65v] Report of the King's speech, May [1]:

I had no intention to speak in this business in this day. The impeachment [*ink stain*] Strafford.[177]

MR. TOMKINS,[178] after long silence, said he was satisfied with High Treason.

Then MR. PYM told it would be necessary.[179]

MR. PEARD is ready for an oath of association.[180]

[MR. GODOLPHIN.] As I conceive you are not yet ripe for this committee.[181]

[f. 63v] Certified to the House:

Knights, citizens, and burgesses, the commons in the House of Parliament finding, to the great grief of our House, that the designs of the priests and Jesuits and other adherents to the see of Rome have been more frequently put in practice than formerly, to the undermining and dangers of the ruin of the true reformed religion in his Majesty's dominions established, and finding also there have been some having just cause to suspect that there still are, even during the sitting in parliament, endeavors to subvert the fundamental laws of England and Ireland and to introduce the exercise of an arbitrary and tyrannical government [f. 63] by most pernicious wicked counsels, practices, plots, and conspiracies and that the long intermission and the unhappy breach of parliaments have occasioned many illegal taxations whereupon the subject has been prosecuted and grieved and that divers innovations and superstitions have been brought into the Church, multitudes driven out of his Majesty's dominions, jealousies raised and fomented between the King and his people. A papist army levied in Ireland and two armies brought into the bowels of this kingdom to the hazard of his Majesty's royal person, the consumption [f. 62v] of the revenues of the crown, and treasure of this kingdom; and lastly finding great cause of jealousy that endeavors have been and are used to bring this English army into misunderstanding of this parliament whereby to incline that army by force to bring to pass those wicked counsels, have thereby thought good to join ourselves in a declaration of our united affections and resolutions and to make this ensuing protestation.

[f. 65] It cannot stand with any man's honor or discretion to take an oath and not know what it means.

MR. MAYNARD from the [*blank*] May 3d 1641.

According to your order and command the committee have resolved of a protestation:[182]

I A.B., in the presence of almighty God, do promise, vow and protest to maintain with my power, life, and estate to defend the true Protestant allegiance, and, according to the duty of my religion, the King, pursuant the lawful rights and liberties of the subject. And, to my power, by all good ways and means to bring to condign punishment those that they shall endeavor by practice or force to do anything contrary to anything contained in this protestation's contents. And that I shall endeavor in all just and honorable ways to maintain the peace and unity between his Majesty's kingdoms of England, Scotland, and Ireland and shall not for any fear, hope, or other respect be drawn from this protestation.[183]

[f. 64v] SELDEN and VAUGHAN said that there was no man's heart went more with the protestation, but desired might be referred to committee of the whole House.

MR. TREASURER. I am of opinion that this protestation is an oath to the end we aim at is unity. If you have every man that we may take the protestation in pieces and break it into parts and debate them throughly, those that have attained the pitch and highest pinnacle/

[f. 37] Mr. M. I do for myself make the same protestation.

I Will. Drake[184] do make the same protestation as Mr. Speaker has made before me really and sincerely.

[*Illegible*] to put men's hands into other men's purses begets others' malignity.[185]

[f. 37v] Mr. Speaker, I William Drake do make the same protestation as you have made before me according to all the [*illegible*] particulars contained of [in] the paper read freely and sincerely.

There are two things inconsistent which makes the difficulty: the furnishing present money and the avoiding doing it in an extraordinary way.[186]

[f. 39v] At the latter end of the preamble it is expressed that it is for the repressing and the better discovery [and] punishing [of] popish recusants. We have suffered no less of late time by superstitious innovators that professed themselves Protestants and therefore I desire it may be added "superstitious innovators" and "introducers of illegal ceremonies".

[f. 40] That it is for the "better discovery and punishment of popish recusants". Therefore, I shall humbly move that these words may be added after the words of "popish recusants": and other innovators and introducers of rites or ceremonies without an authority of parliament.

A bill for the taking the oath.

[f. 64v] May the 4th

Resolved upon the question that the sentence of the Star Chamber taken against John Lilburne is illegal and [a]gainst the liberty of the subject and also bloody wicked and well barbarous and tyrannical.[187]

Ordered that a letter should be sent to the army[188] and sent to the Lord General, Earl of Holland, and desire his Lordship's letter to be sent with this to make a right understanding to him at parliament.

[f. 64] [Letter of the House of Commons to the Army]

> Sir, we have had some cause to doubt that some ill affected persons have endeavored to breed a misunderstanding of the intentions of the parliament. To take away all misapprehensions [189] in that kind, though this in a general consideration tha[t] the distempers and distractions this commonwealth is groveling under is to be assigned to the plots and practices of the priests and Jesuits. Yet in a more particular notion and consideration we may well apply the distempers to the introducing of arbitrary and illegal enemies by some of our prelates.[190]

[f. 38] At a conference [with the Lords].[191]

The occasion of that conference was so visible as he should be brief in his relation.

3 particulars the King commanded him to declare: 1, the assembling in an unusual and tumultuous manner; 2ly, that finding a multitude in the palace yard they declared to them that they should have satisfaction.

Questions who chose the men, whether he was privy to the men by whose command he [illegible]. His Majesty commanded him to receive an 100 men under one Captain Billingsley, Coronet of a troop of horse under my Lord of Strafford in Ireland.

[f. 38v] 4° Maii

A petition from the City to have leave to make the protestation made by the parliament. Many were to give them free liberty to take.

MR. VAUGHAN conceived it very inconvenient; for he said that we might do that which was good and proper and what was in our power, but how we can in any capacity show an inclination to warrant them, it being a thing foreign to ourselves, he made a great doubt.

If a man should doubt whether he should receive his next half year's rent or whether he should be certain whether to receive his next crop or not/

What addition of advantage we may have for the present without foundations we may lay for the future.

[f. 62] May 5th

A letter read[192] importing strange designs and that the ordinary praying in the army was from the devil and parliament. Good Lord deliver us.

[f. 39] Mr. Speaker, I[193] conceive, Sir, the end that we all aim at in this solemn protestation we have made is to fortify [4 words illegible] and secure the reformed Protestant religion and the laws and liberty of the subject against any that shall ever by practice or force attempt anything against them.

Truly, Sir, seeing we have gone so far and the Lords have joined with us, I should desire, Sir, that we may endeavor to cause this protestation as general and universal through the kingdom as we could. Therefore, I shall humbly move, Sir, that, especially considering what aims there have been to corrupt the fountains of the kingdom, especially by the Archbishop of Canterbury, Doctor Laud, [f. 39v] I think, Sir, for the universality no man doubts it, but truly, Sir, his aims were upon the Inns of Court, too. And pray, Sir, give me leave for I think it upon this occasion my duty to tell you what I observed being once at the High Commission where there was one Mr. Barnard at that ti[me]./

We have had a conjunction of the Lords with us.

[f. 61v] May 5th

That the House has received such information as may give them just cause to suspect that there have been secret practices to draw up the King's army towards London, and therefore desire their Lordships to join with us in examining such witnesses.[194]

[10 May 1641 – Afternoon]

[f. 60v] [TREASURER.] Upon reading the Scottish paper Earl of Bristol made his close thus: told us they had signed the cessation.[195] So we see so good hopes of it, let us sit to the business and not let it go out of our hands until some be brought to some good conclusion.

VANE. It is judgment and equality that must preserve the reputation of this House. If we suffer every cobbler to heap up all good order by the heels/

The laws sit violently and suddenly. What have been made by the answer of the last? The business is to be tenderly and dealt withal yet so we have some fruits and effect.

[f. 61] TREASURER VANE. We cannot lay the charge upon the poorer sort and hope to have it paid; having laid this for a ground then we must consider how we may lay it upon the better sort of man.

Let's consider by what particular ways and means we may raise and levy this 7 hundred thousand pound. After you have provided this as a stock then the other considerations will be proved how.

That the great business of the Earl of Strafford has so taken up the time that it could have no progress.

[12 May 1641]

[f. 59v] [Dr. Bargrave.] We present all humble thanks to this House.[196] It is our disadvantage that we cannot apply our discourse rule. We knew upon weighty consideration of state the resolution was had.

Desired in a cause of so great importance they might have counsel speak for them.

We had/

D. Hacket. Our certain expectation that we should have been heard by counsel makes us come not so prepared as otherwise we would.

1. To the objection that they were useless/

1. God's house was called the House of Prayer. That the use of public prayer/

It is grown so full of art and tunes and music that man's ear [f. 59v] is rather ticked than God glorified.

Objection: This may be performed in other places. That in the more places God is worshiped the better, and in the more public manner.

Some have scandalized lecturers, it shows their ignorance. That there may be every Lord's day two sermons in every cathedral church and one lecture read elsewhere.

Wits begin to be so fanciful that [illegible] follow compendiums. Booksellers. In Ignatius's and Augustine's time there was everywhere assistance of presbyters to the bishop, confessed by Hacket.

It is the testimony of an adversary which is the best testimony. [2 words illegible] Aug[ustine] said that we preserve something of advancement to add a splendor and strength to their head.

[f. 58v] A civil kingdom delights not only in the sounds of drums and trumpets but in softer and milder tunes. You may look upon the colleges and cathedrals, they are not the enclosures but the commons of the republic. It is not every man's fortune to be an elder brother. He may if he use vigilance and industry better his fortunes.

That they had/

Some of one coat have committed foul and flagitious crimes as great and big as treason.

It is a snare to man to devour that which is holy. That great [*illegible*] and supporter of all the faction, the staff of their strength.

[13 May 1641 – Afternoon]

[f. 41] Sir Philip Stapleton coming from Portsmouth.[197]

I shall make you a short report:

Mr. [Henry] Jermyn came to Colonel Goring at 12 of clock at night in Portsmouth on Thursday night last and asked the governor whether he did not hear that he was charged with treason by the parliament.

2,000 barrels of powder.

300 soldiers [*illegible*] officers.

For Colonel Goring, him, we administered him an oath which he took chiefly that he should keep the town.[198]

[20 May 1641 – Afternoon]

[f. 42] At a committee of both Houses.[199]

Earl of Bristol began: 75 thousand a month it comes to. The purpose of our meeting is to treat and debate about the disorders of the army.

Let's state the particulars whereupon we shall go step by step. 1st consideration would be whether you have made an estimate or not. The sum is likely to rise to [*illegible*] the disbanding with. 430 thousand propounded as necessary towards this, in ready monies 420 thousand pounds.

1 proposition with Lords to get the Scots/

The result that arises from this point of the debate/

[f. 43] Bristol. I hope to make a proposition to you that will drive the business to some issue.

If we put them upon this dry hope that they shall have only their arrears I am afraid we shall advance little. For this being already due, it is to be conceived they will expect a viaticum.

Treasurer Vane. Let's clear this point, otherwise we shall spend a great deal of time and get not a step forward. They say it is objected very materially by my Lord of Bristol.

[f. 43v] That the whole arrear of the 120 thousand pound be presently paid to the Scots out of which the due debts to the counties are to be deducted, and for the brotherly assistance it shall be settled and fully secured unto them.

It shall be likewise settled by the kingdom unto the army that the deduction of the debts to draw more monies than the Scots can spare from the disbanding, that then the debt may be taken upon the kingdom and the whole 120 thousand pound shall be allowed them for their present disbanding.

[f. 44] Bristol. There must be an open and free dealing with them which will bring us home to our end sooner.

Hampden. There can be no prejudice suffered by making the propositions for the facilitating the disbanding; for we conduce a general sense of the House we should propound them.

Money has a magnetical virtue in it; it draws men's hearts and our hands after.[200]

[f. 45] May 22, 1641

Report from the committee of the customers by MR. HOLLES.[201]

He told them he could make them [a] broken and disjointed report.

There is the great farm, and the petty farm consisted of / The great farm was in the hand of Sir Henry Garway, Sir John Wolstenholme. They had a clause that they should be no losers, as if the profits should not come to 10 thousand, only some gain for their labor and hazards, the King was to allow them for it 2,400 thousand and odd.

3,000l. given to L[ord] Treasurer for a New Year's gift, 20 to his gentleman for his solicitor. They gave 8 percent for interest and gained 80 l. per centum by bribing great courtiers. [f. 45v] Sometimes they were foxes and went by art and fraud and cozenage; sometime[s] they put on the lions' skins and backed themselves with the prowess of all the great officers both of state and court. Nay, not so much as the servants of the Barons of the Exchequer's servants but were bribed.

TREASURER VANE. This is a very knotty, sticking point and therefore let's debate it thoroughly that we may find where the loss will fall.

[1 June 1641 – Afternoon]

[f. 46] Mr. Lisle's report.

June 1.

Committee of the Lords.

Debts since the 16 of October they would pay out of 20,000l. We have agreed through all the articles such conditions with this condition: Our agreement must not bind us up but with the assent of both Houses of parliament.

BRISTOL. There is one agreement suitable to this agreement. Draw you a formal cause, formal counterances [*sic*]. Let's in the meantime take what light we can by all ways. It is fit we debate and not leave it as a *individuum vagum.*

MR. PYM. The satisfaction in that point, an agreement of that now will destroy your work. Committee for reasons to the Lords.

TREASURER. What expedient will you find for this inconvenience? I'll propose the expedient I conceive will be proper.

[2 June 1641]

[f. 57v] SECRETARY VANE.[202] I was extremely startled at the answer of the City that they in these exigencies and straits/

I should rather expected that they should have done as the City of Edinburgh, that melted their gold chalice and their plate.

CULPEPPER.[203] If we leave not a stock of money, trade will fall and consequently lands and all other commodities. Therefore made a proposition for the bringing in and coining of plate.

HYDE objected. If you have the plate brought in will be ten weeks here we can have it made money, treasury being not able to mint above 20 troy a week.

[3 June 1641]

[f. 46v] Of dishes.[204]

Whosoever shall bring in his dishes, saucers, and trencher plates shall have 8 per cent and shall be allowed for every one after the rate of 5s the ounce.

To be brought into the chamber of London.

[4 June 1641]

[f. 46v] 24 bishops have dependence upon 2 Archbishops and they take the oath of canonical obedience. There is no reason that they should have legislative power, the lives, honors, and estates [of others] being but for their lives.[205]

[f. 47] Episcopacy.[206]

A committee for.

[MR. PIERREPONT.][207] 1. Because it is a "hindrance", or, as Hampden would have it, go up with their greater strength, he would have it "inconsistent".

2ly. Because they do vow at their ordination, not canonical obedience.

3ly. Because councils and factious canons deal all against their meddling in secular affairs.

4. They/

Time and usage is not convenient with lawmakers, for the abbots had votes but were taken from them by parliament.

L[ord] of Falkland would have it in the vote.

[7 June 1641]

[f. 57] Holles would have customers held to their agreement.

William Strode. Tale of the calf. I am totally of opinion that they ought to perform this agreement but if you [illegible] them beyond their ability you will fail of your end. There have been other propositions started, as that of plate.

[f. 56v] Greene preached at Aldgate; Nathaniel Robinson, Cantibes.[208]
A Garlick Hills The /
John Spencer preached at one Mr. Hericks.
If they had had presbyters /
MR. PYM. Baptism only. They had the spirit of prophesy.
Adam Bancks.

[f. 58]]ANONYMOUS.] Mr. Speaker,[209] there is one thing [2 words illegible] with me which truly I am satisfied in I cannot give my vote, which is if you take away this inconvenience from learning, as will be taken away I conceive, Sir, it will be necessary by a law to provide that there be not such a number of scholars as have been, for you do mark what inconvenience follows. The active part of life being in proportion to the contemplative had more scholars being bred than preferment can take of. You fill the state full of indigent idle persons and then if *sceler proclinis egesiae* (?) be true, then consider how much more dangerous [they] will be with the advantage of learning.

[f. 55] They have considered of remedies; the sole way is disbanding.

Bristol. They think fit to incite you to as much care as is possible. I am further to let you know that the Scotch commissioners told us at last meeting that it was well taken. They are very/

[9 June 1641]

[f. 55] Mr. Price and Sir William Widdrington's case.

Keeping his voice to the last VAUGHAN said it did not appear to him that it was an adequate offense in these two, if it were necessary to bring in lights. [210]

[f. 54v] In this strange discovery things of greatest importance would be first taken into consideration – the Navy. The islands next France, that they be put in a good state of defense and to see that the governors be sound to the commonwealth that the French may not have opportunity to practice with them. Then the Tower and City of London. That there may be a present course taken to see how the several counties of the kingdom stand provided for necessary defense and to make speedy supply of what defects shall be found.

[12 June 1641]

[f. 53] Report from the close committee. [211]

3 heads resolved on.
To preserve the bishops' votes; that the Irish army should be disbanded till the Scots/
To keep up the King's revenue to such a proportion as formerly gained.
It was a brisk letter but not wisely penned. [212]

[f. 67] [ANONYMOUS.] We cannot conceive how the peace can be durable in Scotland unless episcopacy be abolished in England. It were to be wished that there were a uniformity, but the alteration would be so great.

That the Houses of parliament have in consideration all things that they may conduce to the peace of the Church.

That his Majesty commands us to adhere to his former answer and wishes you to acquiesce therein. That none/

You might differ [in] what is just and what is prudentially and politically fit.

When I find general custom of [*illegible*] they too are apt to the passions of flattery and I should be glad to divest of all these humors.

Another question taken at them/

Mr. Cromwell for/
Let us keep all conveniency of defense.

[16 June 1641]

[f. 53] Goring's examination.[214]

Suckling said that Goring was fit to command in chief.

Davenant said the/

Capt. Chidley/

If there should be any rioting about London the Queen would come down to Portsmouth for her safety.

Strafford to Lieutenant: Without your connivance I know I cannot escape but if you will incline thereunto you shall have 2,000/

[f. 53v] Mr. Northcote's note:[215]

Mr. Attorney	15*l.*		
His man	8	15*s.*	0
Privy Seal and Privy Signet	16	3*s.*	4*d.*
Great Seal	64*l.*		
Striking tallies	22*l.*	14*s.*	0

[22 June 1641]

[f. 47v] Instructions given by the Earl of Montrose and other Lords in Scotland.[216]

He did but crumb bread for your own porridge.

[24 June 1641]

[f. 48] [MR. PYM.] 1 head.[217] The disbanding of the armies, 5 regiments for whom money is/

2 head. K[ing's] journey into Scotland. That his Majesty will allow a convenient time that the armies may be disbanded.

3 head. His Majesty's counsels and ministers of state: such as may be placed as are faithful. Great contributions of gold and silver.

4. The Queen.

5. The children.

6. Those that [*illegible*][218]

That the trained band may/

That the Cinque Ports may be grant[ed] into good hands. I shall humbly desire us to this head of the Cinque Ports you will join the islands that lie next to France to have care that they be in faithful hands and well fortified that the French may not [*illegible*] by practice or force to attempt to open them.

[f. 48v] About sending for a popish priest, Phillipps.[219]

TREASURER. I am in a great strait what to do. If you send for him you are where you were, and wise men look at some end in all they do. I desire we may go by the King or Lords to the King; heats on either side will not be for the good of the commonwealth. When we may go in a smooth, fair way let's not go in a rugged.

[f. 49] MR. PYM'S report, what the Lords do.

The course they have agreed upon is this: A letter to be sent to the committees by the Lord Keeper for the Lords and by the Speaker for us. Instructions from/

They are not without some matters correspondence here.

[f. 51v] Lord Privy Seal told us that their Lordships desire there may be a conjuncture of counsels and actions between the two Houses. The business of our now meeting we may consider in the first place, upon the points whereupon we shall go.

Bristol. We conceive it fit in the first place to make a dispatch by an express messenger that the King may not have it only by hearsay.

Now we are well to communicate our senses one to another.

NOTES

1. The King's speech is printed in full in the *L.J.*, IV, 142; see also Osborn fb161, ff. 26–28v. Concerning other versions of the speech see Notestein, *D'Ewes*, 279–280, nn. 11–15. Preceding the Speech in the MS. are several illegible marks.

2. The last two lines are written upside down in the MS. and are not part of the King's speech.

3. See George Peard's report from the committee of courts of justice, Notestein, *D'Ewes*, 281, n. 2.

4. The first five words of this day's entry may be Drake's excuse for arriving late. The remaining portion of the entry appears to pertain to the joint conference appointed this day with regard to the reprieve of John Goodman, priest. *L.J.*, IV, 146; Notestein, *D'Ewes*, 289–290. The statutes referred to are 27 *Eliz.* I, c. 2 (*S.R.*, IV, pt. 1, 706–708) and 1 *Jac.* I, c. 4, pt. 5 (*Ibid.*, IV, pt. 2, 1021).

5. On 29 Jan. the petition submitted to the House by London merchants concerning the use of gunpowder was referred to the committee for monopolists (chaired by George Peard) which had been ordered to meet on the following Monday (1 Feb.) at 2 o'clock in the Star Chamber, *C.J.*, II, 75. Drake's notes are undated; see also Notestein, *D'Ewes*, 299–300. The committee met again, probably on 8 March, see below, p. 24.

6. Mountjoy Blount, first Earl of Newport, had held the position of Master of the Ordnance since 1634 and Thomas Meautys held several government offices, among them that of Muster Master General. Aylmer, *King's Servants*, 231, 133–134.

7. I am following the D'Ewes Journal in placing the next seven speeches on 8 Feb. Notestein, *D'Ewes*, 335–336. Rushworth, *Hist. Collections*, IV, 183–184, dates them 9 Feb.

8. Two illegible and possibly crossed out words are interlined in the MS. following *know*.

9. In a marginal note Drake attributes the story of the hen to "Bacons *Ad.*, 258", although I do not find it in the *Advancement of Learning*. In the set version of the speech in Rushworth, *Hist. Collections*, IV, 184–186, the story is correctly attributed to Aesop. *Aesopia*, Ben Edwin Perry, ed. (Urbana, Univ. of Ill. Press, 1952), I, no. 58, p. 344, *Parr Aminta, Fabulae Graecae*. Drake desired to increase his familiarity with these authors. In his commonplace book Ogden MS. 7, no. 31 he includes the entry: "Read emblems, fables political, and Aesop's proverbs. Apothogems, speeches, letters, sentences out of the best historians ancient and modern; for fables read Aesop, likewise Bacon, *De Sapientia Veterum*, and fables in *Advancement of Learning* and essays with the application of various fables by Gregoire Tholosanus".

10. "Religion brought forth wealth (i.e., riches) and the daughter devoured the mother".

11. Fiennes' speech is included in various printed collections, see Notestein, *D'Ewes*, 336, n. 12.

12. Pleydell's speech is not included in the D'Ewes Journal. For notice of printed versions of the speech see Notestein, *D'Ewes*, 336, n. 14.

13. Pym's motion is not included in the D'Ewes Journal. Gardiner (*Hist. of Eng.*, IX, 281–283) indicates that 8 Feb. was "the first day on which two parties stood opposed to one another . . . on a great principle of action which constituted a permanent bond between those who took one side or the other". See also, Introductory Notes, n. 1.

14. The debate concerned the putting of the question of episcopacy. See Notestein, *D'Ewes*, 339–340.

15. D'Ewes does not include Palmer's speech in his finished journal but states in his rough notes (Harl. 164): "*Mr. Palmer no totall extirpation*". Notestein, *D'Ewes*, 342, n. 18.

16. An order allowing Denzil Holles to continue his suit against Cooper was made in the House on 10 Feb., *C.J.*, II, 82; Notestein, *D'Ewes*, 344. For the report on the case, 20 May, see *C.J.*, II, 152. Drake's notes are undated and may have been taken at a meeting of the committee for privileges. Concerning Drake's membership on that committee see Keeler, *L.P.*, 160, n. 221 and *C.J.*, II, 20. See also the Anon. diary (Yale 226), 10 Feb.

17. Treasurer Vane's report on the finances concerning the army was similar to Sir John Hotham's report this day from the committee for the King's army. See Notestein, *D'Ewes*, 344–345; *C.J.*, II, 82.

18. I.e., 37,500*l.* a month. See Notestein, *D'Ewes*, 344.

19. I.e., 12,500*l.* over in partial payment for the second month. Notestein, *D'Ewes*, 345.

20. Drake has included a passage on the payment of the army not included in the D'Ewes Journal this day, Notestein, *D'Ewes*, 345.

21. On 10 Feb. the resolutions concerning the supply of the army were passed both in committee and in the House. *C.J.*, II, 82.

22. Possibly one of Drake's philosophical observations. The sentence is separated by a line in the MS.

23. Earle's report dealt with two problems regarding the Irish army: first, the soldiers were restless, demanding back pay owed to them; and secondly, Thomas Wentworth, Earl of Strafford, continued as general of the Irish army although he stood impeached of High Treason by the House of Commons. (Wentworth's trial did not begin until 22 March.) At a joint conference, on 18 Feb., the Lords agreed to petition the King to sequester Strafford from his offices, see below. On the army see Notestein, *D'Ewes*, 346–347, and nn. 4–6. For the report made to the Upper House concerning the state of the Irish army see the Anon. diary (Yale Uncat. 226), 13 Feb. and n. 34.

24. Robert Reynolds was reporting from the committee for the Earl of Worcester which had been appointed on 29 Jan. (*C.J.*, II, 75). Apparently, according to Reynold's report, no

commission granted to the Earl of Worcester could be found. See Notestein, *D'Ewes*, 348–349 and n. 20. The report itself is not included in the *C.J.*, II, 83.

25. It is difficult to tell whether this is a fragment of a speech or one of Drake's philosophical observations.

26. Pym's motions are not included in the version of Pym's speech recorded in the D'Ewes Journal. He spoke following Alderman Pennington's affirmation that the City would lend the needed 15,000*l.* if the Commons desired. Notestein, *D'Ewes*, 351.

27. Rowland Wilson. On 27 Nov. 1640 John Glynne had reported from the committee of grievances that a petition complaining against Wilson and several others had been presented to the Lower House. *C.J.*, II, 37. Wilson was ordered taken into custody by the Serjeant (*ibid.*) and then granted bail on 3 Dec. (*ibid.*, 44, and see also, 70). On 13 Aug. 1641 he was voted a delinquent by the House for sealing a quadripartite indenture imposing 40s. a tun on wines. *C.J.*, II, 254.

28. It is unclear whether Drake is reporting from the committee of grievances or from a select committee concerning either impositions, vintners, or projectors (see the remarks regarding the beaver makers project, below). On 10 Feb. Pym had moved that monies might be raised from projectors and particularly wine projectors (see Notestein, *D'Ewes*, 345). Pym was to report concerning wines on 13 Feb. but did not (*ibid.*, 357). On 11 Feb. Pym is the first listed of eleven new members added to the committee originally appointed for the King's army and on that day assigned the additional task of considering the impositions on wines. It was appointed to meet at 7 am, 12 Feb., in the Treasury Chamber, *C.J.* II, 83; apparently Drake attended the session. I am unable to find any other report of it.

29. The King's assent to the Triennial bill created such joy in both Houses that they urged ringing of bells and bonfires throughout London and Westminster. *C.J.* II, 87; *L.J.*, IV, 163.

30. *a moderate* has been crossed out in the MS. following *go*.

31. Apparently there was a long debate in the Lower House on the procedure for the expression of thanks to the King for his speedy and gracious assent to the bill. The debate was interrupted by messengers from the Upper House urging Commons to join with them in giving thanks to the King that afternoon. Notestein, *D'Ewes*, 366; *C.J.*, II, 87; *L.J.*, IV, 163.

32. The message of thanks to the King from both Houses read by the Lord Keeper at Whitehall in the afternoon of 16 Feb. following the King's assent to the Triennial bill. *C.J.*, II, 87.

33. None of the following remarks included by Drake on 17 Feb. are included in the D'Ewes Journal. After Hyde's committee report and some discussion, it was ordered (*C.J.*, II, 88) that the committee last appointed (*C.J.*, II, 34) for the relief of the northern parts and the maintenance of the King's army meet at 2 pm this day in the Treasury Chamber to discuss further the means for raising money for the army. Some of the speeches recorded by Drake may be part of the afternoon session. The Treasurer's reference is to the King's speech of 23 January, see above, n. 1.

34. Oliver St. John, M.P. for Totness, Devonshire. Concerning legislative power, see Pym's speech, 20 February, Notestein, *D'Ewes*, 382.

35. John Glynne and John Maynard were the only speakers from the Lower House this day at a conference with the Lords concerning whether or not counsel should be allowed to Strafford. Notestein, *D'Ewes*, 388. See also the excerpts from the Peyton diary, *ibid.*, 387–388, nn. 6 and 14.

Warner reports, f. 25, that: *The Commons moved at a conference, that the L. Strafford might answer without counsel, and not by writing, which was entered upon debate that day but put off to the next.*

36. For the committee appointed to examine those particulars against bishops passed in former parliaments, see *C.J.*, II, 91; Notestein, *D'Ewes*, 389–390.

37. A committee had been appointed 14 Dec. 1640 (*C.J.*, II, 50) to examine the misdemeanors of lord lieutenants and deputy lieutenants. Although I find no indication in the *C.J.* or in the diaries (D'Ewes, Moore, Peyton, and Harl. 1601) that this committee met on 23 Feb., neither have I found any evidence to the contrary. Therefore, I have followed Drake's dating in the chronological placement of these notes. The report of the committee to the House concerning the E. of Bridgewater was made on 4 June, see *C.J.*, II, 167. Reports of this case are included in the Ellesmere Manuscripts, nos. 7670, 7693, 7695 and 7697 (Huntington Library).

38. Drake's first two entries for this day seem to be part of the account of the proceedings against Dr. John Bastwick in Star Chamber, reported to the House by Alexander Rigby. Concerning Dr. Bastwick, see Notestein, *D'Ewes*, 399–402. A resolution was passed 2 March that satisfaction be made to him for damages sustained by his Star Chamber sentence. *C.J.*, II, 95. See also S.P. 16/478:62.

39. According to Notestein, *D'Ewes*, 400–402, many spoke this day regarding the Archbishop of Canterbury and his activities dealing with cases in the Star Chamber.

40. The articles against the E. of Strafford and his responses are printed in Rushworth, *Hist Collections*, VIII, 22–32; Notestein, *D'Ewes*, 403–407, and in the Anon. diary (Yale 226), pp. 15–27.

41. This paragraph may belong with the preceding anonymous speech.

42. I am following Drake's sequence here although the placement of this speech seems questionable. Conrad Russell suggests that this and the two preceding paragraphs are part of Strafford's defense.

43. The committee to take into consideration the whole matter of the customs and customers, etc., was appointed on 24 Feb. to meet on 25 Feb. at 2 o'clock in the Exchequer Court. *C.J.*, II, 92. Although Drake's notes on the customers, ff. 83v–83, are undated they are placed in the MS. adjacent to material concerning the E. of Strafford which we know was read in the House on 25 Feb. The committee on customs, etc., met again 1 March, see below.

44. Giles Green, M.P. for Corfe Castle. Keeler, *L.P.*

45. William Toomes had been one of the surveyor-generals of the customs at London. *Cal. S.P. Dom., 1639–1640*, p. 544.

46. The work of this day was "to know what monies might be had" for the supply of the King's army. Notestein, *D'Ewes*, 417. However, heated discussion arose concerning a paper drawn at the order of the Scottish commissioners concerning episcopacy in England. See *Ibid.*, n. 11 and Gardiner, *Hist. of Eng.*, IX, 296–297. The debate continued on 3 and 5 March, see n. 49, below.

47. Probably Sir Gilbert Gerard (Gerrard), M.P. for Middlesex. The middle initial is unclear in the MS. and the diarist may have confused Sir Gilbert with Mr. Francis Gerard. Keeler, *L.P.*

48. There is no way to determine whether or not this remark is part of the day's proceedings.

49. The question of a committee for the matter of the Scottish paper was debated on 5 March. Rudyard's and Hampden's speeches included here may belong with the debates of that day. See Notestein, *D'Ewes*, 445 and n. 10.

50. On 24 Feb. a committee was appointed "to take into consideration the whole matter of

the customs and customers, farmers, receivers and collectors, of the impositions since the last year of King James. . . . *C.J.*, II, 92; Notestein, *D'Ewes*, 398. The committee was ordered to meet on Thursday, 25 Feb., in the afternoon in the Exchequer Court. Neither D'Ewes nor the *C.J.* note the actual meeting; I assume that Drake's date of 1 March (see below, following the queries) is accurate. The report concerning the customers was ordered to be made in the House on 22 May (*C.J.*, II, 153–154, and see below, 22 May), and the votes recommitted; a second report was made 24 May (*C.J.*, II, 155); further debate ensued and on 1 June the House of Commons passed thirteen resolutions concerning the customers. *C.J.*, II, 163. See below, n. 201.

51. Both Sir Job Harby and Pindar (below) were farmers in the new (or reconstituted) syndicate of the great farm and petty farm of wines and currants which was devised in 1640 after the retirement of Lord Goring and his short lived syndicate of 1638–1639. The new syndicate was deeply involved with government finance and by the end of 1640 had lent somewhere between 104,000*l*. and 253,000*l*. to the crown. Ashton, *Crown and Money Market*, 99–105; 111. The names of both men appear frequently in the *Cal. S.P. Dom.* for the period.

52. These were the members of Goring's 1638–1639 syndicate. Ashton, (*Crown and Money Market*, 102) includes also Sir Job Harby.

53. I have been unable to determine why the following four names have been linked together. Perhaps these men were recipients of gifts of wine at Christmastime. Suckling was a military man (and a poet) in the employ of the crown and was declared guilty of treason by parliament in Aug. 1641. Gardiner, *Hist. of Eng.*, X, 2. I am unable to identify Cooker. Freeman had lent money to the crown in 1624 (Ashton, *Crown and Money Market*, 41, 165) but I find no evidence of any financial dealings by him in the early 1640's. Sir William Acton was a London Alderman in 1640 (*Cal. S.P. Dom., 1640–1641*, pp. 95, 107, 115).

54. I have been unable to identify Mr. Lad. The name is difficult to read in the MS. and may be Mr. Had.

55. Harrison was also one of the new syndicate. See above, n. 51.

56. The reference is to the 1635 Book of Rates. *S.T.C.* no. 7695. Sir John Jacob was a member of the new syndicate. See above, n. 51.

57. Sir John Wolstenholme was a collector of pretermitted customs. (*Cal. S.P. Dom., 1639–1640*, pp. 337, 497) and a member of the new syndicate after his father's death in 1638. Ashton, *Crown and Money Market*, 105 and n. 70.

58. Perhaps Mr. Edward Abbot was a relative of Sir Morris Abbot (brother of George Abbot, late Archbishop of Canterbury) and prominent merchant mentioned in Ashton, *City and Court*, 26, 35, 184, 199.

59. Lord Goring had controlled (1638–1639) a syndicate of customs farms from which he retired in 1639 opening the way for the creation of a new syndicate in 1640. Ashton, *Crown and Money Market*, 100–105. Goring, however, maintained his tobacco interest after retirement from the syndicate. Notestein, *D'Ewes*, 267, 311, 540.

60. See Ashton, *Crown and Money Market*, 19, 45, 86, 96–98.

61. Perhaps Sir Edmund Sawyer is meant. In 1628 Sawyer was turned out of the Lower House, declared incapable of ever sitting in parliament again, and committed to the Tower during the pleasure of the House for having made a new Book of Rates. See *Commons Debates 1628*, IV, 401–420, *passim*. Dawes, also a Customs House official, had been implicated by Sawyer in the 1628 business but was exonerated by the House of Commons. See also Russell, *Parliaments 1621–1629*, 386–387.

62. A name squeezed into the margin before the word *whether* appears to be the name

Trelawney. Robert Trelawney, M.P. for Plymouth, was not a member of the committee (*C.J.*, II, 92) but may have attended the session.

63. An illegible three word marginal note is next to this sentence in the MS.

64. On 1 March the committee for Irish petitions was ordered to sit in the afternoon in the Treasury Chamber. *C.J.*, II, 95. Apparently this committee discussed a decision in Star Chamber made 8 *Car.* I concerning the Londonderry plantation. The committee met again on 20 May (*C.J.*, II, 152) and on 21 July the committee was ordered to sit twice a week to hear other petitions following the completion of the Londonderry business. *C.J.*, II, 219. Mr. Whistler reported the Londonderry business to the House on 26 Aug. *C.J.*, II, 272. Whistler's report is also printed in Rushworth, *Hist. Collections*, IV, 379–380.

65. Sir William Russell, deputy lieutenant of Worcestershire, was complained of in a petition submitted to the House of Commons by Francis Haslewood, Esq. *C.J.*, II, 50 and Hamilton, *Northcote*, 57–58. On 14 Dec. 1640 that petition was ordered to be handled by the committee on lord lieutenants appointed that day. I am unable to find a report to the House concerning the petition or petitions against Russell. What may be a second petition against him was, on 4 Jan. (*C.J.*, II, 62), referred to the committee on the petition of Sir Lewis Dives which met in the afternoon of 4 March. Notestein, *D'Ewes*, 440–442. The business was again in agitation on 9 March, *Ibid.*, 461–463.

66. Sir Robert Pye's speech was not recorded by D'Ewes. For further information regarding the Turkish pirates see Henry Percy's report to the House, 6 Mar., *C.J.*, II, 97–98; Notestein, *D'Ewes*, 434–444

67. Drake has not made clear to what particular fen business his fragmentary notes relate. The committee appointed 3 Dec. (*C.J.*, II, 44) was ordered to meet 4 Dec. and then 5 March to consider Dr Tomson's petition concerning fen drainage, *Ibid.*, 97. On 9 Mar. members were added to the committee. *C.J.*, II, 99; Notestein, *D'Ewes*, 461. Another committee concerning fens had been appointed following the submission of a petition to the House on 3 Mar. from "divers inhabitants of Cambridgeshire against the draining of the fenns". Notestein, *D'Ewes*, 429 and n. 3; however, no notice of this petition is included in the *C.J.* Cf. S.P. 16/480:87.

68. The Commons select committee concerning the impending trial of the Earl of Strafford met on 3 March, in the afternoon (*C.J.*, II, 96) and Bulstrode Whitelock reported back to the House on 6 Mar., *C.J.*, II, 98. The Upper and Lower Houses met in a joint conference on the morning of 8 Mar. to discuss propositions concerning the trial. Warner reports, ff. 46v–47, that: *The Commons desire the Lords that the evidence against the L. Strafford be managed by members of their own; 2ly, that all the House of Commons may be there present; 3ly , that it may be in the Court of Requests, and, lastly, that he may answer without counsel. They are to receive an answer the next day.*

The joint conference was reported in the Lower House on 11 Mar., *C.J.*, II, 101.

69. I.e., Mr. Holles, Sir Simonds D'Ewes, and others. See Notestein, *D'Ewes*, 454.

70. Sir Thomas Jermyn, M.P. for Bury St. Edmunds. Keeler, *L.P.*

71. The committee on gunpowder had met 1 Feb., see above, p. 1 and n. 5. On Friday, 5 Mar., the question of the gunpowder monopoly was discussed in the House (Notestein, *D'Ewes*, 444), although there is no indication of the debate in the *C.J.* On Monday afternoon, 8 Mar., (the regularly appointed time for the meeting of the monopolies committee) the subject of the saltpeter commissioners, etc., was discussed. Notestein, *D'Ewes*, 456 and n. 20.

72. Concerning the case of Francis Vincent, deputy saltpeter-maker, see *Cal. S.P. Dom.*, *1639–1640*, pp. 473–474, and Notestein, *D'Ewes*, 456.

73. Sect. Vane was not a member of the committee on monopolies but was involved in the case, see above, n. 72.

74. I.e. Sect. Vane.

75. Vincent's costs (these may be Wilford's costs, see Notestein, *D'Ewes*, 456) incurred in his imprisonment were originally assumed to be 10*l.*, although they grew to 15*l.* before the end of the business. Notestein, *D'Ewes*, 456.

76. Following the discussion of the saltpeter case the committee evidently turned to the questioning of Sir John Heydon, Lieutenant of the Ordnance. The examination of Heydon is not included in the D'Ewes Journal.

77. The business concerning Herbert and Wilde had been deferred from 27 Feb. to 6 Mar., to 9 Mar. C.J., II, 94, 97, 100. For the account of the friction between them see Notestein, *D'Ewes*, 461–463.

78. D'Ewes gives a fuller account than Drake of Crew's report from the committee on the ministers' remonstrance which had added new members on 9 Feb., (C.J., II, 81). See Notestein, *D'Ewes*, 458–461; 467–470. I have followed Drake's design in keeping the 9 and 10 Mar. proceedings together.

79. John Moore reported that it was decided by vote not to go into committee. Notestein, *D'Ewes*, 465, n. 6.

80. I have been unable to identify the next speaker or speakers. The reference to the Turk in Hungary is to the battle of Mohacs, 1526.

81. *Irish army* has been crossed out in the MS.

82. On Saturday, 13 Mar., it was ordered that the House would take up the consideration of disbanding the Irish army after the conclusion of the report from the committee on Strafford. C.J., II, 103; Notestein, *D'Ewes*, 482. The debate on the Irish army began on Saturday and continued on Monday, 15 Mar., when the Commons resolved to present the Lords with a declaration concerning the disbanding. C.J., II, 104.

   I find no speech in D'Ewes similer to the one included in Drake's notes. Because of the subject matter is is possible that it could have been made on 13 Mar., however, the opening sentence suggests Monday the fifteenth. Conrad Russell has suggested that given the form and content, the speaker may be Sir Benjamin Rudyard.

83. "if it may stand with the conveniency of this House, by the same former committee". C.J., II, 104.

84. Following the debate concerning the Irish army the House turned to consideration of the four papist servants to the Queen: Mr. Walter Montagu, Sir Kenelm Digby, Sir Toby Matthews, and Sir John Winter. Notestein, *D'Ewes*, 488–490. The debate continued on 16 Mar (*Ibid.*, 492–493), the speech may have been given that day.

85. According to the D'Ewes Journal (Notestein, D'Ewes, 451) *Sir Roger Palmer* (M.P. for Newton, Lancashire) offered loan security, not *Geoffrey Palmer* (M.P. for Stamford, Lincolnshire). Sir Roger Palmer, one of a family of courtiers and officeholders, seems less likely to have offered security than Geoffrey Palmer. Geoffrey was active in this session, sitting on the committee for the ministers' remonstrance (C.J., II, 81) and managing the Strafford trial 1–3 April, L.J., IV, 204–205. It was not until summer (after the protestation of 3 May, which he signed) that Geoffrey apparently rallied to the King's side. Keeler, L.P.; D.N.B.

86. On 16 Mar. the Commons resolved to join with the Lords to petition for the removal of papists from court. C.J. II, 106.

87. The Articles of Marriage sworn to by Charles, Prince of Wales at the time of his marriage to Henrietta Maria, 20 Nov. 1624. There is a copy of the Articles in Landsdown Ms, 93, no. 37 and in Ellesmere 7715, (Huntington Library).

88. The debate was whether the statutes of 35 *Eliz.* I, c. 2, *An act against popish recusants*, and 3 *Jac.* I, c. 5, *An act to prevent and avoid dangers which may grow by popish recusants* should be read first, or a paper containing the King's answer to the fifth article of the 1625 petition concerning recusants, wherein he stated that he provided in the marriage treaty with France that no popish recusants should be attendant on the Queen. Rushworth, *Hist. Collections*, I, 181–186.

89. Probably Sir Gilbert Gerard. Francis Gerard was M.P. for Seaford from the time of the borough's restoration, 4 Feb. 1641, until 1648; he was not a knight. See the Anon. diary (Yale 226), 4 Feb.

90. The House agreed to begin the debate regarding papists by reading the fifth article of the 1625 petition (see n. 88 above). An autograph copy of the article was produced by the clerk and is described by D'Ewes as "of moore waight then the Journall booke it selfe of that Parliament . . . with which all were abundantlie satisfied". Notestein, *D'Ewes*, 494.

91. Sir Henry Vane, Jr., a Treasurer of the Navy. According to D'Ewes, Edmund Prideaux chaired the committee of the whole House to discuss the provisioning of the Navy. He had no sooner taken the chair when Nathaniel Fiennes returned from the Lords with a message that the Upper House was ready for a present conference on the matter of the Irish army. Debate on the provisioning of the Navy was then postponed until after the conference with the Lords; following the conference Prideaux again took the chair for a committee of the whole. Notestein, *D'Ewes*, 498–501.

92. Moore and Peyton give the figure as 3*l.* 6*s.* 8*d.* per man per month. Notestein, *D'Ewes*, 499, n. 5.

93. I.e.; Sir William Russell, a Treasurer of the Navy and close friend and executor to the Earl of Bedford. He is not to be confused with Sir William Russell, deputy lieutenant of Worcestershire, who was complained of in a petition submitted to the House on 18 Feb.

94. Following the debate on the Navy a message was sent from the Lords requesting the Commons to attend a present conference on the matter of a paper submitted to the Upper House by the Scottish commissioners (the paper is printed in Notestein, *D'Ewes*, 502; *L.J.*, IV, 187) requesting that the previously agreed on relief for the northern counties be paid.

   Warner, ff. 51v–52, states that this day: *the Lords sent to the Commons that the Scots army were in such distress that they must think how to make provision for them for meat and money.*

95. This committee prepared the heads reported on 20 Mar. by Mr. Hyde (*C.J.*, II, 109) and discussed in a joint conference the same day, see *L.J.*, IV, 193.

96. The report from the committee on monopolists concerning Browne was made to the House this day. Notestein, *D'Ewes*, 503–504. The *C.J.* does not record the report. It is unclear why Drake entered the date 1634 in his notes. In July 1635 the Attorney General had been ordered to prepare a bill granting the sole making, selling, and transporting of iron ordnance, shot, iron pots, backs for chimneys, etc., to John Browne (*Cal. S.P. Dom.*, 1625–1649, p. 504) by way of answer to his petition for the same. *Ibid.*, 1635, p. 288. See also Aylmer, *King's Servants*, 341, n. 1.

97. According to Harl. 1601 Russell was willing to advance "5 or 6,000*l.* for the settinge out of 20 shipps, if he may have a foundation of creddit from what is in arreare". Notestein, *D'Ewes*, 506, n. 6.

98. According to D'Ewes (Notestein, *D'Ewes*, 66–67) Mr. John Harrison, son of Sir John Harrison, the customs official, had (to his father's dismay), in November 1640, offered to advance 50,000 *l.* of his father's funds on bonds from fifty men. Also see Ashton, *Crown and Money Market*, 176.

99. For a list of costs in victualling the Navy, see Notestein, *D'Ewes*, 505, n. 5; concerning the cost of furnishing ships, see S.P. 16/478:97.

100. Apparently Hampden interrupted Vane's speech in which Vane was describing what had transpired at the select committee meeting.

101. Sir John Heydon, Lieutenant of the Ordnance, apparently had been examined by the select committee.

102. I.e., the quantity or number of ordnance given for each ship named.

103. The House resolved this day that a bill should be drawn for the passing of a subsidy of tonnage and poundage. *C.J.*, II, 107.

104. On this day the act against usury was read the second time and committed. *C.J.*, II, 108. The bill, which was to reduce the rate of usury to 6*l.* per centum, raised a great controversy in the House and, according to D'Ewes, "divers spake against it supposing if 6*l.* per cent, it would decay trade, etc.". However, more spoke for it than against it and the bill was committed. See Notestein, *D'Ewes*, 511 n. 9.

105. After several speeches on the problem of the relief of the north the House turned into a committee with Hyde in the chair. See Notestein, *D'Ewes*, 511–512; *C.J.*, II, 108. I cannot determine whether the Treasurer spoke in the House or in the committee.

106. I have been unable to find a copy of the petition. D'Ewes includes the names of Sir Robert Pye, Sir George Wentworth, and Mr. Hugh Potter in addition to those listed in Drake. Notestein, *D'Ewes*, 515 and nn. 8–9.

107. The Notestein edition of *The Journal of Sir Simonds D'Ewes* ends with the final entry for 20 March. In annotating the remaining portion of Drake's notes I have referred principally to unprinted manuscript materials relying heavily on the notes of Sir Simonds D'Ewes (Harl. 163 and 164), and the journal of John Moore (Harl. 476, 478) for business relating to the Lower House. Occasionally I have cited to the diary of Sir Thomas Peyton (Univ. of Minn.) and the anonymous diary, Harl. 1601. For proceedings in the Upper House I have continued to cite to Warner (Harl. 6424), although he includes no report of the trial of the E. of Strafford. In each case I have quoted from the fullest account.

108. According to D'Ewes (Harl. 164), f. 142, the trial began about nine o'clock when *the Lords in their robes, being set in a place built in Westminster Hall, and divers of the House of Commons, being placed on the scaffolds built there for them on either side of the upper end of Westminster Hall, Thomas, Earl of Strafford, Lord Lieutenant of Ireland, was called for by the Earl of Arundel, etc., and was brought to the bar. . . . The King, Queen, and Prince were present. The Prince sat in his usual place and robes, the King and Queen in a private place made at the upper end of the stage on which the Lords sat. The Lords and judges all sat in the same posture as in the Upper House, only the spiritual Lords were not there.* Whitelocke, *Memorials*, I, 120–133 also includes a description of the trial.

109. On 19 March the E. of Arundel had been chosen Steward for the trial. Regarding his duties Warner, f. 53, states that: *The Steward may do what the Speaker may in case of misdemeanor. The indicted being at the bar, the Steward asks the Commons whether they will manage their evidence. While the Commons manage their evidence the indicted is to have no counsel. If any judge, the prisoner, or the Commons, shall desire anything to be propounded, they must publicly speak it to the Steward, and he to propound it. There is no debate to be made openly upon any question, but they must go aside. Every morning the Lords are to go from the Parliament House two and two and so to return. The Commons are to be at the place of trial first. The peers are to be at the trial in their robes and none, no, not the Commons, to be there covered. The prisoner may desire the Steward to cross interrogatory witnesses, and they to speak upon oath.*

Warner's diary does not include the proceedings at the trial itself because the bishops did not attend. His notes end on this day and begin again on 6 April. Osborn fb 159, no. 6, gives orders and directions for the trial. Accounts of the trial are printed in Howell, *S.T.*, III, 1381–1536; Rushworth, *Hist. Collections*, VIII, 1–778. A pamphlet entitled *Depositions and articles against Thomas Earl of Strafford* was printed in 1640. *S.T.C.* 25247. Various manuscript sources for the impeachment proceedings and the trial itself are extant: S.P. 16/480:9 is a brief anonymous journal (1 Mar. – 3 May) concerned primarily with the trial; Powis Papers, P.R.O. 30/58/13 is a daily account of trial proceedings. Two accounts of the trial are in the Kenneth Spencer Research Library, Univ. of Kansas, MSS. Q11:4 and Q11:5; Harvard Univ. f. MS. Eng. 916; B.L., Add. MS. 41,688 contains an account as does Harl. 2233 (the notes of John Robartes, first E. of Radnor), and Lansdowne 209, no. 4, to list a few. The printed depositions and articles against Wentworth, interleaved with notes by Denzil Holles, are in Harl. MS. 6865. See also H.M.C., *Fourth Report*, Appendix, sub Strafford.

110.   Following the E. of Arundel's introductory speech (which Drake reports as fully as D'Ewes), Mr. Browne, Clerk of the Parliaments, read the articles charged against the E. Strafford, and his answers. (The articles and answers are printed in the Anon. diary (Yale Uncat. 226), pp. 15–27.) Then, reports D'Ewes (Harl. 164), f. 142: *These being finished between one and two of the clock in the afternoon the said Earl of Strafford stood up and desired leave to speak, but Thomas, Earl of Arundel, etc., told him seeing it was too late for the House of Commons to begin their charge against him the Court held it not fit for him to speak, but that they would proceed tomorrow morning at eight of the clock in the same trial. And then he adjourned the Court to their own House whither all the Lords retired presently.*

111.   For the Lords' preparation for the conference see *L.J.*, IV, 194.

112.   At the opening of the proceedings on 23 March it was ordered "That the E. of Strafford is not to be admitted to speak at his trial before the House of Commons have fully managed their evidence against him". *L.J.*, IV, 195. Pym then proceeded to bring the charges against Strafford and to introduce witnesses. Pym's speech is described briefly in Howell, *S.T.*, III, 1417–1418. For the names of witnesses introduced this day see *L.J.*, IV, 195. Drake frequently refers to the E. of Strafford, Lord Deputy of Ireland, as *Deputy*.

113.   The E. of Strafford took exception to Sir Peirce Croseby, the first witness sworn and examined by the Lower House. *L.J.*, IV, 195. According to Moore (Harl. 476), f. 82a, Croseby had been sentenced for killing a man in Ireland.

114.   Mr. Nicholas Barnewell claimed that for voting against a bill preferred by Sir George Ratcliffe the E. of Strafford had threatened him with the keeping of 500 soldiers. Moore (Harl. 476), f. 83.

115.   The E. of Strafford excepted against the reading of the Remonstrance drawn up by the Irish parliament on the grounds that it was not included in the list of charges against him. However, the Remonstrance was authenticated by the Lords Digby and Baltinglass and all of the Lords voted to have it read by the Clerk, which was done. Moore (Harl. 476), f. 83a. The House of Commons then requested that a copy of the Remonstrance be sent to them to read, which was also done, the Commons averring that *this has been for his [Strafford's] justice. Ibid.*

116.   According to Moore (Harl. 476), f. 83a, *Strafford did say that he being charged with treason there was a correspondence and confederacy with Ireland.*

117.   Lionel Cranfield, Earl of Middlesex.

118. Henry Cary, Viscount Falkland, Lord Deputy of Ireland from 1623–1629. Aylmer, *King's Servants*, 320.

119. The E. of Strafford sought to refute some of the evidence presented by Pym and wanted time to answer. The court, after debate of the matter, agreed to let Strafford answer but, according to Moore (Harl. 476), f. 83a, *if he did not presently make answer he was debarred to speak hereafter.*

120. The E. of Strafford claimed to be surprised by the introduction and reading of the Irish Remonstrance, *L.J.*, IV, 195.

121. I.e., Pym.

122. The letter, according to Moore (Harl. 476), f. 85, was produced by the E. of Strafford in order to show that the King himself borrowed money from the Treasurer and therefore borrowing in itself could be no crime; *then he produced the King's letter wherein the King does command the Treasurer to lend him 40,000 l. for 3 years.*

123. Drake's account of this conference combines information from the reports of the conference 22 March (*C.J.*, II, 111; *L.J.*, IV, 194) and 23 Mar. (*L.J.*, IV, 196).

124. These may be Strafford's responses to the Lower House's accusations presented this day by Maynard. Drake's notes on f. 24v are so fragmentary that it is difficult to date them. The reference to the commissioners may relate to the early part of Maynard's speech dealing with the substance and branches of the first article against the E. of Strafford wherein he discusses Strafford's misuse of a royal commission and his assumption of "regal power". There is a reference in the same speech to the E. of Strafford's collection of customs on flax and tobacco, although no direct mention is made of his cousin. Moore (Harl. 476), f. 88a. Maynard's speech is not included in Howell, *S.T.*, see Rushworth, *Hist. Collections*, VIII, 128–136.

125. Robert Kennedy and Richard, Earl of Cork (and others) were sworn on 25 Mar. *L.J.*, IV, 197. Neither Moore nor D'Ewes report any of the trial proceedings for this day.

126. The words printed in italics have been underlined in the MS.

127. Dominick Sarsfield, Viscount Kilmallock. Sarsfield became Chief Justice of the Common Pleas, Ireland, in 1612. *Cal. S.P. Ireland, 1611–1614*, p. 265. Strafford was charged with the third article this day. For the reference to Jehu in Glynne's speech, below, see 2 Kgs. 9:20.

128. I.e., the E. of Strafford, who requested leave to cross-examine Lord Ranelagh (Roger Jones, Viscount of Ranelagh) regarding his hearing of causes upon paper petitions for titles of lands. The Lords, fearing that L. Ranelagh might accuse himself of a criminal matter, requested that the business be debated in their House before answer be given. Consequently, the Lord Steward adjourned the Lords to the parliament chamber above the trial proceedings in Westminster Hall, where they met as a House, and then adjourned into a committee to discuss Ranelagh's pending testimony. After some debate the House resumed and "it was resolved, That the Earl of Strafford is to examine whether it has been done by the custom of other deputies of Ireland or no; but no man to be examined against himself". *L.J.*, IV, 197–198.

129. MS.: *Lords with 16 House.* See the Anon. diary (Yale Uncat. 226), 25 Mar. Neither D'Ewes, Moore nor Warner include an account of this conference. *L.J.*, IV, 198; *C.J.*, II, 113.

130. The fourth article stated: "That the Earl of Strafford would have neither law nor lawyers dispute or question any of his orders; and that he would make the Earl of Cork and all Ireland know, so long as he had the government there, any act of state there made, or to be made, should be as binding to the subjects of that kingdom as an act of parliament". *L.J.*, IV, 199.

131. According to Moore (Harl. 476), f. 96: *Then, after Strafford had a little perused his notes, he then began as follows and showed a certificate, as he said, under some of the counsel['s] hands, to show that he had not time to procure his witness[es] and papers. But we [the Commons], opposing the reading of it, the Lords were pleased to lay it aside.*

132. The order was made 5 Feb., see *C.J.*, II, 79; Notestein, *D'Ewes*, 329.

133. Moore (Harl. 476), f. 96, reports that: *He said that the Council Table in Ireland is a court of record, and proceeds by bill and answer, replication and otherwise, and it is not a subverting of the law, but a diverting. And if I should not take that course the Protestant clergy and the English planters would be in a far worse course. . . .*

134. The E. of Strafford sought to prove that the actions alleged against him had been *the constant practice of that kingdom, both for plantation and church.* Moore (Harl. 476), f. 96a. He requested that a journal book of a parliament held in Ireland when Sir John Denham was Chief Justice of King's Bench in Ireland (apptd. 1612; *DNB*) be brought in to support his case. However, at this point the Commons opposed the reading of the journal. Later, on 30 Mar., the Lords ordered Mr. Raylton, the E. of Strafford's solicitor, to bring the book to the House the following morning presumably for perusal to determine if it was admissible. We hear nothing further about this business until 8 April when it was ordered that Baron Denham's book and another belonging to Lord Viscount Falkland are "not fit to be given in as evidence, being private books, and no records". *L.J.*, IV, 210.

135. 1 E. VI, c. 12, *An act for the repeal of certain statutes concerning treasons, felonies, etc.* This act states that "from henceforth none act, deed, or offense being by act of parliament or statute made treason or petty treason. `. .shall be taken, had, deemed or adjudged to be high treason or petty treason but only such as be treason or petty treason in or by the act of parliament or statute made in the xxv year of the reign of. . .King Edward the Third. . .".

136. Apparently Lord Kilmallock in his testimony had called Sir George Ratcliffe "the E. of Strafford's echo". Moore (Harl. 476), f. 97a, relates that *my Lord Digby, to vindicate the Lord Kilmallock for calling Ratcliffe the Earl of Strafford's echo, said: 'My Lords, I hope if he should have called him his bosom friend therefore you will not say he is in his bosom; yet, my Lord[s], I conceive he could not have given him a more proper name'.*

137. Moore (Harl. 476), f. 99a, reports that: *the Lord Steward gave the Lieutenant of the Tower [Sir William Balfour], a check for making us wait so long before he came.* Balfour answered that the tide was against him. D'Ewes (Harl. 162), f. 367.

138. The fifth article stated:"That the Earl of Strafford, in time of full peace, did, in Ireland, give, and procure to be given, against the Lord Mountnorris, a sentence of death, by a council of war, called together by the Earl of Strafford, without any warrant, or authority of law, or offense deserving punishment, etc.", *L.J.*, IV, 200.

139. The Moore account (Harl. 476), ff. 99a–100b, of Mountnorris's testimony is as follows: *Mountnorris said upon the 11th December 1635 he was warned to appear, by a pursuivant, the next morning by 8 a clock, where he coming he found many of the Council of War, amongst the rest the Lord Valencia. And Mountnorris asked what the cause of their meeting should be, but they all declared they did not know. And presently the Lord Lieutenant came, and sitting down, and so all the rest. . .and then he said, 'My Lords, I have called you together to right my self upon the Lord Mountnorris', whereupon he pulled forth a paper forth of his pocket and read the words and asked Mountnorris whether he were guilty or no. And he [Mountnorris] demanded he might have the benefit of a peer of the land, and have the accusation in writing, but he [Strafford] denied it. . .then the Lieutenant produced the King's letters, which no little troubled me [Mountnorris], and I*

told his Lordship that his Majesty was misinformed, and he answered, 'No, for I gave the information, and I do not use to misinform his Majesty'. And still I [Mountnorris] desired to have the liberty of a peer and subject. . .and then I was commanded to withdraw, and after half an hour's time I was called in again and then was compelled to kneel as a delinquent and Sir Charles Coote pronounced the sentence of death upon me. And then the Earl of Strafford made a very invective speech against me, but at length he told me that he would move the King for my life, and he would rather lose his hand than I should lose my life. . . .

140. Robert, Lord Dillon. Both Robert, Lord Dillon and Thomas, Lord Viscount Dillon were sworn this day. L.J., IV, 200.

141. L. Dillon answered that *he also does not remember whether the Lord of Strafford gave them thanks or no, but in civility; and he does not remember whether he sat bare by or no.* Moore (Harl. 476), f. 101.

142. I.e., the Earl of Strafford.

143. L. Ranelagh testified that *he asked whether his Lordship [Strafford] would be pleased to withdraw one of the articles [against Mountnorris] or no, and he [Strafford] answered, 'I demand justice in both. . .'.* Moore (Harl. 476), f. 101a.

144. Moore (Harl. 476), f. 101a, reports that: *Then Strafford demanded whether he [Strafford] said anything while Mountnorris was away or no, to which he [Ranelagh] answered, 'He did speak, but he does not remember whether Strafford was bareheaded or no. . .'.*

145. *Denickell* in Moore (Harl. 476), f. 102: *Denewitt* in Rushworth, Hist. Collections, VIII, 196.

146. According to Moore (Harl. 476), ff. 102–102a, Lord Viscount Dillon testified concerning Thomas Deneville. Dillon said *there was a man hanged by martial law, and that he and another nobleman were suitors to Strafford's lady for the sparing of him, but could not prevail. . . . He said it was pretended for running from his colors, but he was brought by the mayor and aldermen for stealing of a piece of beef. Patrick Clough [another witness sworn this day] said he was a soldier at that time and that that man was hanged, some say for stealing a piece of beef, others for running from his colors. Ranelagh said he came short of the sentence and there being some controversy. . .the Lord Deputy was pleased to put the case to him, which was that he [Deneville], demanding his pay, the officer bade him go and be hanged, whereupon he went his way and left his musket with his corporal, and therefore he would have him turned to the law, but for all that he was hanged by martial law, though the Lord Conway opposed him [Strafford].*

147. Sir Charles Willmott, first Viscount Willmott of Athlone, appointed General and Commander in Chief of the forces in Ireland in 1629. Cal. S.P. Ireland, 1625–1632, p. 474.

148. See above, n. 134.

149. The letter was from the E. of Strafford himself and the Council of War to Sect. Coke, 13 Dec. 1640. The reading of the letter was overruled. Rushworth, Hist. Collections, VIII, 199.

150. On Thursday, 25 Mar., both Houses had agreed to send a joint committee to the City of London the following Saturday (27 Mar.) with regard to a loan from the City. L.J., IV, 198; C.J., II, 113. See above, n. 129; and see also Pym's undated speech in the Appendix, below.

151. Following the conference of 30 Mar. the committees of both Houses met and agreed to join together in giving security. L.J., IV, 202.

152. The speech is undated but its content suggests that it was given at the time of the second reading (1 April) of the Act to restrain bishops. . .from intermeddling with

secular affairs, and supports the commitment of that bill. For those added this day to the committee for the bill, see C.J., II, 115.

153. John Stewart, Earl of Traquair. Articles 20–24 were lumped together because according to the court they were in content dependent on each other. (For the articles, see below, pp. 15–27.) The E. of Strafford requested that the court might not proceed with all of the articles at once but proceed in order with one or two articles at a time. Glynne responded to the E. of Strafford's request saying, *that it was never said that it was never seen that a prisoner at the bar, especially charged with High Treason, should direct how the evidence against him should be managed. The request was denied.* D'Ewes (Harl. 164), f. 152v.

154. Marginal note: "Then by the counsel: Whether there were any others that were of another opinion".

155. The E. Morton (William Douglas, seventh Earl of Morton) being sick, was not able to testify in person. His deposition had been sworn to earlier and was now read in the court. See H.M.C., *Fourth Report*, Appendix, 44.

156. According to Moore (Harl. 476), f. 157b, Sir Henry Vane, Sr., the Treasurer of the Household, had proposed a defensive war and the E. of Strafford an offensive one.

157. According to D'Ewes (Harl. 164), f. 152v, The E. of Northumberland's testimony was also read, he being sick. H.M.C., *Fourth Report*, Appendix, 31.

158. This question was directed to Sir Henry Vane. D'Ewes (Harl. 164), f. 152v, records that: *The Bishop of London [and the] L. Treasurer witnessed the same in effect, and said that afterwards the rest of the Council agreed in the main with him [Strafford]* .

159. The bracketed words have been supplied from Moore (Harl. 476), f. 158.

160. *Strafford replied that if they would not supply him the King was quit before God and man, and the King might take some other course to supply himself, though it were against the will of the subjects.* Moore (Harl. 476), f. 158b.

161. MS.: Majesty Majesty.

162. Sir Geroge Wentworth was the E. of Strafford's brother. By order of the Lower House, 26 Feb. (C.J., II, 93) George was the only person allowed to visit his brother during the course of the trial without obtaining prior permission from the House.

163. Moore (Harl. 476), ff. 159b–160a, reports that the E. of Bristol said *that he heard the Earl of Strafford say that in this great distress of King and kingdom the parliament had denied to supply the King in an ordinary way of subsidy and therefore the King must provide for the safeguard of his kingdom by what means he can, and that salus reipublicus was suprema lex, and that the King was not to be pulled by or mastered by the forwardness of his people, and that he meant it upon the parliament, being in discourse thereof, and that the best way for the King was upon the heart and purse of his subjects. And these words were spoken after the dissolution of the last parliament, I telling him that the only way to pacify all these tumults were by calling another parliament.* For Bristol's further remarks, see Rushworth, *Hist. Collections*, VIII, 541.

164. Apparently this is Drake's personal comment.

165. Moore (Harl. 476), f. 160b, reports that here Vane said: *that he has heard the E. of Strafford say to the King, 'Your Majesty, having tried all ways, and [they] refusing in this extreme necessity to assist and supply your wants, you are loosed and absolved from all rules of government, and you are acquitted before God and man, and you have an army in Ireland you may employ to reduce this kingdom'.*

166. *And these were spoken after the dissolution of the last parliament, and he said that either those words positively, or words to that effect were spoken, and it was at the committee of eight.* Moore (Harl. 476), f. 160b.

167. The following speech comprises the E. of Strafford's answers to the charges brought this day. The court did not hold session on 6 April but resumed again on Wednesday, 7 April, as the E. of Strafford had *desired to have a day given him to revive himself a little.* Moore (Harl. 476), f. 170b. It was after six o'clock when the court adjourned on 5 April. D'Ewes (Harl. 164), f. 155v.

168. The trial proceedings of 10 April had ended in confusion as the Commons sought to bring in fresh evidence concerning the Irish army to support the charges in article 23. Strafford countered the Commons' request with a request of his own to bring in new evidence which, the Lords stated, by the impartiality of the court proceedings, they could not refuse if the Lower House request were granted. (See S.P. 16/478:22). Shouts of "Withdraw" came from the scaffolding where the Commons sat and cries of "Adjourn" rang from the Lords' benches. Gardiner, *Hist. of Eng.*, IX, 327. *Thereupon, according to Warner, f. 54v, the Lord of Southampton (as it is free for any one Lord) called to have the House adjourned, and so it was, where the Lords sat till 6 of the clock expecting the Commons who never came to them. This afternoon the Commons made ready a bill to present unto the Lords against the Lieutenant, thereby to cast him without trial upon evidence.* (See also the letter of N. Tomkyns to Sir John Lambe, *Cal. S.P. Dom. 1640–1641*, pp. 539–540.)

Upon reassembling, the Lower House called upon Mr. Glynne to show what new evidence had been collected against Strafford. C.J., II, 118. D'Ewes (Harl. 164), ff. 162–163, gives the following account:

Then Mr. GLYNNE showed that the committee for the Earl of Strafford thought fit to acquaint the House what evidence they would have produced today to the 23 article and desired that Sir Henry Vane, the younger, and Mr. Pym might be enjoined by the House to declare all that they know. . . .

SIR HENRY VANE, the younger, his testimony: In last October found a paper dated 5 May [while] searching for other writings in a cabinet, and Mr. Pym came to him just as he was transcribing it, to visit him being sick. He then delivered [a] copy to Mr. Pym – duty and son of commonwealth. Sent to Mr. Pym to burn the paper.

MR. PYM's testimony: Agreed that he wrote out a copy with his own hand of it and cut that in pieces Sir Henry Vane delivered him, but did not burn it as he [Vane] desired.

MR. TREASURER. [Sir Henry Vane, Sr.] said that till Thursday last he did not know of the means how this paper was come by, not officious or busy in this kind to accuse Earl of Strafford. That King commanded him to burn his paper, which he did before this parliament. Said an unhappy son of his had brought all this trouble upon him.

MR. PYM read so much of the paper as concerned the said 23 article and then stopped. It was much in the same words of the 23 article at the end.

Thereupon ensued a long debate whether that which remained should be read or not at this time, especially seeing a messenger stood at the [door] from Lords. At last upon the question it was overruled upon question that it should be read, and so it was. . . . Then it was moved that Mr. Treasurer might be enjoined by this House to show whether he did not think this paper read to be in substance with [the] same with what he left. It was ordered he should, and he did, and said he thought they did agree. And [he] showed that when he burnt the said paper by the King's command he took some notes of it.

A motion was made for reconciling Mr. Treasurer with his son, divers much commending his son's care of the public good which outswayed private respects.

MR. PEARD moved that the House would command him to do it, and that it might be so ordered, but others opposed that and thought it much fitter to leave Mr. Treasurer to a voluntary reconciliation with his son, he having now seen both the sense and desire of the

House. See also S.P.16/452:31. H.M.C. *Third Report,* Appendix, 3, 81; H.M.C., *Cowper,* II, 252.

169.   According to D'Ewes (Harl. 164), f. 164v, Mr. Cogan testified that: *in the said Mr. Treasurer Vane's House, being also Secretary of the State, near Charing Cross, he had two studies, of the one of which he [Cogan] had the key, being an upper study in which was a cabinet covered with black velvet. That young Sir Henry Vane, the said Treasurer's son, having the keys of the lower study to search evidences and writings, did ask him if there were not a cabinet in the other study, saying he had order from his father to look in it for writings. Whereupon he [Cogan] went up into the said upper study and fetched down unto him a cabinet covered with black velvet.* See also Verney, pp. 36–38; Whitelocke *Memorials,* I, 124–125.

170.   I.e., the others mentioned in the Council Board notes.

171.   After the Treasurer's request to be excused from further examination his son was questioned again. As reported in D'Ewes (Harl. 164), f. 164v: *Sir Henry Vane, the younger, said he thinks he showed Mr. Cogan the letter his father sent him [asking him to search for some writings]. He [Vane] showed him [Cogan] a key and asked him if there were any cabinet he had which that key would open, and he said he had; and thereupon sent down a cabinet covered with black velvet to him, into the lower study, which he opened desiring to find some writings in it which he could not find in the lower study, where he found the paper mentioned which, out of his duty to the public, he thought himself bound to copy.*

   Mr. Cogan, being called in again, denied that young Sir Henry Vane showed him any letter sent him from his father. For showing him any key, he did not remember it, but confessed that he had never spoken with Mr. Secretary Vane about it since nor had heard or sent anything to him since about it by letters, message, or otherwise.

172.   Maynard read three heads, prepared by the committee appointed for the managing of the evidence against the E. of Strafford, to be discussed at a conference with the Lords that afternoon. Following Maynard's presentation the heads were discussed and voted on by the House. For the perfected heads, see *C.J.,* II, 119.

173.   The Commons wished to include the paper originally belonging to the Treasurer as new evidence in the trial. In order to do this they sought Treasurer Vane's authorization of the paper they had in hand as a true copy of the original. D'Ewes (Harl. 164), f. 165v, reports that: *Upon the first head before set down, being read and debated, Mr. Treasurer, upon some motions was twice drawn to declare, concerning the said paper found by his son, that he first moved his Majesty that he might burn it, and so he [the King] commanded to do it; and secondly that he was not possibly able to speak further to it till he had considered deliberately of it.*

174.   The Commons had returned to their own House on the morning of 10 April confused and angry about the questions concerning the introduction of new evidence at the trial. See above, n. 168. It was decided after much debate in the Lower House to proceed further by the drawing of a bill of attainder against the E. of Strafford. The idea of proceeding by way of attainder had been broached as early as 26 Feb. but had been rejected. Notestein, *D'Ewes,* 410–411 and n. 7. Moore does not record the debate preliminary to the reaching of this decision and D'Ewes (Harl. 164), f. 163v, notes that *Divers spake whether we should proceed by way of bill of attainder or as we had begun [i.e., by judgment in the High Court of Parliament].* After several paragraphs dealing with the Scottish problem and the cessation of arms D'Ewes further reports that: *Then [the] bill for attainder of Earl of Strafford was brought in. Debate whether it should be read; divers spake. I [D'Ewes] moved that it might be read presently. The distraction of [blank]. An act for the attainder of Thomas Earl of Strafford of High Treason*

read 1ª vice. (The bill is printed in Rushworth, *Hist. Collections*, IV, 262–263.) See also C.J., II, 118; S.P. 16/479:27. The bill was read for the second time in the Lower House on 14 April (C.J., II, 120), and for the third time on 21 April (*Ibid.*, 125). According to D'Ewes (Harl. 164), f. 171, on 14 April, after the second reading of the bill, there was *long debate. . .but the question was at last put that the said committee should sit at two of the clock in the afternoon and it was ordered that all the lawyers of the House should be present.* (This folio has a line struck through it in the MS.) D'Ewes's account of the afternoon committee meeting (Harl. 163), f. 45, is as follows:

Mr. Peard being called into the clerk's chair took it. The order made in the morning was read touching our agitating the said bill of attainder in a grand committee. Then the Clerk read the bill, after which Mr. Peard took it and read the first part of it, by which it was declared that the said Earl of Strafford had endeavored to subvert the fundamental laws of the realm and to bring in an arbitrary and tyrannical government. This he read twice and when I thought, after so long and clear proof, that we should presently have passed it upon the question divers stood up and opposed it, some alleging that they desired first to know whether this were treason; whether, though the particular acts he was accused of were proved, that yet those acts did tend to the subversion of the fundamental laws of the realm; whether the army of Ireland were intended for England; and some also doubted what were the fundamental laws of the realm; others also said they were unsatisfied that he had endeavored the subversion of the law, for to do actions against law is not presently a subversion of the law, with many other trifling objections, which they did only to keep off the question from being put. (I was much amazed to see so many of the House speak on the Earl of Strafford's side.)

The bill of attainder was carried up to the Lords by Pym on 21 April but not first read in the Upper House until 26 April. It was read the second time on 27 April and pased on 7 May. The Upper House records of the readings of and orders concerning the bill of attainder were expunged from the record and are not included in the printed edition of the *Journals of the House of Lords*. These records, although they have been crossed out in the manuscript, are still readable and have been edited by Paul Christianson. See "The 'obliterated' portions of the House of Lords Journals dealing with the attainder of Strafford". *Eng. Hist. Review*, April 1980, 339–353.

175. These are words from Rudyard's speech of 12 April, see above.

176. According to Moore (Harl. 477), f. 24b: *Then was reported from the committee of the Forest of Dean some heads for the preserving of timber in the Forest of Dean and that Mr. Treasurer shall present them to his Majesty and to desire that a commission may issue forth to examine the abuse of cutting of timber.* D'Ewes (Harl. 163), f. 121, identifies Geoffrey Palmer as the M.P. reporting on the Forest of Dean. The Anon. diary (Yale Uncat. 226), lists those men responsible for the destruction of timber. The orders that followed this report are printed in the C.J., II, 131. The committee for the forests was ordered to sit on the following Monday (3 May) at 2 o'clock in the Court of Wards.

177. The King's speech given in the Uppper House on Saturday 1 May was reported this day in the House of Commons by their Speaker, William Lenthal. For the speech see *Cal. S.P. Dom. 1640–1641*, pp. 567–568, and Rushworth, *Hist. Collections*, IV, 239; D'Ewes (Harl. 164), f. 194.

178. Moore (Harl. 477), f. 27a, reports Thomas Tomkins, M.P. for Weobly, as saying: *Mr. Speaker, I was in the country when the bill against the E. of Strafford was passed, and I am so fully satisfied in my conscience that this Earl has gone about to take our lifes, our liberties, and our properties, and therefore my opinion is that he is guilty of High Treason and I desire that we may have a conference with the Lords.*

179. I.e. necessary to pass a bill of attainder against Strafford. Moore (Harl. 477),. f. 27b,

contains a lengthy speech by Pym in which, after noting that the King's interference with a matter still in question in parliament (i.e., that of Strafford) is a breach of privilege, he stated that: . . . *truly, Sir, I am persuaded that there was some great design in hand by the papist[s] to subvert and overthrow this kingdom, and I do verily believe the King never had any intention to subvert the laws, or to bring in the Irish army, but yet he had counsel given him that he was loose from all rules of government.*

180.   I.e., as in 27 *Eliz.* I, according to Moore's account (Harl. 477), f. 28a. On association see G.R. Elton, *The Tudor Constitution* (Cambridge 1960), pp. 79–80.

181.   After a motion by Sir Henry Marten for a committee to draw the heads of an association for the defense of King and Church, Mr. Godolphin, according to Moore (Harl. 477), f. 28a, spoke against it, *lest it breed a jealousy.* Moore (Harl. 477), f. 28b, reports that: *Then we named the committee* [see *C.J.*, II, 132] . . . *and after their several protestations for secrecy, they went forth into [the] Inner Court of Wards to draw up a declaration of the unanimous consent and resolution of this House for the defense of the King's person, the religion established, and the liberty of the subject, be it by oath or otherwise as they shall think fit.*

182.   *C.J.*, II, 132.

183.   The protestation, after amendment in committee, was resolved on by the House of Commons to be taken individually by its members and then sent up to the Lords House. *L.J.*, IV, 233–234; and see also S.P. 16/480:6. Verney, pp. 66–71, includes an account of "Proceedings Upon Taking the Protestation".

184.   It is through William Drake's name on the protestation that I was able to identify these notes as his. For the names of members who took the protestation on 3 May, see *C.J.*, II, 132–133; others took the protestation in the course of the next few days, see *C.J.*, II, 137, 138, 139, 140, 141, 142, 144, 145, 148, 149, 158, 159, 171, 178. Rushworth, *Hist. Collections*, IV, 244–249 and Camb. Add. 90, ff. 42–43, contain a list of all those members of both Houses who took the protestation.

185.   This is probably one of Drake's philosophical observations.

186.   It is unclear why Drake includes this remark about supply here, although a proviso to the subsidy bill had been read earlier in the day, see *C.J.*, II, 132.

187.   On 13 Feb. 1638 John Lilburne had been sentenced in Star Chamber for printing Puritan books at Rotterdam, see Howell, *S.T.*, III, 1326–1327. Francis Rouse reported to the House this day on Lilburne's sentence, that he had been *sentenced to be whipped at a cart tail, and to stand upon the pillory, and that he should be imprisoned with irons on his hands and feet, and that no man should have recourse unto him (and that hereafter that any man that shall be sentenced by the Star Chamber shall have his garments searched lest they should have any papers or other scandalous libels about him), and they also put a gag in his mouth for the space of one hour, at the least, for then blood issued forth of his mouth and he had 200 stripes, and fined a 400l. only for dispersing a book.* Moore (Harl. 477), f. 31b.

The House of Commons resolved that the sentence was illegal, etc. [see the Anon. diary (Yale 226) and *C.J.*, II, 134], and further resolved that reparations should be given to Mr. Lilburne for the imprisonment, suffering, and losses sustained by this illegal proceeding. Moore (Harl. 477), f. 31b.

188.   The House of Commons, concerned about rumors of a plot within the army, sent the following letter to Sir Jacob Astley, Commander of the Foot Soldiers and Sir John Conyers, Lieutenant General of the Horse. The letter was to be carried into the country by Commissary Willmott, see *C.J.*, II, 134.

189.   *between the army and the parliament* has been crossed out in the MS.

190. The last sentence in Drake's version of the letter does not appear in the copy of the letter included in Moore's journal (Harl. 477), f. 32a. The letter is printed in Rushworth, *Hist. Collections*, IV, 252. On 8 May the Commons sent a second letter to the army (*C.J.*, II, 140) and the Lords sent a letter of their own. *L.J.*, IV, 242; Rushworth, *Hist. Collections*, IV, 261.

191. This day following debate regarding the state of the kingdom the protestation drawn by the Commons on 3 May was subscribed to by the Upper House. *L.J.*, IV, 233–234. Warner, f. 60, reports that: *The Commons desire a conference about the affairs of the kingdom wherein they present unto them a protestation. . . . This protestation, the commons said, had passed with them nemine dissentiente and [they] desired the Lords to make the same. Hereupon the Lords first voted that the protestation should pass, which passed unanimously. Then every Lord read openly and made the same protestation and afterward subscribed it with their names. It was wished that all the Lords absent would do the like when they came to the House. It was moved by the L. Essex, Mandeville, and Saye that [those] who refuse to take this protestation should have no votes in the bill against L. Strafford; but was finally ordered that [those] who refused the protestation only in point of doctrine of religion might vote; but who upon any other point, should not.*

192. I have been unable to identify the speaker. Besides the protestation passed on 3 May (and alluded to at the beginning of this speech) the House was working toward passage of a bill against recusants and for the security of the "true religion". See *C.J.*, II, 135.

193. A letter which came from Yorkshire to Mr. Henry Darley (M.P. for North Allerton, Yorkshire) concerning a plot within the Army was read in the Lower House this day. *C.J.*, II, 135. Mr. Holles was sent to the Lords to read the letter to them and to request their participation in an examination of the facts. Moore (Harl. 477), ff. 37a–37b, reports: *Mr. Holles was sent to the Lords with a message . . . that our House has received such information as doth give them just cause to suspect that there have been, and still are, secret practices to discontent the army with the proceedings of parliament and engage them in some design of dangerous consequence to the state by some other mischievous ways to prevent the happy success and conclusion of this parliament. And because the discovery, remedy, and prevention of these dangerous plots doth so surely concern the safety both of King and kingdom they desire your Lordships would be pleased to appoint a select committee to take the examination upon oath of such persons, and upon such interrogatories, as shall be presented unto them by the direction of the House of Commons, and in the presence of such of the members of that House as shall be thereunto appointed, with injunction of secrecy as a business of this nature doth require. They have ordered that such members of their House as shall be thought fit shall upon notice be ready to be examined and they desire your Lordships would please to order the like for the members and assistance of your own House; and further, it is desired that your Lordships forthwith send to his Majesty to beseech him in the name of the parliament, upon this great and weighty occasion, and that no servant of his Majesty's the queen and the Prince may depart the kingdom, or otherwise absent himself, without leave from his Majesty with the humble advice of this parliament, until these examinations be perfected.*

The Lords appointed a committee of 10 *amongst which there is no bishop*, to make the examinations. Warner, f. 62; *L.J.*, IV, 235.

Warner, f. 62v, reports that: *The King wished the E. Holland to let them know that he is forthwith to go to the army to put them into good order or to disband them as occasion shall serve, and that therefore they might have a conference with the Commons; which the Lords heard but gave no answer thereunto, but went to the L. Strafford's business.*

194. The Lower House appointed a committee of six this day (Holles, Pym, Hampden,

Strode, Fiennes, and Clotworthy) to prepare heads for a message to be sent to the Lords concerning the army plot. *C.J.* II, 135. On 7 May (*Ibid.*, 138) Sir Philip Stapleton was added to make this a committee of seven by which name the committee was known (also called the close committee, Rawl. 1099, f. 85), although its membership came to exceed seven. Sir Wm. Lewis and John Lisle were added on 15 May (*Ibid.*, 147). On the army plot see Gardiner, *Hist. of Eng.*, IX, 357–361; 384–386; and see below, no. 198.

195. *They have voted* has been crossed out in the MS. following the word *cessation.* Treasurer Vane reported the 10 May conference with the Lords to the Lower House on 11 May. Moore's account (Harl. 477), ff. 55a–55b, includes Bristol's introductory remarks and also a copy of the paper from the Scottish commissioners (printed in *L.J.*, IV, 243–244), but does not include Vane's remarks following the report of the conference.

196. Drake makes no mention that this was the day that the E. of Strafford was beheaded. See the anon. diary (Yale 226), 12 May and n. 143. D'Ewes (Harl. 163), f. 165, states that this day *Dr. Bargrave, Dean of Canterbury, began and first gave great thanks to the House for the favor showed the deans and chapters because we would hear them speak before we proceeded further against them.* Both Moore (Harl. 477), ff. 60b–61a and D'Ewes (Harl. 163), 165–167, include a long report of Dr. Hacket's speech this day.

197. Sir Philip Stapleton and Sir John Clotworthy were appointed 7 May (*C.J.*, II, 138) by the Lower House to go to Portsmouth and examine the Governor with regard to his military affiliations. The *L.J.* (IV, 238) and Warner, f. 65, state that L. Kimbolton accompanied Stapleton and Clotworthy. On 13 May Stapleton reported on the journey to Portsmouth but the report itself is not included in the *C.J.*, II, 146, see D'Ewes (Harl. 163), f. 175. Jermyn fled rather than testify. S.P. 16/480: 20, 28.

198. Goring was subsequently, on 11 and 16 June (*C.J.*, II, 173, 177), ordered to attend the House for questioning concerning a plot to draw the army to London. A report from the committee of seven on his examination was made in the House on 21 June, *C.J.*, II, 182. D'Ewes (Harl. 163), ff. 326–328, contains an account of Goring's examination. See also Rushworth, *Hist Collections*, IV, 291–292; HMC, *13 Report*, Appendix, 15–23 (Portland MSS.)

199. For the members of the committee of the Lower House, see *C.J.* II, 152. The particulars agreed on at the joint committee meeting 20 May were resolved on in the Lower House the following day. *C.J.*, II, 153; *L.J.*, IV, 255.

200. Perhaps one of Drake's philosophical observations.

201. *C.J.*, II, 154. The report itself is not included in the *C.J.* Sir Henry Garway had come a farmer of the great customs in 1621 and headed his own syndicate in 1637, backed by the Earl of Dorset. Ashton, *Crown and Money Market*, 92, 100. For Wolstenholme, see above, n. 57. On 1 June the Commons passed 13 resolutions concerning the customs farmers, *C.J.*, II, 163. For the report see, D'Ewes (Harl. 163), ff. 219–222; Verney, pp. 78–79 contains a brief account of the report; Rawl. 1099, ff. 3–6v.

202. D'Ewes (Harl. 163), f. 254, does not record Vane's speech. See Rawl. 1099, ff. 31–32.

203. According to D'Ewes (Harl. 163), f. 255: *Sir John Culpepper moved about coining of plate. This proposition held debate a long time. Divers spoke about it.* See Rawl. 1099, ff. 32v–33v. A committee was appointed (*C.J.*, II, 164) "to consider of some way for the bringing in of the plate of the kingdom", and was to meet at 6 o'clock the following morning (3 June) in the Star Chamber to prepare a bill.

204. Drake's entry regarding *dishes* may relate to a proposition made at the committee

which met on the morning of 3 June and reported to the House on 4 June (C.J., II, 168), although it is difficult to place the entry exactly. In the debate on coining plate which took place on 4 June D'Ewes (Harl. 163), f. 267, notes that: . . . *Mr. Treasurer made his report from the committee that was appointed to consider of the means to raise money. Then divers spoke to the matter of coining of plate: Mr. Charles Price began and said it was a new way and that which our ancestors had never used and therefore wished that we might decline it. Sir John Hotham spoke that we might proceed with it and hoped that men would be willing to part with their plate, [it] being but a vanity. Others spoke also, some for and some against the said proposition.* D'Ewes himself followed the other speakers with a long speech on the disgrace of having to resort to coining plate to get ready money. Hotham was himself known for his frugality and "narrow living". J.T. Cliffe, *The Yorkshire Gentry* (Univ. of London, 1969), 123. D'Ewes notwithstanding, the House resolved that the monies from the plate should be used for the disbanding of the armies. C.J., II, 168.

205. This paragraph is included by D'Ewes (Harl. 163), f. 264 and C.J., II, 167 as item four in Pierrepont's report containing a list of reasons why bishops ought not to have voice in parliament.

206. The words *Pierrepont said* have been crossed out in the MS. following the word *Episcopacy.*

207. Pierrepont reported the nine reasons why bishops ought not to have voices in parliament that were drawn up by the committee on episcopacy. After considerable debate the reasons were resolved on in the House of Commons this day (4 June). C.J., II, 167.

208. John Spencer, John Greene, Nathaniel Robinson, and Adam Bancks were lay preachers who were given a "sharp reprehension" by the Speaker this day and warned that if they should offend the House again they would be severely punished. C.J., II, 170; see also Rushworth, *Hist. Collections,* IV, 282. A similar entry in Cobbett, *Parl. Hist.,* II, 817, includes John Durant or Durance. On Spencer, Greene, and Durance see Brook, *Lives of the Puritans,* III, 529, 31–32; 34–37

209. I have been unable to identify this speaker.

210. Mr. Herbert Price and Sir Wm. Widdrington had on the previous evening (8 June) taken candles from the Serjeant without permission of the House. D'Ewes (Harl. 163), ff. 301–302, reports that: "He [Price] *therefore stood up and in his place confessed that he had not been long a parliament man and therefore he might be ignorant of the orders of the House, and therefore desired the pardon thereof if he had transgressed. That his intention was only to advance the service of the House in what he did, for, many desiring to have the question put touching the Lord Digby, and it growing late and candles being called for and brought in, when he perceived that they were likely to be carried out again he stepped out of his place to the Serjeant and took one of the candles from him and set it down on the House floor that it might have been of use to all.*

After he had spoken he withdrew into the Committee Chamber and then we fell to debate the business. MR. HYDE excused the fact as done with a good intention and said that others were as faulty as he who would have thrust the Serjeant out of the House when he brought in the candles, and said that the Serjeant did well in bringing the same candles into the House when it grew dark. . . .

Divers spoke after him and agreed that the Serjeant ought not to bring in lights without the consent and order of the House. . . .

Sir William Widdrington came in after him [and], the Speaker having told him his offense at which the House took exception, he thereupon stood up in his place and excused himself confessing that he indeed took the candle from the Serjeant desiring to hold it that himself might be seen because he intended to speak.

So being bidden to withdraw by the Speaker and divers others he went up into the Committee Chamber. Then we fell in debate of both their offenses, and the Serjeant of the House being commanded to relate the whole circumstance – who took the candles from him and who pulled off his cloak – stood just in the place where the bar used to be laid cross and there made a full relation of it.

About eleven of the clock, soon after the Serjeant had ended, Mr. Treasurer returned and divers spoke to the matter of the offense and the manner of it. Some excused it as an error only and so thought that a sharp reprehension was sufficient for them standing in their places. But others said that it was done with much violence and that if God had not prevented it it might have occasioned blows and bloodshed. . . .

Ordered that Sir William Widdrington and Mr. Herbert Price, after the votes given in (Ayes – 189; Noes – 172), shall for their offense to this House be sent to the Tower during the pleasure of the House. (Rawl. 1099 gives the figures for the division as Ayes 182, noes. 175.)

Price and Widdrington petitioned the House on 12 June (C.J., II, 173) for their release (the petition was not read until 14 June, *Ibid.*, 175) which was granted. An account of this business is printed in Cobbett, *Parl. Hist.*, II, 818–819.

211. On Sat., 12 June, Fiennes's report from the committee of seven (see above, n. 194) was ordered postponed until the following Tues. morning. C.J., II, 174.

212. Holles this day reported on a letter received by the E. of Northumberland wherein Northumberland's brother, Mr. Percy, related news concerning a second army plot. The letter is printed in Rushworth, *Hist. Collections*, IV, 255–257. For a more complete account of the business see C.J., II, 174, 175. According to Whitelock's *Memorials*, I, pp. 134–135, some officers in the English army formed a junta and drew up heads for a petition to the King incorporating in it the three points listed above in Drake. Part of the petition is printed in Gardiner, *Hist. of Eng.*, IX, 399; the points listed in Drake are not included there.

213. The bill for abolishing episcopacy was brought into the House on 27 May (C.J., II, 159) and debated in committee on 11 and 12 June (and again on 21 June). Sir Henry Vane spoke on 12 June of "the improbability of settling any firm or durable peace so long as the cause of the war yet continues . . .". Cobbett, *Parl. Hist.*, II, 826. Drake's notes are undated.

214. On Goring's examination, see above, n. 198. According to D'Ewes (Harl. 163), f. 291, Strafford had offered the Lieutenant of the Tower 22,000 *l.* for help with the escape. See also Verney, pp. 94–97 and Gardiner, *Hist. of England*, IX, 366. See also Rawl. 1099, ff. 70–72. Goring was re-examined and a report made 21 June.

215. I have been unable to determine to what the note pertains.

216. By 22 June information concerning a Scottish plot against Charles I led by the E. of Montrose was known in England; rumors had circulated for about a month prior to this date. See Gardiner, *Hist. of Eng.*, IX, 395–401; Rushworth, *Hist. Collections*, IV, 290–291. Charles in his speech to both Houses this day (L.J., IV, 283) chose not to enlarge on the issue of the plot. On 23 June the instructions by Lord Montrose were to be examined by committee. Rawl. 1099, f. 83v.

217. On 24 June Pym reported the heads concerning the safety of the kingdom which had been drawn up by the committee of seven. The heads were read and resolved on question to be the basis of a conference with the Lords this day. The complete heads

are printed in C.J., II, 184–185. For a report of Pym's speech at the conference (and another copy of the heads) see L.J., IV, 285–287. See also Rawl. 1099, ff. 87–89.

218. The 6th head concerned papists at court. According to D'Ewes (Harl. 163), f. 347, there was some discussion by Thomas Tomkins and Herbert Morley that the Queen Mother *might be sent away as well as the priests and Jesuits*.

219. See Anon. diary (Yale Uncat. 226), n. 166.

APPENDIX A

Undated Speeches[1]

[f. 92v] MR. PYM[2] moved that for the better continuance of the good correspondency with the City that they might not be moved in anything that should corner difficulty from them but what may have a smooth and easy passage.

MR. HAMPDEN[3] being set in the chair for the ministers' remonstrance first read the order then said we will, if you please, proceed where you last left and then read how far they voted; and so began upon the next article.

[f. 90v] [ANONYMOUS] 1. There are two powerful and effectual [*illegible*] to preserve all governments and to keep them from/
    The one as often to reduce and recompose them to the rules of their first institution.[4] For the first we have laid a very good foundation by one triennial parliament which will give us an opportunity of repairing the breaches that shall be at any time near us – human frailty and corruption. For the second means let us look into [*illegible*] entirely [*illegible*] Roman state, a pattern of best government and we shall find a father not only sitting in judgment and condemning his sons to death who were enemies to the state but also present and assisting at their execution. You have one of them before you [f. 90] who did what in him lay not only to inflame us to an arbitrary government but with a black, formidable judgment to prefer misery, even for the children born to show mercy to such will be to show cruelty to ourselves and those that come after us.
    I am not so inconsiderate but to object to myself that it is somewhat improper to produce an ancient and foreign example in this place, but to refrain altogether what is but [*illegible*] ourselves of the wisdom of forgoing [*illegible*] what surely/

[f. 91] I hope we shall set us those martyrs to prosperity that shall make the successors of those judges so careful how they run us and themselves upon these rocks.

74

A man/

[f. 66] [ANONYMOUS.][5] The obstacles you will find will [be] doubts and fears of a man. He that takes away obstacle[s] does as good service as he that [*illegible*] helps. I cannot wonder at the answers of the people that you have represented to you. Things of greatest burden, as the ship money, would be taken off.

[f. 92] [*Illegible*][6] by Lord of Falkland to consider of [*illegible*] themselves to any objections that shall be made to the Lord. As let the City see that he is a great man but the E. of [*illegible*] not us see that he is a great man then, for what [*illegible*] is propounded not little of heart. There was no writing dated till Richard I time. The poet [*illegible*] said men in their youth may study for emulation and glory but when they come to years those considerations are all drowned in utility and interest.

[f. 74] SIR BENJAMIN RUDYARD[7] said that we should make so many examples that we should leave none to take example. It is of ill consequence in a commonwealth if you make *multis utile bellum*. In letting of ground consider what will feed me: how many cattle or [*illegible*], how many loads of hay.

[f. 74] SIR FREDERICK CORNWALLIS said he that is bad shall be made worse than he is, he that [is] rich shall be made richer than he is, and he that is good shall be made better than he is.

[f. 66v] At a committee for the supply.[8]

Mr. Pym propounded to have it put to the question whether we should go in an extraordinary way or go by subsidy. Subsidies are valued at 50 thousand pounds apiece.

Mr. Vaughan said that the crisis of the parliament and the crisis of the commonwealth depend upon what you have now [in] debate. 1. Consider what you have to do by way of counsel; 2ly, consider what difficulties and obstacles you may meet in this way and labor to remove them.

All your counsel that you apply to delinquents is accidental and contingent and we had need to apply them to a certain way that may not fail us. For the way by/

[f. 67v] This last article has been a very pregnant and teeming article, it has produced much more. Devise what may be final to engender a/[9]

My lord has commanded me to represent you that the first thing is a uniformity of the Church government.

TREASURER. That both the Houses are in consideration of it, the neglecting Cinque Ports. He said that the King would have them acquiesce therein. When we say agree we do not intend a final agreement but with relation to the parliament. That his Majesty desires the disbanding the Irish army and desires you would take it into your cares.

FALKLAND. If Earl of Strafford had not been sick last summer he would have had a pluck [*illegible*]. A man made drunk with prosperity and transported with passion/

CULPEPPER. We cannot cure a wound unless we search it to the bottom.

[f. 94v][10] [*Illegible*] upon ourselves if we put the question. They preach orders sometime to be referred to the patentees [*illegible*] to the Attorney General.

We [*illegible*] you as far for this particular as we can, let us go to the next consideration. It concerns us both in honor, confidence, and interest. One post will not uphold the fabric, many will; as I take there is an old time and a new. Whether it will not be fit to consider the strength of the state and the Protestant army and if it be not of considerable strength it may be reinforced to meet with such accidents as may happen in case this new army should stand at defiance and refuse to disband.

NOTES

1. The following sixteen speeches or fragments which are undated in Drake I have been unable to place.
2. Pym was a strong proponent of the policy to encourage the City's financial support of parliamentary activities. On 11 Feb. he spoke for the "speedy dispatch" of City money. See Drake, n. 26.
3. I find no other evidence that Hampden chaired the committee for the minister's remonstrance.
4. Six judges were charged with treasonous activities, particularly with regard to the ship money case, by the House of Commons in February 1641. The reference to a "black, formidable judgment" and the admonition concerning the "successors of those judges" would suggest that this speech had been given during the course of the proceedings against the judges. See Notestein, *D'Ewes*, 352–353, for the articles against the judges.

5. The sentiment expressed in the first line of this speech is incorporated in Pym's metaphor of his speech of 7 Nov. 1640. See Rushworth, *Hist. Collections*, IV, 21.
6. The classical reference in the last line provides no clue to the speech.
7. The speeches of Rudyard and Cornwallis are adjacent in the MS.; I am unable to date either speech.
8. Debate on supply occurred on numerous days. These speeches may be part of the proceedings of 12 May.
9. A fragment from Gervase Holles's 26 April speech against the treaty with the Scots for which he was censured by the House. See C.J., II, 128; Cobbett, *Parl. Hist.*, II, 771 and the Anon. diary (Yale Uncat. 226), p. 116. I am unable to confirm that the other speeches on the folio, following the Holles fragment, relate to the same business.
10. The notes on f. 94v are faded and difficult to read; I am unable to place them in any context.

APPENDIX B

Entries from Ogden MS. 7, no. 52[1]

(The're many disadvantages lie lurking under a hasty belief. Guill.)

[17 (?) February]

It is no expiation but a qualification only.

Vane. We cannot apprehend suddenly the consequences and inconveniences of a specious proposition.

The point fell for our debate; we are quite receded from and fallen upon.

Vane. There are two things considerable in the business: the raising credit and getting money on that credit. If you find a way to pass over the first difficulty I shall show you the means to get the money.

[17 March]

[TREASURER VANE.] It is a business that concerns the whole kingdom and therefore I shall humbly move that we may turn the House into a grand committee that so by freeness of debate we may grow to some ripeness of resolution.

At a committee for the Navy.

Treasurer Vane said I am glad to see so general a sense and inclination of the House to speed this business. There is never a prince in Christendom that has not these last twenty years increased in shipping. The first thing that would be taken into consideration would be what proportion of ships would be fit for a guard, then how to raise the money for the setting them forth.

Propositions were made to have ships of divers sizes and capacities fit for variable occasions. Then to speak with butchers, brewers, graziers, fishmongers to learn of them the rates and prices of things.

Let's state the particulars whereupon we shall go by steps. Our first step would be to know what Sir William Russell will advance for this service.

Committee for the necessity of the kingdom.

78

Our stock is almost spent and what we have now in debate is to consider of a way and means to raise monies and to consult how to rid the kingdom of the vast charge that lies upon us. And that there may no inconvenience fall upon the kingdom, whilst the treaty lasts, by either army.

[18 March]

Answer was made that Sir William could not advance present money but that he would give his credit as far as it would go.

The next consideration will be the preparation of victuals and the question will be whether you will go by the great, by contracting with the victualers, or make provision yourselves.

Trinity men call in. Vane said you shall have after the rate of 8d. ob. a man and you shall have half in hand and the other half when your work is at an end.

Vane. There is shortly the state and issue of the business. We can only prepare the contract and report it to the House. You see upon what disadvantage we are brought by not tying things earlier.

Young Sir Henry Vane moved to call in the Trinity men once again and to consult alike with their experience how we may husband things to best advantage. Where their own interest is not concerned it is likely they will deal clearly with us.

I am sorry when we have made so good a step into the business we should let it fall to the ground. Let's speak with Sir W. Russell and set the work agoing. Let's not let ourselves down too low.

[22 March – Afternoon]

Earl of Bristol told us how forward and willing they should be to anything that might conduce to the settling of the great distempers of the kingdom. He conceived that was not the granting of subsidies that would open credit but the settling of a firm peace; the doubts whereof staggered men's minds and their fears of unquiet times made them keep their monies in their purses.

His Lordship said further that their Lordships were agreed with the House of Commons concerning the disbanding of the Irish army. The only difference was *sub modo*. They desiring to limit the joining with this condition: that the old army shall be reinforced.

Let's think of a way to remove those impediments that might give a stop to the loan of monies. We are resolved to see as soon as possible we can the bottom of the Scots' demands, and not to give them above a month *non datum ultra*.

[22 and 23 March]

Bristol said was not the security the difficulty rested in, but the getting of the money. For the Lords, if money may be gotten, they are willing to join with us in giving particular security to such persons as shall advance monies and for their Lordships' indemnity to be countersecured by the security of the kingdom.

[25 March – Afternoon]

At another conference.

Bristol. That which would be first in our eye and consideration would be of the way to furnish a sum of money. For the facilitating of this he thought the removing of the obstacles and impediments would be the first step.

Secretary Vane said we are in a consumption. Unless you cure the lungs it is to no purpose to give all the physic in the world. We plant upon a rock and anchor upon a quicksand, while we are at this distance with the King all we do will come to nothing.

May 28, 1641

At a conference with the Lords in the debate concerning the providing of monies Earl of Bristol told us that they were but the conduits to convey our wiles and pleasures to the Scots and were ready to hear what we had done upon consideration of the last proposition of the Scots concerning their having part of the brotherly assistance of goods.

Treasurer Vane said we should adhere to our terms [illegible] which the Scots seemed satisfied with, but if any new proposition came from them/

[Undated]

There is no means to effect and settle a firm happiness to this kingdom. Then/

Extensively slighted and vilified we are not sensible of the great burden the people sustain.

NOTE

1. See above, Description of the Diaries, n. 15.

II
The Anonymous Diary

Uncat. MS. 226, Beinecke Rare Book and Manuscript Library,
Yale University

[f. 1] Monday 1 February 1640

Before the government of the Church was debated 'twas debated whether
Dr. Eden, Dr. Parry, and Dr. Chaworth, 3 being bishops' chancellors, and
having taken the new oath never to consent to any alteration in Church
government, should give votes or hear the debate concerning Church
government; especially being they have taken an oath as chancellors never
to consent to diminish the prerogative of the Bishop of Canterbury or of
the Prerogative Court.[1]

This was not resolved upon question but it was left to their discretion to
come or forbeare.

[f. 1v] Sir Robert Pye[2] was sent to the Lords to desire [if] the judges
might be examined in the presence of some members of this House
concerning the charge against the Lord Finch and, that they would take
some speedy course for the appearance of and proceedings against my Lord
Finch.

The Lords returned this answer: that it should be done as it was desired.

The part of the ministers' remonstrance concerning Church government was read.[3]

[f. 2] Tuesday 2 Febuary

MR. PEARD reported from the committee for monopolies that Sir
Nicholas Crispe had a patent for redwood, but it was not voted for a
monopoly either at the committee or in the House. But he was voted at
the committee for a monopolist for having a patent for gathering
copperas stones, and a new warrant to choose a new member in his
stead.[4]

[f. 2v] Wednesday 3 February
[*Committee of the Whole House*]

The House debated how much money we shall give the Scots.

Mr. Selden said, being the King had appointed 16 Lords to treat with the Scots, we have nothing to do to treat without commission, but we run into danger by assisting any that have a sword in their hands within the kingdom.[5]

My Lord Falkland said no danger to declare what we are willing to give in this way, that we are willing the Lords should conclude to give money not exceeding such a sum.[6]

[f. 3] Resolved upon question that this House does conceive 300,000*l.* is a fit proportion for that friendly assistance and relief formerly thought fit to be given towards the relief of their brethren the Scots, and that in due time the House will take into consideration the manner how and the time when the same shall be raised.

The Lords sent us this message: that the King's pleasure was that both Houses should attend him at Whitehall this afternoon at 2 a clock.[7]

[f. 3v] Thursday 4 February

Mr. Francis Neville was sent to the Tower during the pleasure of this House for accusing Mr. Henry Belasyse and Sir John Hotham at the Council Table for words spake in the last parliament.[8]

The town of Seaford in Sussex was returned to send burgesses to parliament.[9]

[f. 4] SIR THOMAS JERMYN delivered this from the Queen to this House: that she has been ready to use her best endeavors for a good understanding between King and p[arliament]. She moved with the Lords that petitioned for a parliament. She will always do good offices between King and people. That being Count Rossetti is offensive he shall be removed. Denmark House shall not be frequented to mass as it has been. Her ignorance in the law made her move the papists for money; she will do so no more. [f. 4v] She desires the parliament to look forward and not back and she will repay it with all her power.[10]

Mr. Treasurer Vane was sent up to deliver our vote for 300,000 *l.* for the Scots (in a conference) to the Lords.[11]

[f. 5] Friday 5 February

A bill read for the abolishing [of] idolatry and superstition, and for the better advancing of the true worship of God.[12]

Tis ordered the Lord Keeper should be moved from this House that all the divines in England and Wales should be put out of the commission of the peace. And the same message is sent to the Chancellor of the Duchy by members of this House.

MR. SPEAKER reported the King's speech to both Houses at Whitehall on Wednesday last.[13]

Mr. Stevens delivered a petition with 2 or 3 thousand hands to it from Gloucestershire, against episcopacy.[14]

[f. 5v] SIR THOMAS DANBY made answer in the House (in his place) to the petition against him concerning the execution of 2 persons by martial law in Yorkshire about October last. This business was committed to my Lord Strafford's committee.[15]

The Lords returned the bill for 4 subsidies and the bill for a [sic] triannual[16] parliaments with the alterations which they desire to be amended.

[f. 6] Saturday 6 February

The Usher of the Court of Wards[17] claimed privilege of this House to be freed for [sic] arrests because he and his servants attend in the court to wait upon committees. But the House would not allow him any privilege.

Tis against the orders and privileges of this House to have any of the members examined as a witness or [to] plead as a counsellor before the Lords without leave of this House.[18]

The amendments of the subsidy bill were twice read in the House and committed.

The amendments of the parliament bill were likewise read and committed.

We had a conference with the Lords about the Scottish treaty.[19]

[f. 6v] MR. TREASURER VANE reported from the Lords the Scots' thanks for the 300,000*l*. and for calling them "brothers". The English Lords desire a cessation of arms to be renewed for a month longer.

Resolved upon question that there shall be a continuation of the cessation of arms for a month longer, from the 16 of this Feb. to 16 March, upon the same terms, so as the treaty last so long.

Resolved upon question that Mr. Strode has given no offense in speaking these words: "the sons of Zeruiah are too strong for us".[20]

[f. 7] Monday 8 February

The London petition against bishops and that part of the ministers' concerning Church government was debated 10 hours.[21]

[f. 7v] Tuesday 9 February

Mr. Francis Neville that was committed for breach of privilege did make an humble acknowledgment of his fault and petitioned for liberty.[22]

Yesterday's debate was resumed;[23] and resolved upon question: the London petition, and that part of the ministers' remonstrance about Church government, and such other petitions of that nature as have been read in the House, shall be referred to the committee of 24 with the addition of 6 others, reserving to this House the main point of episcopacy. This committee is only to prepare heads of debate.

[f. 8] Wednesday 10 February

'Twas declared by order that Mr. Holles may proceed in his suit against Sir Anthony Ashley Cooper, notwithstanding he is returned a member of this House, because there is 3 returned for that place and so his election questionable; therefore, till the election is determined, Mr. Holles may proceed.[24]

Mr. Francis Neville[25] acknowledged his offense at the bar on his knees and asked forgiveness and thereupon he was released of his imprisonment.

[f. 8v] SIR JOHN HOTHAM reported there would be 125,000l. due to the King's army the 16 of this February and there will be 52,000l. due to the Scots on the same day for the relief of the northern counties.

[f. 9] Resolved upon question that the first 50,000l. out of the 60,000l. to be provided by the City of London shall be employed for the King's army upon account.

Ordered my Lord General be moved to pay out of this 50,000l. to the country a proportion of a month's billet, and the rest to the soldiers.

Resolved upon question the next 2,500l.[26] that shall be raised shall be disposed for the relief of the northern counties.

[f. 9v] Thursday 11 February

SIR WALTER EARLE reported the Irish army to consist of 7,000 papists and 1,000 protestants, and urged many reasons why we should desire the

Lords to join with us to the King to desire this army may be presently disbanded.[27]

[f. 10] A conference with the Lords about the Scots' treaty.[28]

Reported by MR. TREASURER VANE the seventh article which was to have all proclamations, books, and other things that call them traitors, recalled and abolished; and this article was consented unto by this House.

[f. 10v] Friday 12 February

Resolved upon question that Sir Robert Berkeley, one of the judges of the King's Bench, shall be accused of High Treason and other great misdemeanors; and desire he may be committed presently.[29]

Sir John Culpepper is sent with this message to the Lords; and the Lords did send him, and commit the judge presently.[30]

[f. 11] Mr. Hampden was sent to the Lords to desire a free conference with a proportionable number of the Lords in a committee about the amendments in the bill for triannual parliaments.

The Lords agreed to meet us this afternoon in the Painted Chamber with 22 Lords, and we sent 44 to meet them.[31]

[f. 11v] Saturday 13 February

Mr. Arundel (now a member of this House) sued Sir Gamaliel Capell in the spiritual court, and Capell moved in the King's Bench for a prohibition and had a rule for it, and sent it to Mr. Arundel. Upon this he complained of breach of privilege, but the House would not challenge this for a privilege.[32]

Sir Edward Coke's 11 books are now sent by the King's command to Sir Ranulph Crew, amongst which are these three: *The Jurisdiction of Courts*, the *Pleas of the Crown*, and the *Commentary upon Magna Carta*.[33]

[f. 12] Twas ordered all these books shall be restored to Sir Robert Coke according to the intent of Sir Edward, his father.

The Lords desired a conference by the same committee of 44 to meet the 22 Lords that met yesterday, about the same triannual bill for parliaments, and we agreed to it.

Sir Robert Harley was sent to the Lords to desire a conference concerning the disbanding the new Irish Army, the disarming the English papists, and the banishing the English papists from the court, and particularly those 4: Mr. Walter Montagu, Sir Kenelm Digby, Sir Toby Matthews, and Sir John Winter.[34]

[f. 12v] Sir Walter Earle, Sir John Clotworthy,[35] Mr. Reynolds, Mr. Lisle and Mr. Edward [sic] Waller are appointed to manage this conference.

[f. 13] Monday 15 February

18 members of this House are appointed[36] to move the King this day that he will please to come to the parliament house in convenient time to give his royal assent to the bill of subsidies.

Mr. Treasurer Vane is appointed to move the King that this committee of 18 may have access to the King.

The King answered we should know his pleasure tomorrow.

[f. 13v] Sir Francis Seymour was sent with a message to the Lords to let them know this House had appointed some members of this House to move the King to come to parliament in convenient time to give his royal assent to the bill of subsidies,[37] and that this House desires their Lordships to move the King to come to parliament in convenient time to give his royal assent to the bill for triannual parliaments.

[f. 14] Resolved upon question that the borough of Cokermouth, in the county of Cumberland, shall be restored to send burgesses to parliament.

[f. 14v] Tuesday 16 February

If a bill be read the second time and that any man speak for the committing of it, and the House resolved to cast it out, then the first question must be whether it shall be committed or not; and if the negative carry it, then the next question must be whether it shall be engrossed or not; and if the negative carry it, then it is to be cast out without any further question and this was done in a Mr. Wells his case this day.[38]

[f. 15] A message to the Lords to desire a conference by a committee of both Houses concerning the Earl of Strafford.

Mr. Maxwell (with the Black Rod) came into the House and told the Speaker and all the members that the King commanded us all to wait upon him in the House of Lords.

Upon this we all went up and then the King bid the Clerk of the Crown to read the title of the bill for triannual parliaments, and then the [f. 15v] King made a short speech[39] and commanded him to read it again, and then he did command the Clerk of the Parliament to pronounce these words, [blank], and so that bill did pass.

Then Mr. Speaker, having the bill for 4 subsidies in his hands, made a short speech to the King to let him know the Commons did present him with these subsidies; and then he delivered the bill to some of the Lords to convey it [f. 16] up to the Clerk of the Parliament, and then the King called to the Clerk of the Crown to read the title of it, which being done, the King command[ed] the Clerk of the Parliament to pronounce these words, [*blank*].

And so the bill passed. All the Lords were in their robes, but the King was not.

[f. 16v] Mr. Pym was appointed to manage the conference with the Lords in which we desired the Lords to call my Lord Strafford speedily to answer.[40]

A message from the Lords to let us know they were full of thanks and joy for the passing of the bill for triannual parliaments; and they intended to move the King that they might give him public thanks for it, and therefore they desired this House to join with them in it. [f. 17] And then the messengers did intimate that they intended to move the King that there might be public ringing in all the churches in this City and bonfires to express their joy for the same. We answered we agreed with their Lordships in this.

[Afternoon]

And both Houses did accordingly attend the King in the Banqueting House at Whitehall this present day, and my Lord Keeper did there give the King thanks in the name of both Houses for his grace and favor in [f. 17v] passing the bill for triannual parliaments. Mr. Speaker was present, but my Lord Keeper only spoke in the name of both Houses.

The King made a short speech[41] to desire the parliament to consider the commonwealth and then to do somewhat for his particular person, now he had done so much for them.

[f. 18] Wednesday 17 February

The Queen's jointure was read again and committed.[42]

[f. 18v] Thursday 18 February

Mr. Thomas Coningsby appeared at the bar on his knee as a delinquent for misdemeanors about the election at St. Albans.[43]

A message from the Lords for a conference concerning the sequestration of my Lord Strafford from all his offices.

SIR WALTER EARLE reported from this conference that the Lords would join with us to petition the King to sequester my Lord Strafford from his offices until his trial is passed.[44]

[f. 19] A message from the Lords to desire a free conference by a committee of both Houses concerning the proceedings against the Earl of Strafford.

MR. PYM reported from this conference. The Lords sent for my Lord Strafford to make his answer and his counsel gave divers reasons wherefore the answer was not ready, upon which the Lords gave them till Wednesday next to bring in the answer peremptorily. And that the Lords have allowed him counsel and to put in his answer in writing, and that he has seen the articles against him.

[f. 19v] Upon this report the House appointed a committee to consider of this report and also the proceedings in the Lords House against my Lord Strafford,[45] and what concerns the kingdom in general touching the legality of these proceedings and to consider what tis fit for the Commons to claim in case of impeachments.

[f. 20] Friday 19 February

MR. HYDE reported from the committee for the Court of Honor. My. Lord Marshal's first commission was dated 19 *Jacobi*, but no Marshal's Court; was not heard of till 1 March 1633. But 3 years before that he did do a very hard thing about the complaining against a Herald, Mr. Say, a counsellor, for saying no fees were due. He was called into the court and kept there a long time, and divers other strange causes.

This House resolved upon question the Constable and Earl Marshal's Court had no jurisdiction to hold plea of words.

[f. 20v] Resolved upon question that the Earl Marshal can hold no court without the Constable.

Resolved upon question that the Earl Marshal's Court is a grievance.[46]

[f. 21] Saturday 20 February

Resolved upon question that two subsidies shall be granted for the maintenance of the King's army and the supply of the northern parts.

[f. 21v] Monday 22 February

Lord Russell sent to the Lords to desire a free conference concerning the proceedings against my Lord of Strafford.

The committee appointed about this on Thursday last[47] were commanded to manage this conference. Three things were appointed to be considered by this committee: first, that the Lords have allowed him a copy of the articles against him; secondly, that they have allowed him to answer in writing; thirdly, they have allowed him counsel. The 2 first of these are passed, so the committee did not consider them.

[f. 22] But for the third, about allowing him counsel, tis conceived he ought to have none because 'tis in case of treason.[48] First, if counsel should conceal treason they were in misprision of treason, therefore tis not safe for them. Secondly, there is no precedent for it, but divers against it: 4 *Ri.* 2, Sir Ralph Ferriers case, being accused for treason was allowed as none.[49] 5 *Ri.* 2, *numero* 45, in the case of the University of Cambridge it was denied to the Mayor and commonalty.[50] 5 *Ri.* 2, *numero* 43, Cogan's[51] case, it was denied. And no counsel was ever allowed till 21 *Jacob.*, in my Lord Middlesex['s] case, and he [f. 22v] was not accused of any capital crime.[52] At this time the Lords made an order for it, and 1 *Car.*, in my Lord of Bristol's case, there was counsel assigned and the King sent the Lords word it was against the fundamental law, and the Lords sent him word there was an order made for it. The King replied that his Father's counsel were never heard about it, neither were the judges consulted with about it, but in this case he would admit it, but he would admit it to no other, being against the fundamental law.[53]

[f. 23] Tuesday 23 February

Resolved upon question that no bishop can inhibit any minister that is lawfully instituted and inducted from preaching in his own parish as often as he pleases.[54]

A committee appointed to peruse Bishop Montagu's pardon and prepare a bill to reverse it; and to consider of Bishop Maynwaring's pardon[55] and to inquire by whose means he was preferred and to prepare a bill to take away his bishopric.

[f. 23v] SIR WALTER EARLE[56] reported from the Lords they would join with us to move the King to disband the new army in Ireland, to disarm the papists here in England according to law, to banish Mr. Walter Montagu, Sir Kenelme Digby, Sir John Winter, and Sir Toby Matthews from the court; and 4 of the Lords spoke to persuade us to be favorable to the Queen's servants because she has been very willing to do all good offices between the King and his people,[57] and that she has but ten popish servants in ordinary and but 2 of them of quality, and one of them a woman.

[f. 24] Wednesday 24 February

Mr. Enyon's bill for cutting off an entail of land was rejected.[58]

MR. PYM reports the committee has prepared 14 general Articles against my Lord Archbishop of Canterbury in maintenance of their accusation of High Treason.

1. His endeavor to subvert the fundamental laws of the Kingdom.
2. Printing and licensing books that preached for unlimited power.
3. Corrupting the judges of the kingdom by menaces and otherwise.
4. Bribery to his own use and for building Paul's church, and selling judicial places.
5. Making and publishing canons directly against law.
[f. 24v] 6. Exercising a papal and a tyrannical power over the subjects.
7. Opposition against religion and the articles of this church.
8. Encroaching upon divers great officers in not letting them present to any ecclesiastical livings.
9. Corrupt chaplains of his own, and suffering them to license books.
10. Endeavoring to reconcile this Church to the Roman church.
11. Suppressing preaching over all the kingdom.
12. Causing a division between us and the reformed churches.
[f. 25] 13. Making a division between us and the Scots.
14. Bringing the King into a dislike of parliaments.
These Articles were voted to be engrossed.[59]

[f.25v] Thursday 25 February

We had a conference with the Lords and my Lord Keeper delivered my Lord Strafford's answer to Mr. Solicitor and a copy of it to Mr. Hampden, to the intent that as we read the answer this copy might be examined and the original be returned to the Lords.

We took this course in reading the answer: First we read the first Article and then the answer to it, and so throughout, first the Article and then the answer to that particular Article.

[*Afternoon*]

[The Articles drawn by the House of Commons against Thomas Wentworth, Earl of Strafford, and his responses to them.][60]
1 *Special Charge*: He being made President of York, 8 *Caroli*, the King's
power was diminished by his commission. That he had the same power as
our Star Chamber. That he had power to examine and judge in Chancery,
which others before him had not, or used not, as he did. That he
disinherited divers. That he fined and punished men to their ruin against
the laws. That he would admit no prohibition nor grant *habeas corpus*.

Response: He believes no material difference between his and other
commissions and if any alterations be they are rather for explanation than
enlargement of power. He was no procurer of the enlargement of his
commission. He joined the best lawyers in the land when he sat in
judgment and followed former precedents. He executed only according to
law: Darcy and Bourchier were fined accordingly. The rest he denies.

2 *Article*: He procured a new commission larger than the former. On the
Bench he told the people that the least finger of the King's should be
heavier than the loins of the law.

Response: He says his words were clean contrary: That the least finger of
the law was heavier than the King's loins.

3 *Article*: He did in a public speech before the greatest [*blank*] of Ireland
say that Ireland was a conquered nation with which the King might do
what he would; that their charters were nothing worth.

Response: He denies the words as they are alleged but confesses he said
Ireland was not governed as England, the reason of their many different
customs; that many of their charters were void did highly extoll the King's
goodness to them, else it might be worse.

4 *Article*: He threatened the Lord Cork that he would have his lands, that
he would make any act of state as binding as any act of parliament and did
arrogate to himself power above law.

Response: The order against the L. Cork was legal and according to
former precedents. He remembers no such threatening words, but if the
Lord Cork did disobey the act of state he would imprison him. That he
said the acts of state should bind, but compared them not to the acts of
parliament. That he governed according to law.

5 *Article*: He did extend his power to the goods and lives of subjects. In
1635 he did sentence Mountnorris to death. In 1638 he did sentence
another to death, and executed him without law.

Response: He had a commission as other deputies and lieutenants had
before him to use martial discipline, yet no soldier in his time had suffered

death thereby. Mountnorris had used mutinous words in Dublin against the Deputy [Strafford] for which, and breach of other articles, he was sentenced to death by the unanimous consent of 20 the chief officers of war, which judgment was wholly left to them; yet he sued and obtained his pardon from the King which he [for] either contemning or neglecting was again committed. The other person which he is said to have executed being neither named nor described he cannot make answer unto.

6 *Article*: Without legal proceedings he dispossessed Mountnorris and three others of their lands and tenements.

Response: The causes having depended long in Chancery he, assisted by the learned judges of the law, relieved the plaintiff against Mountnorris and so dispossessed him.

7 *Article*: Upon the case of tenure he did procure the judges to give their opinions and thereby dispossessed Dillon and others of their freehold to the ruin of hundreds without legal trial.

Response: With the Council of State he proclaimed that all should bring in what they held by statute in that tenure, whereupon Lord Dillon, the judges having drawn up the case, gave judgment against him; the rest he denies.

8 *Article*: He did upon the petition of Gifford imprison the Lord Loftus, made him to resign the seal. He imprisoned Kildare, made him to resign his land; so threatened a lady to make her relinquish her estate, and divers others, under pretence of disobedience in an arbitrary course.

Response: The Council Board having power to hear such causes as Gifford's, they sentenced against Loftus; after it was heard in England by the King, and the sentence ratified by the whole Council Board. The seal was required upon order made at the Council Board, upon disobedience whereof he was committed, which seal after he delivered upon the King's command. Kildare kept away writings contrary to award, which cause being by the King referred to the Council he was committed for contempt of the order. But after performance upon the King's letters he was relieved. He never imprisoned any but as his predecessors had done.

9 *Article*: 12 *Caroli* he gave power to commit such as should refuse to answer.

Response: He did nothing above law nor otherwise than his predecessors had done who gave unto bishops such warrants; and yet he in this kind gave only a warrant to the Bishop of Downe, after which, finding to be too large, he recalled the same.

10 *Article*: He improved the customs of Ireland to his own use, as *Caroli* 9 he overrated the goods of Ireland above a fifth part as hides, tallow, etc.

Response: The Lord Treasurer told him that the customs were let at 13,000*l*. per annum, but wished him to advance them, who told the Treasurer that some would give 15,000*l*. per annum with 8,000*l*. fine for 14 years, so as Strafford would be partner with them, which the Treasurer wished him and the King commanded him to do whereby to advance the King's profit. But he raised not the rates of customs but dissuaded the same; neither hides or tallow, etc., overrated.

11 *Article*: *Caroli* 9° he did for his own gain restrain the carriage of goods out of the land; and afterward for money gave license for the same, as vessel staves are raised from 5*l*. 10*s*. to 10*l*. the thousand.

Response: He denies he did anything for his own gain and says it was fit to restrain the exportation of these staves for saving of ship timber; and by the King he was commanded to lay a charge of 30*l*. per thousand upon the same, which brought to the King 1500*l*. per annum without any benefit to himself, which to other deputies had been worth 500*l*. per annum. Yet this charge was no hindrance to the country, for it was not paid by the native but by the exporter.

12 *Article*: 13 *Caroli*, under a color, he made a proclamation against bringing in tobacco, yet after imported it to his use and bought it all at his own price and set 6*d*. upon every pound to seal tobacco. The opposers he fined, imprisoned, and whipped, by which he raised an 100,000*l*. per annum and bought tobacco from 6*d*. to 3*d*. and raised divers monopolies.

Response: Tonnage and poundage are the inheritance of that crown. In King James['s] time there was 2*s*. set upon tobacco: 6*d*. poundage 18*d*. importage which was desired by the Commons in parliament. This was hired at 5,000*l*. per annum for the first five years and 10,000*l*. per annum for the six years following. By the King he was made partner with the contractors who have not in two years received above 8,000*l*. for their pains and great sums of money which he lent them. He denies whipping or imprisoning and says that for 18*d*. set for impost he has taken but 3*d*. The planters have better prizes in Ireland than in England, as 2*s*. or 2*s*.4*d*. per pound. Much tobacco is brought in to help the poor planters and sellers. The monopoly of starch was before him but fell after him; iron pots was granted without him; glasses granted to Sir Robert Mansel; tobacco pipes granted without him from England. He never countenanced bringing in monopolies nor was benefitted by them.

13 *Article*: He proclaimed the dressing of flax the native commodity and making of cloth to his own use.

Response: He ordered the making of linen cloth for the public good and thereupon acts of state were made and proclamations to make good cloth.

He bought flax seed from foreign parts. He bought their yarn, set up looms at his own charge, whereby to set the people on work. He never seized anyone's cloth but restored it again; he was no gainer but a loser hereby to a 1,000*l.*

14 Article: He imposed an oath upon boatmen to give a true account of what goods they received or carried out, and thereupon made a proclamation.

Response: This was done by the advice of lawyers, at the instance of the farmers, but never heard any to refuse or complain thereof.

15 Article: He devised to subdue the subjects to his own will, therefore, 8 *Caroli*, he taxed divers and great sums of money upon several towns by force of arms and, 12 *Caroli*, he sent soldiers to lie there where refusal was made for payment and this by warlike force; and did raise troops of horse and foot to expel Butler and 100 families else from their houses, and imprisoned them until they had surrendered their estates; and has levied war against the King.

Response: He has not taxed any such sums of money in such manner as is supposed, but in 1626 agents from Ireland to treat with the King granted 120,000*l.* to be paid unto him in 6 years, and by them agreed that the same contribution should be paid not to the Exchequer, but that the Deputy should distribute the same proportionably to several captains, which payment, if refused, they might forcibly recover the same, which was begun in Lord Falkland's time and so continued. St. Leger had commission to receive part of this money but I never heard any force used, though in this and the like cases it had been usually done, and so at Council Board it was decreed to be against them as rebels. He says that no soldiers were laid upon any place for his use or end without the consent of the Council Board. The rest he denies.

16 Article: He made an act that no complaint should be made unto the King but first unto himself, and thereupon made a proclamation that all Irish should reside in their own kingdom, and thereupon did imprison divers nobles and others for going into England to complain of him to the King.

Response: Such an order was made at the Council Table in England that justice might be done upon the place where the fault was committed, and for divers other reasons, but no way to suppress the subject; and so it was entered in England the third year before his going into Ireland that noblemen of Ireland should there reside and not go out without leave; yet he never denied leave to any but to Cork and Mountnorris because they had causes depending at that time in the country. Parry was committed for contempt.

17 Article: He, in scandal of his Majesty's government in England, said that Ireland should be made a pattern for the government of the King's other dominions.

Response: That the King was so pleased with their soldiers he said that in respect of them Ireland should be a pattern. The rest he denies.

18 Article: He increased the number of papists for his own end and power; raised an army of 7,000 papists who were well paid. He made compositions with them at low rates and discharged them from all courts.

Response: Lord Cork had seized upon mass houses and, before his coming to Ireland, had converted them to his own use, after which Kildare and others claimed such, and after 2 years trial no ground being found of their seizure of these houses he restored them to them from whom they were taken. The 7,000 soldiers he raised at the King's command but left the care to other generals; neither knows he whether they were papists or not, but conceives it is hard out of Ireland to raise such a number but the most should be such. Yet the most part of the captains are Protestants. He ordered all the old army to be Protestants and preferred no papist, though he found many. He was absent when the payment was made to the soldiers. The permission of the profession of their religion is no otherwise than usually has been; they do not compound for lower rates than heretofore, nay, in four years he has raised the composition from 2,300 per annum to 11,000 or 12,000 and by it has brought to the King an 100,000*l*., which is more than ever was received in Queen Elizabeth or King James his time, or more than England yields, and by this means he has lost the love of the papists.

19 Article: He framed a new oath that all should submit themselves to the King's commands whatever they were. Hereto forced the Scots there and imprisoned such as refused, fined some at 3,000*l*., others at 5,000*l*. apiece, adding, that this oath bound to ecclesiastical rites and that he would prosecute all refusers of it to death.

Response: He found in Ireland an 100,000 Scots while the King was at Berwick and thereupon put them to an oath devised by the Council and which the Scots desired thereby to clear themselves. That the Scots (except few) took it willingly, some refusers were sentenced and he confesses that he used his best endeavors that the Scots should take the oath or leave Ireland, but not to bring them into hatred or the observation of the ceremonies but for their allegiance.

20 Article: In the 15 and 16 *Caroli* he begets an ill opinion in the King of his subjects, the Scots: he is an incendiary, calls you rebels and traitors, would root the Scots out of Ireland, seized the Scottish ships thereby to hasten the war.

Response: He advised the King as a councillor and found it fit to raise an army when the Scots had one; moved the King to call a parliament in England and gave reasons for the same, whereupon the parliament was called. One Lord moved and all the rest consented that the coventers' demands could not be granted and therefore they must be forced to it. Hereupon a Council of War was called and borrowing of money till the parliament. He denies he called them all rebels except perhaps such who opposed the King. He did seize their ships to reduce them to obedience but denies that ever he intended to root them out of Ireland.

21 Article: He caused the King to break the pacification and to make war upon the Scots and if the parliament would not relieve the King he would cause the King to dissolve it.

Response: The pacification was broken before his coming into England; he moved for a parliament to a good end and said if the parliament would not relieve the King he would serve him some other way, meaning that which was lawful and just, for the King would take no other.

22 Article: He procured a parliament in Ireland and raised an army against the Scots and said if the parliament would not relieve the King he must use his prerogative to take what he would from the subject.

Response: He gained 4 subsidies for the King in Ireland, freely granted in parliament. He raised 8,000 for to secure that Kingdom and to keep the 100,000 Scots in obedience and to hinder Argyle's coming into Ireland, or if Argyle should go on towards England then that this Irish [blank] should be poured into Argyle's country thereby to reduce it. It was given out indeed by way of disguise that this army should land in Cumberland, but the Marquis Hamilton, the E. of Northumberland knew, and (the King presently affirms so much) that this army was not to go out of Ireland except as is before said in Argyle's country.

23 Article: The parliament meeting in England, Strafford and Canterbury having the chief trust thereof they two urged the parliament to subsidies and caused 12 subsidies to be demanded for the release of ship money. They two procured the King to dissolve the parliament. He stirred up the King against his best subjects and added that the King was to do what he would; told him that he had an army in Ireland to reduce them to his will.

Response: He denies that the King put more trust in him or Canterbury than in others, or to dissolve the parliament, but confesses that he coming to England 10 days after the parliament had sat he moved the Council to assist the King how to get money for the war, and so advised the King to lay down ship money thereby to get (if he could) 12 subsidies. Yet Strafford desired the King if he could not get 12 to take 8, and this Sir

Henry Vane was to have made known for the King to the best of the Commons, nay, said Strafford, would we could get 6. After the King had sat with his Council half an hour (the day of the last dissolution) Strafford coming to the House asked the E. Berkshire what was the business, who told him the dissolution of the parliament. To which, said Strafford, God forbid! and desired the King that the matter might be debated again, and withal that they might hear those of the Privy Council that sat in the Lower House, whereupon Secretary Windebank and Sir Henry Vane affirming that the Commons would give nothing unless their grievances be first redressed, these two first voted for the dissolution and so did Strafford among the rest. And there being 20 at the Council at that time all assented but 2 or 3, after which dissolution he confessed that he said that in case of absolute necessity, and to repel an enemy, the King was absolved from ordinary ways and might use all moderate means for the defense of the land, provided always that it must be upon extreme necessity not to make a precedent of it hereafter; and that the King is bound to give satisfaction to the people afterward, and reparation. He denies to have incensed the King against refusers to pay ship money or the rest.

24 *Article*: The parliament having forsaken the King he said the King might provide for the kingdom as he would, therefore caused a scandalous [blank] to be printed against the Commons called the Declaration, which was done by Canterbury and the Keeper.

Response: He spoke nothing of the parliament neither caused that book with the help of Canterbury to be printed, neither knows who did it, he then being sick.

25 *Article*: After the dissolution he pressed and counseled the King to sue for ship money and to borrow 100,000*l*. from the Londoners together with the names of such who were able to lend; that the refusers might be fined, and put to their ransom, nay, added that they who denied deserved to be hanged.

Response: He persuaded the ship money to be gently gathered, conceiving it was lawfully judged and never caused any to be troubled therefore. He said that London should execute and not dispute ship money; that they deserved to be fined and ransomed who refused to lend, but denies the rest.

26 *Article*: He projected to seize upon the money in the mint and to embase the King's coin. He told the Londoners that they had dealt ill with the King in refusing to lend him money and were rather helpful to the Scots than to him. He said that the French King would examine the

wealth of the merchants and take their money from them.

Response: He denies the stay of any money in the mint or to embase the coin, only added that it would be a less mischief to the kingdom to have money embased than to enhance the value; and said that the E. of Leicester had written a letter to him out of France declaring what the cardinal had done with their merchants, which letter he showed to the L. Cottington blessing God that it was not so with us.

27 Article: He being General at York, upon his own authority he made a tax upon the country to pay to every soldier 8*d*. per diem and threatened to commit refusers.

Response: The trained bands being dismissed, save the 2 regiments of Richmond and Cleveland, he propounded it in the Great Council whether he should not make such a tax, which they approved, but not to be done by force.

Note that the King himself in parliament said he thought he was herein mistaken, for he was rather encouraged to it than advised and divers of the Lords, as Essex, Bristol, Berkshire, Mandeville, etc., said that he did propound it unto the Council but they gave no assent but left the manner to a further debate.

28 Article: The Lord Strafford suffered Newcastle to be lost, not defending it; and wrote to Lord Conway to fight at the time, though Conway said they were not able.

Response: In the sickness of the E. Northumberland, the General, he was made Northumberland's deputy, he being at London when the Scots were coming in. He persuaded the L. Conway by letters to secure Newcastle, and the passages, and to resist them before they came over the Tyne that by delaying the Scots the English might receive more force, and the L. Conway having 11,000 foot and 3,000 horse then near Newcastle. The army was under the L. Conway and Sir Jacob Astley, who were advised by divers letters from the King to keep the Scots out, he wrote as a friend to the L. Conway as a General telling him how much he suffered in his honor for not repelling the Scots before they came over the Tyne, for hitherto the L. Conway followed the direction of the King by his secretaries, and not the Lord Strafford's who, when he was going toward Newcastle to take the command of the army, at Darrington he found the English soldiers retreating, Newcastle being taken by the Scots, which English army he found complaining that they had neither bullet, match, powder, nor victuals where, though himself were, he sat up all night to provide the soldiers' victuals who had eaten nothing in two days before, and to use means how to convey the soldiers to York there to join them in one body for offense and defense. When he came for London in the time of parliament, hearing he should be there questioned, he came the 9th day and was committed the 11th of November.

He, in the close of his answer, desires competent time wherein to fetch such writings from Ireland as thereby to make good his own answers and to disprove the accusation. He desired the Lords to consider the statute made in the 25th of *E.* 3 which determined what should be treason, and none else; and that of 4 *H.* 4, *cap.* 10, and the 1 Queen Mary 1st, which say no treasons shall be but what is expressed therein; and 25 *E.* 3, and the statute of 11 Henry 7, *cap.* 1, where is said that no subject for serving the King shall be attainted.

[f. 26] Friday 26 February

Tis ordered the answer of my Lord Strafford be committed to the committee appointed for draw[ing] up his charge.[61]

We had a conference with the Lords, and delivered in the 14 Articles in maintenance of our accusation of High Treason.[62]

[The Articles drawn by the House of Commons against William Laud, Archbishop of Canterbury, and his responses to them.]

The Archbishop being at the bar, the Articles were read in the Lords House:

1. That he traitorously endeavored to pervert the laws of the land and to bring in an arbitrary government, to that end advised to levy money without the consent of the subject.

2. Caused divers books, sermons, treatises, and other things to be printed which might deny the law and establish that arbitrary way, and himself was a protector of such writers.

3. By his letters and other powerful means to the judges he hindered the course of the law and justice.

4. He sold justice in causes wherein himself sat judge, and corrupted others by selling places of judicature.

5. He caused lately canons to be made and executed wherein the prerogative of the King, laws, parliaments, and proprieties of the subjects are impeached.

6. He has usurped papal power in temporals and spirituals; challenges to himself the King's jurisdictions as incident to his bishopric.

7. He altered the true religion established, set up popery, urged new ceremonies, and punished refusers.

8. He abused the power that was entrusted unto him by promoting

prelates, priests, chaplains which were either popish or unsound in religion or manners.

9. He chose his own chaplains such as were disaffected to the true religion whereby many dangerous books were licensed and printed.

10. He labored to reconcile England unto Rome, kept intelligence with the Pope, countenanced his priests and messengers, and the Romish hierarchy.

11. Both in his own person and by his deputies he persecuted Godly preachers without cause, whereby ignorance and profaneness is crept into the Church.

12. He has caused many divisions betwixt ours and other reformed churches, vexing and troubling the French and Dutch here in England.

13. He plotted to stir a war with Scotland to that [illegible] induced many innovations here tending to popery. He advised the King to subdue the Scots, he forced the Clergy to a contribution towards a war against them, and censured the pacification as being a thing weak and dishonorable.

14. To preserve himself, being in all these things guilty, he incensed the King against parliaments and alienated the King from his subjects.

After the Articles read, the Archbishop speaks:

That the accusation indeed is a heavy one, but upon his knees he thanks God that it is not such to him, for the noise abroad is great but the cry within in his own conscience is not weighty. Generals, he says, make noise but particulars bring weight; and error *contingit descendendo*, which will appear by the discovery of particulars. He will speak only to two things wherein he must deliver nothing but truth as a dying man.

1st. The canons making had as much freedom from all coercion or fraud as any canons ever in the Christian world. The [illegible].

2nd. General, he says, is that he is accused for being popish, wherein he desires them, if he should forget himself, to weigh what St. Jerome said: that a man ought not to be patient when he is accused of heresy. But separation being so strongly on foot in the Church must easily bring on such an accusation against him, wherein if he were guilty, being now 68 years of age, and to dissemble with God and the world in point of religion he would profess himself a villain and a beast if he were any way guilty directly or indirectly. And to clear himself herein he would give some probable motives: 1. That he has kept as many back from Rome and called from Rome as many of quality and learning as ever any clergyman did. 2ndly. After a conference had with Fisher, the Jesuit, he in print has published to the world his opinion of the Church of Rome, wherein if he should deal hypocritically, being in this place and at these years, he could be no less than a villain. 3rdly. That the papists both abroad and at home take him for their greatest enemy, yea, he has been advertised from abroad that Conn or some others have endeavored to take away his life for standing in their way. 4thly. If he were popish why should he keep in England? He has no wife nor children to make him stay, neither could the honor of the place keep him for his conscience; if it had been corrupted, he knew well enough how to have dealt with the Archbishopric. Neither was he of so mean a quality but that he persuaded himself he might have been entertained by Rome, and let him have but victuals and raiment, nothing could make him go against conscience. He has been daily libeled most shamefully and certainly had he been a papist he would not have stayed any longer here. He ends all with this protestation: in the presence of God, to whom he shortly must go, that he never had purpose of resolution to alter the religion established in the Church of England. He never had any intelligence or practice with the pope by priests, agents, or messengers directly or indirectly, yea, when he was requested by great persons, yet he would not admit it so much as an outward civil correspondence with Father Con. He concludes with this request: that having been now 10 weeks under restraint in Mr. Maxwell's house he may by their favor be continued there until his trial, giving them sufficient bail either in money or life for life. But if this may not be granted then, Sunday drawing on so near, that he might continue there till Monday.

Which motions, he being withdrawn, were severally debated. The E. Warwick moved to have him presently sent to prison and to be sequestered from all ecclesiastical power. So Paget, Brooke, and Lord Andover added that they ought to show no compassion to him who showed none to others. It was at last ordered that Mr. Maxwell, undertaking for him he should continue with him till Monday and then go to the Tower, he, being called in, thanks them for this last favor and desires he may have a copy of the charge and may be admitted to retain counsel. The first of these is granted and the 2nd to be answered upon his petition. Some Lords are to move the King for the sequestering of him from his ecclesiastical power.

[f. 26v] Saturday 27 Feburary

Whensoever the House is divided and the negatives and the affirmatives happen to be of an equal number, then the Speaker must give his voice and divide it; otherwise he is to give no voice.

Further, if the affirmatives go out and it happen that any member that gave his voice affirmatively happen to stay in the House, yet he is not to be questioned for it, but he must be accounted for a negative.[63]

[f. 27] Monday 1 March

If a committee be named of 16 or more, then any 8 of them may sit and hear the business; but if there is not 16 named then the major part of them may[64] sit and hear the business. And though there is very many of a committee, yet any 4 of them may adjourn it.

In the 16th year of King Stephen the papal decretals came first into England by the name of Rogations and from thence came the name of our Rogation weeks.

[f. 27v] Tuesday 2 March

Tis an order of the House that no man should name above two persons of one committee.[65]

[f. 28] Wednesday 3 March

Resolved upon question that no petitions shall be received into this House nor new matters moved for 14 days because the House is so full of business.

Resolved upon question that all those that sit in the several chairs of every committee shall have power to receive all petitions that are proper for that committee.

11 *Hen.* 3, New Salisbury was made a city.[66] The election of citizens for the city of New Salisbury is confirmed to the 24 aldermen and 48 burgesses.

[f. 28v] The Lords sent us 5 bills.[67] The Lords sent us a message for a free conference concerning the moving the Scottish commissioners to make known all the several parts of their 8th article and to conclude a firm peace as soon as possibly may be.

[f. 29] Thursday 4 March

[f. 29v] Friday 5 March

Resolved upon question that the King shall be moved to send six of his ships of the second, third, and fourth rank to guard the western coasts against the Turks. And that the King shall be likewise moved that any of his subjects may take any Turkish pirates without any letters of mart or reprisal, and without paying any duties to the King or Lord Admiral for the same.

[f. 30] And that the King likewise moved that his subjects may make gunpowder and bring it in, at their pleasures, according to the law.[68]

[f. 30v] Saturday 6 March

The committee that was appointed the 26 Feb. last to peruse my Lord Strafford's answer commanded MR. WHITELOCKE to report:[69] That tis not fit to put in any replication in writing to L. Strafford's answer, for that will prolong the time by examination of witnesses and otherwise. But we were desired to send this message to the Lords, that we have considered my L. Strafford's answer and do aver their charge [f. 31] of High Treason against him and intend to manage the evidence against him by members of our own House, and desire a free conference by a select committee of both Houses to consider of some propositions and circumstances concerning the trial.

The Lords appointed 24 of themselves to meet us on Monday in a free conference as was desired.

[f. 31v] Monday 8 March

A bill to disable all the clergy from bearing any temporal or lay office in England or Wales. This is the second reading, and this bill was committed.[70]

MR. WHITELOCKE reported from my Lord Strafford's committee that these 2 should be the heads of the free conference: first, that a place should be appointed that all the members of this [f. 32] House may be present at the trial or else they cannot be satisfied in conscience to give their votes to demand judgment. And also that there be convenient places for witnesses, and for the counsel, and that there be order taken to exclude all persons that ought not to be at the trial, and that there be a convenient place for the prisoner.

[f. 32v] 2 head: That whereas we intend to manage the evidence by members of our own, we do not expect any counsel to be allowed to my Lord Strafford to manage the evidence at the trial.

We went to the Lords with these 2 heads and they told us they would send to us by messengers of their own.

[f. 33] We had another conference with the Lords in which we consented to take away all the fortifications at Berwick and Carlisle, and that the Scots should be pressed to bring in all the eighth article at once, that a peace may be speedily concluded.[71]

[f. 33v] Tuesday 9 March

MR. CREW reported from the committee for the ministers' remonstrance those three heads first:

Secular employments, by which he meant their legislative and judicial power in parliaments and their judicial power in Star Chamber, and commissions for the peace, and at the Council Table and temporal offices.

Secondly, sole power in ecclesiastical things, by which is intended ordination and censures.

Thirdly, the greatness of the revenue of deans and chapters, the little use of them, the inconveniences that come by them.[72]

[f. 34] We had a conference with the Lords to renew the cessation of arms from 16 March to 16 April, if the treaty last so long.

Resolved upon question that we do agree to it.[73]

[f. 34v] Wednesday 10 March

Ordered that no motion shall be made to get any member of this House leave to go into the country until it be past nine of the clock.

The first head of Mr. Crew's report yesterday was debated, *videlicet*, in 3 particulars: first, that the secular employments of bishops and ministers, by which is intended their legislative and judicial power in parliaments. Secondly, their judicial power in the Star Chamber and commissions of the peace. Thirdly, [f. 35] their sitting as Privy Councillors at the Council Table, and their temporal offices.[74]

Dr. Brownrigg, Dr. Hacket, and divers other divines desired the House to hear them upon this head. But the House did refuse to hear them because this concerns only secular matters, and not ecclesiastical.

[f. 133v] [MR. SELDEN.] Bishops sit not [*words faded*] 100 years not 5 [*word faded*] for in H. 8 time [*words faded*] changed.

Oxon, Peterborough, Gloucester made by H. 8 but [*words faded*] abbots sat only being they were barons but there did not but bishops sit because there were diocese.

[f. 133][75] Suffragan bishops had no voices, they sat not as bishops; but if they have a diocese and jurisdiction then they sit in parliament/

In a vacancy the guardian[s] of the spirituality are called to parliament and then the barony is in the King's hand. The 26 bishops represent the body of the clergy. In criminal causes bishops made———[76] proxies, and the proxy had voices.

HOLLES. No profession as a profession has a vote in parliament but for his freehold. They represent not the body of the clergy because the clergy does not choose them.

[132v] ST. JOHN. All the judges have resolved that bishops do not represent the clergy but the proxies are chosen by themselves. Bishops are neither chosen nor elected.

MONTAGUE.[77] If bishops sit as a representative body and the Lords out vote them and the law pass, then the law binds them and the whole clergy, which it ought not to do without their consent. And laws have been made good when they have deceived; *ergo*, they represent not the clergy.

GLYNNE. No breach of privilege to vote this more than to vote [f. 132] any Lord guilty of treason, for that takes away their vote in the Lords House as well as this. The guardian of the spiritualities for York and Canterbury is the dean and chapter. Now York is dead; *ergo* the dean and chapter should now give their votes in parliament.

The Convocation represents the clergy; if the bishops did so too then they were twice represented, which is not allowed.

PYM. Bishops sit not in a representative way because they can make proxies, for representers cannot do so. [f. 131v] No profession makes a man uncapable of sitting in parliament but clergymen are excluded because they cannot choose; for none can be chose[n] that have not a voice to choose.

PALMER. Barons are tried by their peers but bishops are not; *ergo* they are not barons.

CAGE. The Book of Ordination says they vow never to meddle with secular things; *ergo* 'tis inconsistent with the function of a bishop.

[f. 35v] Resolved upon the question that the legislative and judicial power of bishops in the House of Peers in parliament is a hindrance to the discharge of their spiritual function, prejudicial to the commonwealth and fit to be taken away by bill, and that a bill be drawn to that purpose.[78]

[f. 36] Thursday 11 March

A bill committed, entitled thus: To abolish all trials by battle and joining of issue by battle in all writs of right.[79]

[f. 131] [MR. WHISTLER.][80] [*Illegible*] they ought by the statute of 3 *Hen.* 7, *cap.* 1, but one bishop be called to the Star Chamber, and he is no judge neither; there is but 4 that sit as judges.

[MR. BAGSHAW.] *Hen.* 3 time, about an° 1260, all [that] were bishops, and the Irish bishops, do decree that no clergyman shall be a justice. Thomas Becket sent up the seal when he was made Archbishop of Canterbury; 2 time—Thomas Arundel did the like.

DIGBY. We cannot judge upon any evidence which we hear not *in curia*.[81]

Resolved upon the question that for bishops and other clergymen whatsoever to be in the commission for the peace, or have any judicial power in the Star Chamber, or in any civil court, is a hindrance to the discharge of their ecclesiastical function, prejudicial to the commonwealth, and fit to be taken away by bill, and that a bill be drawn to that purpose.[82]

[f. 36v] We had a free conference with the Lords concerning the trial of my Lord Strafford.[83] At the conference 8 March last we made 4 propositions to the Lords for the place, the person, manag[ing] of the evidence, and use of counsel. First, for the place: the Lords conceived the Blanch Chamber to be unfit because the floor is not strong enough to bear such a multitude. But they conceived their own House, if the bar were removed higher and the lower part scaffolded, they thought it a fitter place [f. 37] and the less room would serve the Lords, being the bishops desire to be absent at the trial.

The Lords desire us to explain whether we intend to come to the trial with the Speaker, as an House, or a[s] particular members of the House. And to explain what we mean by managing the evidence, whether it be applying and marshalling the proofs only. And the Lords desire precedents concerning the place for the trial and our being present at the trial.

[f. 37v] Then for counsel: they will allow my Lord Strafford none in mere matters of fact, but in law they will allow him counsel and they will be judges what is matter of fact, and what is matter of law. Next, they desire us to explain what we meant by these words at the conference: "We desire to be present at the trial the better to satisfy our consciences to give our votes to demand judgment".

[f. 38v] Friday 12 March

An answer to be sent to the Lords concerning the conference we had yesterday about the 4 circumstances about my Lord Strafford's trial.[84] First, the place. Though the bar in the Lords House were removed and the lower part scaffolded, yet there would not be room enough for the members of this House; *ergo*, desire the Lords to appoint some more convenient place for the trial. And urge this precedent, that 1 *Ri.* 2, in Comines and Weston's case, the parliament did sit in the Blanch Chamber.

[f. 39] Secondly, the persons. My Lord Strafford being impeached by the Commons, the Commons may come to the trial as an House, if they please; but for some special reasons we resolved to come as a committee to this trial; thirdly, and to appoint some particular persons of our own members to manage the evidence. This is to order and apply the evidence according to the truth of the fact.

[f. 39v] Fourthly, concerning use of counsel. The Commons saving to themselves the right and course of proceedings agreeable to the law and course of parliaments, they desire the Lords to explain whether during the time of giving the evidence they intend to allow my Lord Strafford's counsel to plead, for tis against the law and course of parliaments that any counsel should be allowed until the evidence is fully managed and if his counsel should offer to plead before the Commons have finished, [f. 40] then the Commons must desist for it will not stand with the honor of this House to let any of their members plead against any other counsel.

[f. 41] Saturday 13 March

LORD DIGBY[85] reported from a conference. The King desired a care to be taken to regulate the army in the North by a commission of oyer and terminer, but this way would not redress many inconveniences. Therefore he desired some other way might be taken that might well regulate the army and not cross or weaken the Petition of Right, and the Lords desired a free conference in convenient time concerning this business.

[f. 41v] We had a conference with the Lords concerning the 4 particulars resolved upon yesterday about my Lord Strafford's trial, and in another conference the Lords did concur with us concerning these 4 particular circumstances.

[f. 42] Monday 15 March

We desired a conference with the Lords to desire the present disbanding the new Irish army of 8,000 papists. But for the reinforcement of the old army we leave it, being unfit to engage ourselves in that business. And we desire the papists in England and Wales may be presently disarmed according to law, and that Mr. Walter Montagu, Sir Toby Matthews, Sir Kenelm Digby and Sir John Winter should be presently removed from court.[86]

[f. 42v] This conference was put off till tomorrow morning.

The Lords sent to us for a conference concerning the time of my Lord Strafford's trial, and some circumstances about it.

MR. WHITELOCKE reported from this conference that the place for the trial should be Westminster Hall, and the time should be on Monday next at nine of the clock, and that whereas the Lords of the great Council at York were [f. 43] injured by my Lord Strafford's answer to the 27th article, in that he declares that they did advise the King to levy money in Yorkshire without parliament, they have entered a protestation against it, and it is unanimously received in their House, and they had a command to give the House of Commons notice of it.[87]

[f. 43v] Tuesday 16 March

An act for confirming the subsidies already given and to explain some doubt in the subsidy bill.[88]

We had a conference with the Lords, and we transmitted Dr. Cosin and some others to the Lords concerning Mr. Smart's business.[89]

[f. 44] Wednesday 17 March

This day we went up to the Lords to a conference concerning the Irish army and other things resolved upon on the 15 March.

MY LORD DIGBY[90] reported from a conference with the Lords concerning the affairs of both the kingdoms. That a paper was delivered to the commissioners which they now send to us, 'tis to this effect: that there is but 18,000 l. paid of the 80,000 l. and they cannot be trusted any longer. They desire the arrears may be paid and they desire to know the time and [f. 44v] the manner of payment of the 300,000 l. that the parliament had given to the relief of the Scots, and also they desired a speedy conclusion of the treaty.

[f. 45] Thursday 18 March

Resolved upon question that we hold it fit a bill should be drawn for the passing a subsidy of tunnage and poundage for 3 years and to be presented to this House, according to a book of rates agreed upon by this House.[91]

[f. 45v] MR. WHITELOCKE moved the House that Mr. John Gower should be sent for as a delinquent by a Serjeant at Arms for going out of town, being my Lord Strafford's committee enjoined him not to go out of this town till my Lord Strafford's trial was passed, he being a witness against him.

And this was ordered accordingly.

Ordered that if any Commoner that is a witness in my Lord Strafford's cause shall venture to go out of this town until [f. 46] my Lord Strafford's trial is passed, it shall be taken for an high contempt and he shall be punished accordingly.[92]

[f. 46v] Friday 19 March

A bill for bringing money to six in the 100 was committed.[93]

Sir John Rainie's[94] bill to confirm the lands that he bought of the King, at the second reading was rejected.

[f. 130v] [MR. PYM.] Fay,[95] Okellie, Sir Charles Coote. Okellie never indicted but Fay was, 2 horses stolen. 5 Esqrs. and a knight for bail, [ac]quitted by jury. Judge Barrie bound them over to the Castle Chamber and jury fined 2,000 *l.* apiece, put out of all office, committed for 16 months, never give testimony; a mitigation, but a 4th part must be paid to the Clerk of the Council.

The Earl of Meath purchased divers lands and a good stone house worth 400 *l.* for 6,000 *l.* Strafford would [*illegible*] it and Meath put out of possession. He kept away all the writings, a 4th part denied to Meath and all divided amongst Lieutenant and his friends. [f. 130] Meath complained that meaner men than himself that [were] ill taken, and a submission forced from him.

Lord Viscount Nettersfield and Mary his wife, Lady Hibbots,[96] 1,600 *l.* and 2,250 *l.* more offered. Then 2,500 *l.* was demanded and agreed unto and writings sold and 2,000 *l.* paid. Sir Robert Meredith urged to revoke the bargain and he should have 3,000 *l.*

A complaint against Lady Hibbots at the Council Chamber, in her answer instead of 99 years expresses for her life. The counsel brought on his knees, an order to forbid the judge to pass the [*illegible*] fine and Thomas Hibbots was to be examined if she would be bound by it. The Lady Hibbots would not, refuse[d]. [f. 129v] Then committed and 500 *l.* fined and so doubled every month; the major part of the Council for the lady.

Strafford angry and told us he would make a party, but however the reference came from him to the Council and would/[97]

[f. 47] Saturday 20 March

My Lord Strafford's committee is appointed to manage the evidence against him at the trial.

Mr. White and Mr. Prideaux are appointed to take notes at the trial and the committee is to appoint 2 others to help them.

SIR JOHN CULPEPPER reports from the committee that was appointed to view the place of my Lord Strafford's trial, and the circumstances of it.[98]

[f. 47v] 1, the scaffolds are safe; 2ly, that all the members should come to the trial from their several lodgings and not from the House of Commons; 3ly, that no strangers shall sit amongst the members of this House; 4ly, that the members of this House are to be at the trial by eight of the clock in the morning; 5ly, that the serjeant attend within the bar there, and his men without the bar to execute the commands of those that shall manage the evidence; 6ly, that the Speaker shall be there [f. 48] as a private member, but there must not be any order made for his being there; 7ly, that every member bring a ticket of his name and the place for which he serves.

And this committee is appointed to receive the tickets and to see that none but the members of this House come in at the trial.

[f. 48v] A message to the Lords to desire them to sit as an House this afternoon, being we have resolved to sit to consider of the affairs of the kingdom and perhaps we shall have occasion to confer with their Lordships about it.

MR. BELASYSE reported from the Lords, that their Lordships would sit this afternoon as we desired.

[f. 129] [illegible][99] That if our pet[titioner], finding it necessary at his trial to desire the favor of this honorable House for/

Some members thereof to be used as witness for him.

His humble suit is that the persons hereundernamed may be present at the said trial to be used as witnesses as aforesaid:

The humble petition of Thomas, E. of Strafford, his Majesty's Lieutenant General of Ireland: To the K[nights], C[itizens], and B[urgesses] of the honorable House of Commons assembled in parliament/

[f. 49] A petition from my Lord of Strafford was read, in which he desired leave of this House to examine Sir Thomas Jermyn, Sir Arthur Ingram, Senior, Sir William Pennyman, Sir Robert Pye, Sir George Wentworth, and Hugh Potter, Esquire, members of this House, as witnesses at the trial, and that the persons above named may be present at the trial.

The House leaves them to themselves to do therein as they think fit, without offense to the House.

[*Afternoon*]

[f. 49v] Ordered that the committee appointed to manage the evidence against my Lord Strafford shall ask if any of the witnesses examined on my Lord Strafford's behalf have been sworn, and if they find they speak upon their oaths, then the committee shall proceed no further till they have reported it to this House and received their resolution therein.

[f. 50] Ordered that no new petition or other new matter be received into this House for this month.

The petition against Mr. Lane is referred to the committee for the judges.[100]

[f. 50v] Mr. Whitelocke went to a free conference with the Lords with this saving:[101] Whereas the House of Commons did formerly declare to their Lordships that the Earl of Strafford, being impeached by them, they do conceive it does belong to them to resolve in what manner they would be present at the trial, and that of right they may come as an House if they please but for some special reasons upon this occasion they are resolved to send their own members as a committee of the whole House, to be present at the trial and [f. 5] that some particular members of this House shall manage the evidence. The House of Commons do still continue their resolutions in every part thereof and therein, and in the matter of allowing counsel, and their Lordships' reservation to their judgments what is matter of fact and what is not, the House of Commons do save unto themselves, as they have formerly done, all rights that do appertain to them according to law and the course of parliaments, and do declare that the proceedings in this case shall not be drawn into precedent to the prejudice of the House of Commons.

[f. 51v] Heads for a conference with the Lords:[102]

This House is very sensible of the want of money in the King's army and the northern parts and have given 4 subsidies and voted 2 subsidies more for these occasions and these 6 subsidies will come to above 300,000 *l.* and there is 120,000 *l.* remaining, but they cannot raise so much to suddenly, therefore they desire to advise with their Lordships in this great exigent concerning the safety of the kingdom.

[f. 52] A message from the Lords that they intend to sit as an House on Monday in the afternoon about the matter of this last conference and they desire we would do the like if it stand with our conveniency.

And we agreed to sit as an House as was desired.

[f. 52v] Monday 22 March

This morning my Lord Strafford was brought to his trial, and the House of

Peers did sit in Westminster Hall, and the House of Commons did sit on scaffolds by them as a committee of the whole House. And our articles against him and his answer to them was read.

My Lord Strafford offered to speak, but my Lord Steward put it off till tomorrow. And at 3 a clock we met, and did sit in our own House.[103]

[Afternoon]

[f. 53] Resolved upon question that for Bishops or any other clergymen whatsoever to have employment as privy councillors at the Council Table, or in temporal offices is an hinderance to the discharge of their spiritual function, prejudicial to the commonwealth, and fit to be taken away by bill and that a bill be drawn accordingly.[104]

[f. 53v] Ordered, that if the Earl of Strafford shall ask leave or have leave to speak anything by way of defense before the committee that is appointed to manage the evidence have begun, that then the committee shall interpose and if he shall have leave granted him, then the committee shall proceed no further till they know the resolution of this House.[105]

[f. 54] Tuesday 23 March

My Lord Strafford was brought again to his trial and Mr. Pym managed the matter of the preamble of his answer, and my Lord Strafford did presently make his answer unto it.[106]

[Afternoon]

And at 3 a clock we met and did sit in our own House, and had a conference with the Lords to appoint a time to go to the King about disbanding the Irish army, and disarming the papists, and banishing Sir Kenelm Digby, Sir Toby Matthews, Sir John Winter, and Mr. Walter Montagu from court, especially considering Montagu appeared yesterday at the trial.[107]

[f. 54v] MR. PIERREPONT reported the matter of the conference we had with the Lords yesterday about the raising money for the present use of the kingdom, and they would desire the Lords of the treaty to finish the Scottish treaty and propounded the calling the City before both Houses to persuade them to lend money, and they offered us they would join with us to remove the grievances and the advisors of them.[108]

We had a conference with the Lords concerning this last conference, and about the northern affairs.[109]

[f. 55] Wednesday 24 March

LORD DIGBY reports from the conference: That the Lords would join with us to go presently to the King about the disbanding the Irish army, the disarming the papists, and banishing the 4 eminent papists from the court, and then a letter from the officers of the King's army in the North expressing their great necessities.[110]

Resolved upon question that this House shall join with the Lords to treat with the City of London about the raising of present money to supply the necessities of the kingdom upon the security of the subsidies.

[f. 55v] Ordered that no member of this House shall confer with the Earl of Strafford during the time of his trial.[111]

This morning my Lord Strafford was brought to his trial and Mr. Maynard managed the first and second article[s] against him, and my Lord Strafford answered to them.[112]

[f. 56] Thursday 25 March 1641

This morning my Lord Strafford was brought again to his trial and Mr. Maynard managed the 3 article against him, to which my Lord Strafford did answer: and the 4 article was begun, and then adjourned till tomorrow.[113]

Ordered my Lord Strafford's committee shall have power to contract and proceed upon such articles as they think fit for the speedy trial of the Earl of Strafford.[114]

The bill for the amendments of some doubts in the late subsidy bill was sent to this House from the Lords when they had passed it and Mr. Speaker presented it to the King and he passed it.[115]

[Afternoon]

[f. 56v] Heads for a conference with the Lords.[116] First, the necessity of having my Lord Strafford's trial, therefore tis desired by this House that the Lords would prevent all unnecessary delays and impertinent speeches of my Lord Strafford that may protract the business; for by these speeches much debates are begotten and frequent adjournments, which this House desires their Lordships to prevent in their wisdoms.

At a free conference the Lords did propound 3 things about treating with the City for money to supply this House presently. First, [f. 57] 1, the persons: 8 Lords and 16 Commoners; 2, the time: Saturday next at noon; 3, the sum of money: 120,000 *l.* to be borrowed, and the Lords would give the City notice of their coming.[117]

A message from the Lords that tis the King's pleasure both Houses should attend him on Saturday about disbanding the Irish army, disarming the papists, and banishing papists from the court.

[f. 57v] Friday 26 March

This morning my L. Strafford was brought again to his trial and Mr. Glynne managed the 4 article against him, and he answered unto it.[118]

[f. 58] Saturday 27 March

This day my Lord Strafford was brought against to his trial and Mr. Glynne did manage the 5 article against him, and he answered unto it.[119]

[f. 58v] Monday 29 March

This day my Lord Strafford was brought again to his trial and Mr. Glynne did manage the sixth article against him, and he answered unto it.[120]

My Lord Strafford desired my Lord Primate of Ireland might be examined as a witness for him and being he was sick, he desired some of the Lords would examine him upon such interrogatories as my Lord Strafford should propound; and this was granted, only the Lords desired leave for the Commons to examine my Lord Primate upon cross-interrogations upon oath.[121]

[Afternoon]

Now being the Commons had not been called to the examination, the committee excepted against the reading of the examinations.

[f. 59] We had a conference with the Lords about these examinations and they consented to suppress those that were already taken and to take new examinations in the presence of some members of the House of Commons who have liberty to cross-examine upon oath.[122]

[f. 59v] Tuesday 30 March

This day my Lord Strafford was brought again to his trial and Mr. Glynne did manage the last part of the 8th article concerning my Lady Hibbotts, and the 9 article against him, and my Lord Strafford answered to them both.[123]

[f. 60] Wednesday 31 March[124]

[f. 60v] Thursday 1 April

[f. 61] Friday 2 April

[f. 61v] Saturday 3 April

[f. 62] Monday 5 April

My mother died.

[f. 62v] Tuesday 6 April

[f. 63] Wednesday 7 April

[f. 63v] Thursday 8 April

[f. 64] Friday 9 April

[f. 64v] Saturday 10 April

[f. 65] Monday 12 April

I came to the House again.

[f. 65v] Tuesday 13 April

[f. 66] Wednesday 14 April

Mr. Prynne's case was reported but not voted for the present.[125]
A bill for the attainder of Thomas, Earl of Strafford, of High Treason was read the second time and committed to a committee of the whole House.[126]

[f. 66v] Thursday 15 April

[f. 67v] Friday 16 April

[f. 68] Saturday 17 April

[f. 68v] Monday 19 April

[f. 69] Tuesday 20 April

[f. 69v] Wednesday 21 April

[f. 70] Thursday 22 April

[f. 71] Friday 23 April

[f. 71v] Saturday 24 April

Resolved upon the question that the commission and instructions whereby the president and Council in the North do exercise their jurisdiction is illegal in the creation and execution.

Resolved upon the question that the court of the president and Council in the North is unprofitable to the King.

Resolved upon the question that the court of the president and Council in the North is inconvenient and a grievance to his Majesty's subjects in those parts.[128]

[f. 72] SIR THOMAS ROE acquainted this House that the King does purpose to send him to the Diet at Ratisbon and, being the employment is likely to last long, he desired the House would give him leave to go and to continue him a member of this House; and this House granted his desire and gave him leave to go.[129]

[f. 72v] Monday 26 April

MR. GERVASE HOLLES, speaking of the treaty of the Scots said that they, like Jacob, went about to take away our birthright and, like Nahash, they endeavored to put out our right eyes, and that their propositions were dishonorable, such as the King could not grant, and yet we not only entertain them, but embrace them,

For those words, after a long debate, he was called to the bar on his knees and Mr. Speaker pronounced this judgment on him, that he was suspended this House during this session of parliament.[130]

[f. 73] Tuesday 27 April

A bill twice read and committed for the cutting off the right hand of [blank] James, for stabbing Mr. Heywood in Westminster Hall when he was in the service of this House.[131]

Yesterday, when Mr. Gervase Holles was at the bar receiving his judgment the mace was not taken off the table and the reason was because he did only withdraw into the Committee Chamber and so was still within the jurisdiction of this House, and being he was a member of the House, the mace was not held at the bar by him.

[f. 73v] A message from the Lords that they will give us a meeting on Thursday morning in Westminster Hall by a committee of both Houses at nine of the clock, there to hear us according to our own offer when we brought up the bill of attainder against the Earl of Strafford.[132]

We returned this answer: that we had considered the message and resolved to give a meeting at the time and place as is propounded.

[Afternoon]

A bill twice read and committed for the fining of all the members of the last Convocation House for making the late new canons and constitutions.[133]

[f. 74] Wednesday 28 April

Resolved upon the question that the fines and penalties laid upon delinquents by prosecution of this House/[134]

[f. 74v] Thursday 29 April[135]

[f. 75] Friday 30 April

[f. 75v] Saturday 1 May

A bill to restrain bishops and others in Holy Orders from intermeddling with secular affairs. Read the third time, did pass.[136]

An act for suppressing of Turkish, Moorish, and other pirates.

These 2 bills were this day carried up to the Lords by Mr. Arthur Goodwin.

[f. 76] SIR HENRY ANDERSON reported the examination of Browne, a priest.[137] Names of such as are to destroy our timber: Sir Bazile Brooke, Sir John Winter, Sir Richard Weston, Mr. Benedict Holland.

Divers collectors for the Jesuits at Douai and St. Omers.

Divers employed to let out the money of Jesuits.

[f. 76v] Monday 3 May[138]

[f. 77] Tuesday 4 May

[f. 77v] Wednesday 5 May

[f. 78] Thursday 6 May[139]

[f. 78v] Friday 7 May

We sent to the Lords to desire them to move the King in this time of danger to make the Earl of Essex Lord Lieutenant of Yorkshire. And the Lords did consent to do as we desired.[140]

[f. 79] Saturday 8 May

[f. 79v] Monday 10 May

The King gave a commission to my Lord Privy Seal, my Lord Lindsey, and my Lord Marshal to pass the bill of attainder against my Lord Strafford, and the bill that this parliament should neither be adjourned, prorogued, or dissolved without consent of both Houses of parliament. And these 2 bills did pass accordingly.[141]

We sent to the King to make my Lord Salisbury Lord Lieutenant of Dorsetshire, and he granted it accordingly.

[f. 80] We sent up a bill to the Lords for 2 other subsidies, with some other bills.

[f. 80v] Tuesday 11 May[142]

[f. 81] Wednesday 12 May

Dr. Hacket and others were heard on the behalf of the deans and chapters, and Dr. Burgess was heard in answer to him.

This day my Lord Strafford lost his head.[143]

[f. 81v] Thursday 13 May

This day the King came to the House of Lords and our Speaker brought up a bill for 2 subsidies, and the King did pass it. And with it he passed a bill about Turkish and Moorish pirates, and a bill about the abbreviation of Michaelmas term, and a bill about the levying and pressing of mariners.[144]

[f. 82] Friday 14 May[145]

[f. 82v] Saturday 15 May

[f. 83] Monday 17 May

[f. 83v] Tuesday 18 May

[f. 84] Wednesday 19 May

[f. 84v] Thursday 20 May

[f. 85] Friday 21 May

[f. 85v] Saturday 22 May

[f. 86] Monday 24 May

[f. 86v] Tuesday 25 May

[f. 87] Wednesday 26 May

[f. 87v] Thursday 27 May

Mr. William Taylor, burgess of New Windsor, in Berkshire, was accused for these words: Mr. Taylor, being asked whether he gave his vote for the bill of attainder against my Lord Strafford, he answered "No", and said further, that those that did give their votes for that bill did murder him with the sword of justice.

Upon this the House did proceed to this judgment, and Mr. Taylor was [f. 88] called to the bar upon his knee to receive it. First, that he should be committed to the Tower during the pleasure of this House, next that he should make an acknowledgment of his fault at this bar, and at Windsor, and be expelled this House and be disabled for ever being a member of this House.

And an order was made for a new warrant for a writ to choose a new burgess.[146]

[f. 88v] Sir Edward Dering brought in a bill to take away all Archbishops, bishops, deans, and all their officers and dependencies out of the Church of England. This was twice read and committed to a committee of the whole House to be debated on Thursday next.[147]

[f. 89] Friday 28 May[148]

[f. 89v] Saturday 29 May

[f. 90] Monday 31 May

[f. 90v] Tuesday 1 June

[f. 91] Wednesday 2 June

[f. 91v] Thursday 3 June

[f. 92] Friday 4 June

[f. 92v] Saturday 5 June

[f. 93] Monday 7 June

Mr. Maynard transmitted our votes of the canons to the Lords in a conference.[149]

[f. 93v] Tuesday 8 June

Resolved upon question that there shall be a cessation of arms continued for 14 days longer from the 14th of this month if the treaty last so long.[150]

[Afternoon]

An act for regulating the Privy Council and taking away the court commonly called the Star Chamber was read the third time and did pass this House.[151]

An act for the repeal of a branch of an act made in the first year of Queen Elizabeth concerning commissioners ecclesiastical did pass.[152]

[f. 94] Lord Digby questioned for these words, speaking of Colonel Goring, "In my opinion he is perjured". He explained it thus: that in the sense that as it appeared by Goring's examination he understood the oath, in his opinion he was perjured.

Then he withdrew.[153]

[f. 94v] Wednesday 9 June

A bill to prevent the dangers that may happen by the recusants.[154]

Mr. Herbert Price and Sir William Widdrington were questioned for taking the candles out of the serjeants' hands last night in a tumultuous manner. Widdrington held one in his hand and Price did let the other in the middle of the House, and this in a violent manner.

Price did withdraw and Sir William Widdrington was sent for. Both these men explained and confessed the fact and professed they intended the service of the House, and submitted themselves.

[f. 95] After a long debate Mr. Price and Sir William Widdrington came to the bar on their knees and received judgment to be sent to the Tower during the pleasure of this House.

Resolved upon question that/[155]

[f. 95v] Thursday 10 June

Mr. Digby came in and sat upon the ladder[156] and the Speaker called to all members to go to their places and told us men use to sit there, as if we were going to execution.

Upon this Mr. King spoke to the orders of the House and told the Speaker those words were not fit to be spoken to a man of that quality.

Upon this he was questioned and withdrew and the business was debated.

Upon this Mr. King was called down and in his place acknowledged his offense and professed his sorrow for it.

[f. 96] Friday 11 June

Resolved upon question that the preamble as it was now read should be the preamble of the bill:[157]

Whereas the government of the Church of England by Archbishops, bishops, three chancellors and commisaries, deans, archdeacons, and other ecclesiastical officers has been found by long experience to be a great impediment to the perfect growth of religion, and very prejudicial to the civil state and government of this kingdom, therefore be it enacted, etc.

[f. 96v] Ordered that Colonel Goring, Colonel Willmott, Colonel Ashburnham, and Mr. Hugh Pollard forthwith attend this House, and that they neither write, send, or speak with Colonel Goring or receive and [sic] message from him, or come into his company until this House take further order, and that they make a protestation to observe this order.

Willmott, Ashburnham, and Pollard in their places did make their protestations carefully to observe this order.[158]

[f. 97] Saturday 12 June

Resolved upon question that the taking away of the several offices of Archbishops, bishops, chancellors, and commissaries out of this Church and kingdom shall be a clause in this bill.

Sir William Savile[159] was committed to the Tower for accusing Mr. Henry Belasye and Sir John Hotham at the Council Table for words spoken in the last parliament.

Mr. Neville was sent to the Tower 4 February last for the same business.

[f. 97v] Monday 14 June

A copy of the letter that Mr. Percy wrote to my L. Northumberland was read[160] and Mr. Willmott, Mr. Ashburnham, and Mr. Pollard, after they had heard it twice read, did withdraw into several places and were not suffered to speak one to another but were called in severally and were not permitted to hear what answers one another made to such questions as Mr. Speaker demanded of them; but [f. 98] still when one was answering the other 2 did withdraw and after they had answered in their places (for they were all members) the House debated the business and committed them all three upon suspicion of High Treason: Mr. Willmott to the Tower, Mr. Ashburnham to the King's Bench, and Mr. Pollard to the Gatehouse.[161]

And the Houses did send a Serjeant at Arms to the [f. 98v] King['s] army in Yorkshire to fetch up Sir John Berkeley and Mr. Daniel O'Neale upon suspicion of High Treason, and my L. General was desired to write to the officers of the army to be assisting to the Serjeant.

Sir William Widdrington and Mr. Herbert Price did petition this House and acknowledged their offense and submitted to the judgment of this House and desired mercy for their offense for which [f. 99] they were committed to the Tower on Wednesday last. Upon this the House gave order for their enlargement.[162]

[f. 99v] Tuesday 15 June

[f. 100] Wednesday 16 June

[f. 100v] Thursday 17 June

[f. 101] Friday 18 June

The poll money was debated and certain rates set upon several men according to their degrees.[163]

[f. 101v] Saturday 19 June

The bill to take away all pluralities did pass this House.[164]

[f. 102] Monday 21 June

[f. 102v] Tuesday 22 June

[f. 103] Wednesday 23 June

[f. 103v] Thursday 24 June

Resolved upon question that Rossetti (the Pope's nuncio) and Robert Phillipps[165] (a Romish priest, and the Queen's confessor) shall be presently sent for to this House, and be kept by the Serjeant in safe custody till they are examined.

[No entries on ff. 104–106v]

[f. 107] Friday 25 June

The Serjeant told us Rossetti, the Pope's nuncio, lay not at his lodging last night, and that yet he cannot find him, and that Robert Phillipps, the Queen's confessor, told him the Queen forbid him coming till he had spoken with the King, and that the King forbid him to come till he was more fully informed, being he was a servant; but for his own part he was very willing to come.

Upon this the House debated in what way to send for him, being he was a servant and kept [f. 107v] himself in his chamber in the King's house at Whitehall. And it was resolved that no place nor office could be any privilege for any man unless he were of the degree of a peer, but he ought to come if this House sent for him. This Phillipps is a Scottish man.

Resolved upon question that Robert Phillipps shall be presently sent for as a delinquent.

And the Serjeant was commanded to go to Whitehall and bring him hither and if he were opposed, or Phillipps [f. 108] kept from him, that then he should repair to the Lord Chamberlains of the King and Queen's house, or any other officers, and acquaint them that this House had sent for Phillipps to be examined in a case of High Treason, and require them to assist him to apprehend and attach Phillipps.

[*Afternoon*]

This day Phillipps came and rendered himself to this House and he was sent for into the House and appeared at the bar on his knees as a delinquent, [f. 108] and then Mr. Speaker reprehended him for his contempt, and he made an excuse that his name was mistaken, for his name is Robert, and not Francis, Phillipps.[166] Then he did withdraw.

And then he was called in again and a letter showed him which he acknowledged to be his letter, and said if any crime were in it he is criminal.

[No entry on f.108]

[f. 109] Saturday 26 June

[f. 110] Monday 28 June

A bet with Mr. Morley of a piece that the poll money will not amount to 60,000 *l*. [167]

[f. 110v] Tuesday 29 June

Sir William Savile was brought to the bar on his knees and was released of his imprisonment in the Tower to which he was committed the 12 of this month for breach of privilege. [168]

[f. 111] Wednesday 30 June

[f. 111v] Thursday [1 July]

Resolved upon question that neither the body of the Lords of the Privy Council nor any one of them in particular as privy councillors have any power to imprison any subject of this kingdom, except in such cases as they are warranted by the statutes of this realm. [169]

[No entries ff. 112–122v]

[18 June]

[f. 123] All widows shall pay a third part according to the degree of her husband. [170]
Serjeants at law 20 *l*.
The King's serjeants 25 *l*.
The King's, Queen's, and Prince's counsel 20 *l*.
Drs. Physic and Civil law 10 *l*.
Popish Drs. must pay double.
Archdeacons, chancellors, and commisaries 15 *l*.
Every office above 100 *l*. per annum to be rated and to be referred to a committee to digest and prepare.
All men able to spend 50 *l*. per annum 2 *l*.
All men able to spend 20 *l*. per annum 5s.
All men that receive not alms and is above 16 years old, if they be not formerly taxed 6d.
[f. 123v] The masters and wardens of the 12 companies in London and such as have fined for it 10 *l*.

The liverymen of these 12 companies 5 *l.*
The masters and wardens of the other companies as have fined for it 5 *l.*
The liverymen of these companies 2 *l.* 10*s.*
The freemen of the 12 companies 1 *l.*
The freemen of the other companies 10*s.*
Merchants strangers Kts. 40 *l.*
Merchant strangers that trade to sea 10 *l.*[171]
Merchant strangers that trade within the land 5 *l.*
Merchants English dwelling in London and not free 5 *l.*
Factors English dwelling in London and not free 2 *l.*
Handicraftsmen or artisan 4*s.*
Strangers, London householder papists 4*s.*
And others shall pay 2*s.*
[f. 124] Dukes 100 *l.*
Marquesses 80 *l.*
Earls 60 *l.*
Viscounts 50 *l.*
Barons 40 *l.*
Baronets 30 *l.*
Kts. of the Bath 30 *l.*
Knights 20 *l.*
Esquires 10 *l.*
All men under Esquire able to spend 100 *l.* per annum 5 *l.*
Bishops 60 *l.*
Deans 40 *l.*
Canons resident 20 *l.*
Prebends 10 *l.*
Parsons or vicars able to spend 100 *l.* per annum 5 *l.*
All recusants must pay double.
Alderman [*sic*] of London and such as have fined for it 20 *l.*
Sheriffs and such as have fined for it 20 *l.*
The Lord Mayor of London 40 *l.*
The deputy Aldermen of London 15 *l.*
The common councilmen of London 5 *l.*
[f. 125] Judges, Serjeants, Drs. of divinity, Privy councillors, the 3 eminent offices, Earls' eldest sons, all Lords' sons, Baronets' eldest sons, widows, mayors, physicians, archdeacons/

[17 June][172]

[f. 124] From 10 No. to 29 June

King's army has had 150,000 due to it more.

The total [remains due to the King's army]; 312,[050]
427,800 [Total due to the King's army and the Scots]

Of this great sum we yet but know of]:
[f. 116v] 100,000 *l.* [from the] old customers
15,000 [from the] new customers
40,000 [from the] City
50,000 [from the] old customers
Total is 205,000 *l.*
302,800 *l.* now to provide
The billet must be trusted and that with the half pay is about 60,000 *l.*
242,800 *l.* must be provided.
Edward Huchison de Wicombsley in con. York.
[f. 125v] Mr. Peard's proposition:
28,400 *l.* Dean and chapter, old rents
8,400 *l.* rectory rents
200,000 *l.* if they are improved at 5 years purchase 900,000 *l.*
Durand a watchmaker in Blackfriars
773,990 *l.*
120,000 *l.* City
150,000 customers
50,000 Merchant Advent.
Total 320,000 ready money
150,000 *l.* Merchant Advent. to be paid beyond sea.

[f. 126] A message from the Lords to desire a speedy conference by a committee of both Houses in the Painted Chamber.

I AY? do willingly make the same protestation that the Speaker has taken to all the particulars contained in this paper.

NOTES

1. Dr. Thomas Eden, Chancellor of Ely; Dr. George Parry, Chancellor to the Bp. of Exeter; and Dr. Richard Chaworth, Chancellor of the Diocese of London. On 1 Feb. the House was preparing to debate the particulars of the ministers' remonstrance when a motion was made by Mr. Henry Marten (M.P. for Berkshire) that those who had taken the oath in the new canons (1640) might withdraw. The debate concerning withdrawal was lengthy but upon Mr. Pym's suggestion "that hee hoped the saied Doctors seeing the sence of the Howse would in ther owne discretions forbeare the Howse whilest this matter was in agitation". Notstein, *D'Ewes*, 307-308. According to Peyton (*Ibid.*, 308, n. 11), the three heeded the sense of the House and withdrew into the Committee Chamber. See S.P. 16/477:2.

2. Mr. Hyde had made a motion for the speedy examination of the judges and witnesses concerning the charge against Lord Finch. When Hyde was nominated to deliver the message he excused himself, "being a gowneman", and Sir Robert Pye, who had seconded Hyde's nomination, was himself nominated to carry the message. Notestein, *D'Ewes*, 307.

3. The remonstrance of the ministers of Kent is printed in Rushworth, *Hist. Collections*, IV, 135; it is paraphrased and discussed in Larking, *Proceedings in the County of Kent*, pp. 28–38.

4. See Notestein, *D'Ewes*, 312, and nn. 4 and 5. Sir Nicholas Crispe had been a member of Lord Goring's 1638–1639 syndicate. See Drake, 1 March. William Smith was elected to Crispe's place. O.R., I, 497; Brunton and Pennington, *Members of the Long Parliament*, 219.

5. D'Ewes has paraphrased Selden's conclusions (Notestein, *D'Ewes*, 318) but he does not include the speech. See *Ibid.*, 318 n. 11 for Peyton's version. In his footnote Notestein has omitted the final line of Peyton's account of Selden's speech which states: *He humbly left to the consideration of the House what kind of act it was, etc.* Peyton, f. 79v.

6. D'Ewes notes, after his paraphrase of Selden, that "This speech having been in parte answeared by two or three but not fullie; Mr. Kirton stood upp. . .". Lord Falkland apparently was one of the two or three speakers following Selden and preceding Kirton not recorded by D'Ewes. Notestein, *D'Ewes*, 319. The resolution concerning the Scots is printed in *L.J.*, IV, 151; *C.J.*, II, 78 and S.P. 16/477:8. The answer was delivered to the Lords by the Scottish commissioner on 5 Feb. and debated in a conference with the Upper House on 6 Feb., see below.

7. D'Ewes gives only a brief summary of the King's speech. Notestein, *D'Ewes*, 321 and nn. 21–25. Warner, ff. 13v–14, reports the speech as follows:
    At 2 of the clock in the Banqueting House the two Houses wait upon the King where the King first gives them thanks for the care they had of the maintenance of religion established, from which he would never swerve, as also for the care of his person and the state. 2ly, that he would give the Jesuits and priests which lurk about his kingdom a month's warning to be gone who, if they should either remain or return into the land should feel the extreme rigor of the law made against them in the 27th of Q. Elizabeth, 1st and 3d of K. Charles [sic]. 3ly, that the Pope's messenger [Count Rossetti] who was here for conference with the Queen about her religion which was granted her in the Articles of Marriage, should in a convenient time be sent away. 4ly, he would take order that his subjects should not so fast flock to masses at Denmark House, St. James, and the ambassadors'. 5ly, that although neither Q. Elizabeth nor K. James did never condemn priest merely for religion, yet rather than he would discontent his subjects he would leave John Goodman the priest to the judgment of both Houses in Parliament and so discharge himself; but withal wished them to consider what inconveniences might arise both to his own subjects and others abroad if they proceed to arraignment. The speech is printed in *L.J.*, IV, 151; Rushworth, *Hist. Collections*, IV, 165–166.

8. Concerning Neville, see Notestein, *D'Ewes*, 322–323. According to *C.J.*, II, 78, this diarist has reversed the order of business, Neville should follow Seaford.

9. Francis Gerard was elected from Seaford. See Drake, 16 March, n. 89. See also Notestein, *D'Ewes*, 321–322, nn. 1 and 2.

10. For a more complete version of Jermyn's speech see Notestein, *D'Ewes*, 323–324, and nn. 7–12.

11. Sir Thomas Barrington had been sent up to the Lords to request a conference (to be managed by Treasurer Vane) concerning the treaty with the Scots. Notestein, *D'Ewes*, 325. Warner, f. 15, records that: *A message from the Commons by Sir Thomas*

Barrington concerning the treaty betwixt the 2 kingdoms, before which meeting the E. of Bristol moved the Lords first, that they might confer with the Commons to consider whether they thought fit they should think of a further cessation of arms with the Scots, being there were but 10 or 11 days now to come of the former truce; 2ly, whether they should move the Commons to settle a standing committee to which the English lords commissioners might impart what concerned the treaty betwixt the two kingdoms. This latter was denied, but the former was presented to the Commons by the E. of Bristol at the present ensuing conference. . . .

12. D'Ewes describes this as "An excellent act [which] was brought in by Mr. Alderman Pennington. . .". Notestein, *D'Ewes*, 327.

13. See above, n. 7.

14. Petitions against episcopacy were received from both Gloucestershire and Hertfordshire. See Notestein, *D'Ewes*, 339 and n. 10. Petitions from the counties concerning episcopacy had been ordered to be read in the House on 25 Jan., *C.J.*, II, 73.

15. In his draft notes (Harl. 164) D'Ewes reports that the petition from Eden Langdale complaining of Sir Thomas Danby's actions was read in the House this day. See Notestein, *D'Ewes*, 329 and n. 10; *C.J.*, II, 79.

16. I.e., the bill for triennial parliaments which passed the Upper House this day, *L.J.*, IV, 152. This diarist consistently writes *triannual* for *triennial*. The bill entitled "An act for the preventing inconveniences happening by the long intermission of parliaments" had been read the third time in the Lower House, passed, and sent to the Upper House on 20 Jan., accompanied by the bill for relief of the King's army. *C.J.*, II, 70.

17. Edward Hanchett. *C.J.*, II, 80; Notestein, *D'Ewes*, 316, 331.

18. See Hatsell, *Precedents*, III, 20–21.

19. Warner, ff. 15v–16, reports: *A message to the Commons for a conference to deliver to them the answer of the Scots commissioners which was: first, to express their hearty and manifold thanks for the great care the Commons had in providing for the reparation of their losses and necessities, but more heartily, that they are pleased to rank them in the number of their brethren. 3ly, that they accept with all love their [the Commons] offer of 300,000 l. and 4ly, it increases their obligation that they have promised to do it in a convenient time. 5ly, as they magnify the providence of God in bringing these things thus to pass, so they hope this shall be a means to settle a firm peace between the two kingdoms.*

    After this the Commons were desired to take into their consideration a further time of cessation of arms upon like conditions. . . .

20. See Notestein, *D'Ewes*, 334, n. 20.

21. Many of the speeches of 8 Feb. concerning episcopacy and the bishops are printed. See Drake, 8 Feb., and Notestein, *D'Ewes*, 335–338, nn. 7–20. The Londoners' petition against bishops is printed in Rushworth, *Hist. Collections*, IV, 93–96.

22. Neville had been ordered to the Tower on 4 Feb., see abve, n. 8.

23. See Drake, 9 Feb., and Notestein, *D'Ewes*, 338–343, and nn. 1– 22.

24. I.e., Denzil Holles was able to proceed with a suit in progress against Cooper in the Court of Wards. Until Cooper's election case (on the Downton election, see Keeler, *L.P.*, 70–71) could be resolved by parliament (as late as 1645 it had not been decided *C.J.*, IV, 260, and was not finally concluded until 1660. Brunton and Pennington, *Members of the Long Parliament*, 3.) he was unable to be admitted to sit as a member and claim privilege of parliament. Notestein, *D'Ewes*, 334; 504–505, and n. 4. Brunton and Pennington, *Members of the Long Parliament*, 22.

25. See above, n. 8.

26. D'Ewes reports (Harl. 164) the more likely figure of 25,000 *l.* to be raised for the relief of the northern counties. Notestein, *D'Ewes*, 345; *C.J.*, II, 82.

27. See Drake, 11 Feb.

28. The conference dealt primarily with the seventh article. Warner, ff. 17v–18, relates: *That to the 7th article of the Scottish demands, as it is already decreed, ordered that such libels, proclamations, as touch upon the disloyalty of the Scots, and printed in Scotland, shall be recalled so that all the like shall be damned both in England and Ireland and, on the other part, what either has been printed by the Scots against the King or the English shall be likewise called in, and that the loyalty of the Scots in the end of the treaty and pacification and thanksgiving be published in all churches in England.*

   The Scots 8th and last demand is that all monuments of hostility be taken away betwixt us and them, namely, and especially, the fortification, garrisons, ordnance, and other things at Berwick and Carlisle may be dismantled and slighted which (say they) K. James so did as being of no other use to us but to serve against the Scots. Hereupon a conference is desired with the Commons that we and they may severally take this last demand into consideration thereby to have a free conference in both Houses and so give answer unto the Scots. . . . The proposition of the Scots concerning their 7th demand and the Lords commissioners' answer is printed in the *L.J.*, IV, 159.

29. Judge Berkeley was judged guilty of High Treason in nine particulars (see Notestein, *D'Ewes*, 352–355; Rushworth, *Hist. Collections*, II, 606–614 cites eleven particulars), primarily concerning his activities in the ship money case, 1637.

30. Warner, f. 18v, reports: *Judge Berkeley accused of High Treason and committed to the sheriff of London.* See also *L.J.*, IV, 161.

31. The conference on the triennial bill was ordered before the business of judge Berkeley. *L.J.*, IV, 160. The conference was reported in the Upper House on 13 Feb., *Ibid.*, 161, and another conference was called for that afternoon. The King gave his assent to the bill on 16 Feb., see below.

32. D'Ewes records that: "this was conceived to bee no breach of priviledge: because the prohibition was not to stopp Mr. Arundel's suite but to bring the matter into the right channell wheere it ought to bee handled; and that the rights of the common law ought to bee maintained". Notestein, *D'Ewes*, 356.

33. *C.J.*, II, 85. Sir Ranulph Crew, one of Sir Edward Coke's executors, was to deliver the books to Sir Robert Coke, Edward's son and heir. According to D'Ewes nineteen books had been confiscated (Notestein, *D'Ewes*, 108) although Samuel E. Thorne, *A Catalogue of the Library of Sir Edward Coke* (London, 1950), p. vi mentions twenty-one. D'Ewes notes (*Ibid.*, 358) that a motion was made that the three works listed be printed, but he records no order to that effect.

34. The speeches delivered at the conference 13 Feb. grew out of the debates in the Lower House on 11 Feb. See Notestein, *D'Ewes*, 346–351. Warner, ff. 19–20, reports the conference as follows: *And then Sir Edward [sic] Earle delivered the insolency of that whole army, which consisted of 7,000 papists and 1,000 protestants drawn from the old army. They set up the Mass, called to it by crews in court halls, etc. and hardly kept out of the churches; they disturbed the preachers. Priests [blank] soldiers' pay, and some priests had as good maintenance as some bishops. Not the like insolencies and tumults since Tyrone's time. All arms are in their hands, they better provided for ever than ever. They quartered along the ports for 150 miles, possessed of all havens and fortresses, in 24 hours can gather together 5,000; they are where the English are weakest; they have 3 several magazines; the people much discontented hereat, as by their petition; the Lieutenant [Thomas Wentworth, Earl of Strafford] is yet General, and all to subdue the kingdom of England.*

Sir Thomas [sic] Clotworthy seconded this. That this army is to force a tyrannical government, for the General has boundless power; for his commission leaves all at his discretion; it is said therein to stay tumults in England, and yet at first they were provided for the northwest of Scotland. Then there are letters to the President of Wales to submit all to the E. of Worcester, in Wales, and the like to the E. of Pembroke. The Lieutenant [Strafford] had power to land his men in Wales. The old Irish army cost the K[ing] 55,000 per annum and this 18 months in arms, but the new army of 8,000 costs 300,000, and it duly paid. It is desired this army of 7,000 papists be disbanded and the 1,000 protestants added to it may be returned to the old army.

And 2d, Mr. Reynolds. The scene is Wales, the commander, E. of Worcester, a papist, who has by the King's command under the letters of Sir John Windebank, Secretary, the sole command of 7 counties in South Wales. In North Wales they have store of corn provided, in Lancashire 15,000 papists, in Monmouth 3,000; able to raise men and money. Priests wrote their [blank] during these stirs to keep every day a fast for the good success. A petition was read at the Council Table against these, yet nothing answered.

And 3d, Mr. Waller. That the papists hold the face of a parliament in England where the Pope's nuncio, the Speaker, the nobles, Commons present. It is desired that all papists be removed but especially these: Walter Montagu, Sir Toby Matthews, Sir John Winter, Sir Kenelm Digby. . . .

35. Clotworthy is not mentioned in the C.J. (II, 84–85) as a manager of this conference.

36. For the names, see C.J., II, 85–86.

37. I.e., An act for the relief of the King's army and the northern counties. The hope was that this subsidy bill for relief of the army and the bill for triennial parliaments would be passed together. C.J., II,

86. Warner, f. 20v, reports that: Thereupon the Lords send to the King to know what time he will appoint to receive both bills, which he determined to be the next morning in the Lords House. . . .

38. Concerning the procedural point regarding the reading and passing of bills, see Notestein, D'Ewes, 363 and nn. 1–3. The point arose on the 2nd reading of a bill for Gilbert Wells.

39. The King's speech and the act itself are printed in Rushworth, Hist. Collections, IV, 188, 189; the speech is in S.P. 16/477:29. See also Notestein, D'Ewes, 364–365. Warner, f. 21 records: Le Roy le voult, i.e., the King is willing. The King speaks and tells them that he had before advised them to eschew 2 rocks: the one not to trench upon his royal power, the 2d not to alter the government of the church and state. And yet against the former he has given way in this bill of parliaments then, which never anything was more forcible for the benefit of the subject. The other rock if they shall avoid they can ask nothing which he will not grant them. That hitherto he had had no encouragement, no, not in the very face of things, for hitherto nothing has been done neither for the state nor him, yea, the very hinges of government is almost on pieces, yet he speaks not this to ill reproach them, but to put them in mind that as in a walk to be mended or cleared though it be taken in pieces yet great care must be taken that not so much as a pin be left out. He concludes that he has done all on his part and trusts them to do theirs, wherein he relies upon their affections. After this the Speaker of the Commons presents the bill of subsidies. . . . See also L.J., IV, 163; C.J., II, 87.

40. Four reasons for bringing Strafford to a speedy trial were presented to the Upper House by Mr. Pym: 1st, since the time of their charge they have conceived new causes of suspicions of new matters which have not hitherto been presented. 2ly, that he is the head of a numerous discontented and mutinous company who, so long as they have hope of him, may break out into flames. 3ly, he continues his great power and places in Ireland and the North, and over

the armies in both places. *4ly, the general fear and discontent of the people which cannot be allayed so long as he stands accused as an incendiary between the two kingdoms.* . . . Warner, f. 21v. See also, *L.J.*, IV, 163.

41. See Notestein, *D'Ewes*, 367. For the speech see also, Osborn fb 161, f. 54.

42. For the committee members, see *C.J.*, II, 87. They were appointed to meet on Friday afternoon (19 Feb.) in the Star Chamber. Drake records the speeches made this day at the committee of the whole House for the army and northern relief.

43. A petition had been preferred against Coningsby by various inhabitants of St. Albans for his "many violent wordes and deedes to hinder a free election ther before this present Parliament and to procurre himselfe to bee choosen a burgesse againe". Notestein, *D'Ewes*, 370. According to D'Ewes Coningsby had sat for St. Albans in the short parliament although he is not included on the M.P. lists printed in O.R. or Rushworth, *Hist. Collections*, IV, 4. See Keeler, *L.P.*, 51. Upon a motion by D'Ewes the House ordered Coningsby to be released upon his own bail. *C.J.*, II, 88.

44. The Lower House was particularly concerned about Wentworth's continuing position as General of the Irish army even after his impeachment. See Drake, 11 Feb., n. 23. Warner does not record this conference with the Upper House.

45. For the committee, see *C.J.*, II, 88. They were to meet this day in the afternoon (18 Feb.) in the Treasury Chamber. Pym's report is not included in *C.J*; a folio has been left blank in the MS. *C.J.* for the insertion of the report.

46. Thomas Howard, Earl of Arundel and Surrey, had inherited the office of Earl Marshal in 1621, although the office was not recognized statutorily as an inherited office until 1672, Aylmer, *King's Servants*, 107. In 1633, "when ther was noe moore hope of Parliaments" and when, according to the D'Ewes Journal, "the Common law was declining in its power and honor", the Earl Marshal, singularly, without the Constable, heard several cases and pronounced judgments on them. Concerning the cases, see Notestein, *D'Ewes*, 375–379 and nn. 3–22. The House ordered reparations to be made to the parties judged by the Earl Marshal. *C.J.*, II, 89.

47. I.e., 18 Feb., see *C.J.*, II, 88.

48. Warner does not record the proceedings at the conference this day but includes an account of the report of the conference to the Upper House the following day (23 Feb.), f. 25v, as follows: *The Commons desire the Lords to admit no counsel for the L. Strafford but according to parliament law, for delay by this means will be ill, 1st by reason of the pressure of time; 2ly, the heinousness of his crime; 3ly, the quality of his person; 4ly, the people's distaste of him. The Lords answer, that no counsel shall be admitted in this case otherwise than the justice and honor of the House shall think fit when his answer is brought in. The Commons desire that there may be expedition of his trial, which the Lords granted.* See Drake, 22 Feb., n. 35.

49. *Rot. Parl.*, 4 R. II, no. 17.

50. *Rot. Parl.*, 5 R. II, no. 45.

51. MS.: *Coggells. Rot. Parl.*, 5 R. II, no. 43.

52. The impeachment proceedings against Lionel Cranfield, Earl of Middlesex, see Howell, *S.T.*, II, 1183–1254.

53. The impeachment proceedings against George Villiers, Duke of Buckingham; John Digby, Earl of Bristol; and Edward, Lord Conway, see Howell, *S.T.*, II, 1267–1450. On 6 May 1626 Bristol was granted counsel to plead his cause. *L.J.*, III, 587. Two days later (8 May) the King sent a message to the Lords questioning the right of counsel in a treason case and requesting the Lords to "proceed with caution" in the matter. *Ibid.*, 588. On 9 May the question of counsel was put to the judges (*Ibid.*, 591), who refused

to give an opinion. *Ibid.*, 595. Bristol was permitted counsel by the Lords in this case on the grounds that it had been appointed before the King's message.

54. The resolution came as the result of an action by the Bp. of Norwich to prevent one Mr. Carter from preaching in his parish church. *C.J.*, II, 91.

55. Richard Montagu (Bp. of Chichester 1628, of Norwich 1638) and Roger Maynwaring (Bp. of St. Davids 1635) were both pardoned in the summer of 1628. Gardiner, *Hist. of Eng.*, VII, 23; *D.N.B.*

56. According to the *C.J.*, II, 91 (23 Feb.) Earle reported from the conference that the business was of great length and that he desired liberty for the reporters to make their reports in the morning (24 Feb.). However, no report of this conference seems to be recorded in either the *C.J.* or Notestein, *D'Ewes* on 24 Feb.

57. D'Ewes records (Harl. 164) that the Earls of Holland, Dorset, Bristol, and Hertford spoke at the conference in defense of the Queen and of her support of the triennial bill. Notestein, *D'Ewes*, 392–393 and nn. 15 and 16.

58. James Enyon. *C.J.*, II, 91.

59. See below, n. 62.

60. I have inserted Warner's account (ff. 27–39) of the Articles drawn by the Lower House against the E. of Strafford and Strafford's responses to them at the bar of the Upper House, with the King present, on 24 Feb. Warner's account is substantially different from and more complete than that printed in Notestein, *D'Ewes*, 403–407 and that in Drake, 25 Feb. According to Warner, f. 39, on 25 Feb. the Lords sent down to the Lower House a parchment containing the E. of Strafford's answers to the Articles, and a copy of the same; the original parchment was to be returned to the Upper House after verification of the copy by the House of Commons.

61. *C.J.*, II, 93. The committee was "to proceed in the secretest and speediest way they can for the advantage of the business, in preparing it for a trial, and for further proceedings".

62. I.e., in the case of the Archbishop of Canterbury. I have inserted Warner's account (ff. 39–42) of the Articles charged against Archbp. Laud and his response to them. Notestein, *D'Ewes*, 413, n. 19, includes the Articles but not Laud's responses. A longer and more formal account of the Articles is printed in Rushworth, *Hist. Collections*, IV, 196–199; see also S.P. 16/477:62.

63. "Upon the division, if the members appear to be equal then the Speaker is to declare his vote, whether he be a *Yea* or a *No*, which in this case is the casting vote. . .". Scobell, *Memorials*, 27. A division in the House occured on Monday 1 March in regard to whether or not Dr. Chafin should be committed to the Tower for indiscreet words used by him in a sermon in Salisbury Cathedral. The no vote was 190; the yes vote 189. See *C.J.*, II, 94; Notestein, *D'Ewes*, 419–420 and nn. 4 and 5.

64. MS: *any.* Cf. Scobell, *Memorials*, 27.

65. I find no evidence of such an order having been made this day. Included at the end of this diary (f.134) are notes of Bagshaw's speech made this day (see Notestein, *D'Ewes*, 425 and n. 5) but, originally written in pencil, they have faded to have become almost unreadable.

66. New Sarum sent burgesses to parliament in 23 E. I. It was first incorporated by King H. III. Oldfield, *Hist of the Boroughs*, III, 124–126.

67. For the names of the bills see *C.J.*, II, 96.

68. See Drake, 5 March and n. 66. The order concerning Turkish pirates is printed in the *C.J.*, II, 96. Concerning gunpowder, see Notestein, *D'Ewes*, 444 and n. 5.

69. See Drake, 6 March and n. 68.

70. For the committee see C.J., II, 99.
71. The conference is reported in L.J., IV, 178. Warner, ff. 46–46v relates: that on 6 March the E. of Bristol had told the Lords that *"he feared the Scots might summer here unless that the Lords take care with the Commons to get them money. The Lord Saye wished them to be tender lest the spurring the Commons out of their own pace might offend them and beget an impediment.* A debate ensued on the question of the treaty with the Scots and Lord Savile complained: *there has been a stop in the business yet no fault in the commissioners but rather that the Commons will give no answer to their last motion whereby to bring the Scots to set forth their utmost demands.*
72. See Drake, 9 March and n. 78.
73. C.J., II, 100.
74. See Drake, 10 March.
75. The notes on ff. 131v–133 are in the back of the diary and are entered upside down. For other accounts of Selden's speech, see Notestein, D'Ewes, 468, n. 10. Mitered abbots, as had episcopal authority within their limits, were "abbots sovereign" and consequently Lords of parliament until the dissolution of the monasteries; Lords priors, exempt from diocesan authority, were also entitled to seats in the Upper House. Coke, First Inst., sect. 137, Cf. also, Coke, Fourth Inst., p. 5.
77. Probably Sir Sidney Montague who spoke the following day (11 Mar.) concerning the Church. Notestein, D'Ewes, 472.
78. This resolution was passed on Ash Wednesday (see Drake, 10 March and C.J., II, 101) and was discussed in the Upper House the next day (11 Mar.). Warner, f. 48, records the following remarks on the subject: *The Commons voted that the bishops shall have no power in Privy Council, Star Chamber, nor Justice of Peace. Vide Statute 1 Eliz., cap. 4, that bishops make one of the states in parliament. 31 Henry 8, that none may sit in the bishop's places in the Parliament House. 25 Edward 3, that bishops (in express words) are peers of this land.*
79. For the committee, see C.J., II, 101.
80. The accounts of the speeches of Whistler and Bagshaw are included at the back of the Anonymous diary with the notes from 10 Mar., see above, n. 75. For a fuller report of Bagshaw's speech, see Notestein, D'Ewes, 472, n. 7.
81. Following Digby's speech is the entry (written right side up): *78,000 l. to the Scots; 500,000 l. to the King's army; 253,000 l., 4,000, Total 282,000 l.; 16 May 357,000 l.*
82. This is the second head in the order presented by the committee for the ministers' remonstrance and passed in the House the day before (10 March). The resolution on 11 March (C.J., II, 102) called for a bill to be drawn. See below, 22 March, n. 104.
83. Bulstrode Whitelocke reported the conference. See Notestein, D'Ewes, 453; C.J., II, 101–102.
84. Whitelocke's report to the House from the committee for the Earl of Strafford. C.J., II, 103.
85. George Lord Digby, M.P. for Dorset.
86. See Drake, 15 March and n. 84.
87. The C.J. account (II, 105) indicates the committee for the Earl of Strafford was to examine the protestation, "how far they make use of it as evidence at the trial".
88. See Notestein, D'Ewes, 491 and n. 4; C.J., II, 105. The bill was presented to the King on 25 March, see below, p. 28, and C.J., II, 112.
89. Concerning the impeachment of John Cosin and the petition of a minister, Mr. Peter Smart, submitted to the Commons on 10 Nov., complaining of Cosins, see Notestein,

D'Ewes (Index); Rushworth, *Hist. Collections*, IV, 208–210, and S.P. 16/472:61.

90. According to the *C.J.*, II, 106, Digby's report, "a paper of great consequence", was read and ordered to be considered the following morning when the business of the navy was ended. See Notestein, *D'Ewes*, 502–503.

91. See Notestein, *D'Ewes*, 506–507. Regarding the Book of Rates, see Drake, n. 61.

92. *C.J.*, II, 107. Gower was sworn as a witness at the trial on 24 Mar. *L.J.*, IV, 197.

93. See Drake, 19 March and n. 104.

94. MS.: *Raymer*. Rainie's bill was rejected before the reading of the usury bill. *C.J.*, II, 107. On Rainie (Reyney), see Notestein, *D'Ewes*, 508–509.

95. Pym was reporting from the committee for the Earl of Strafford. Notestein, *D'Ewes*, 509–511. For a description of the case involving Mr. Edward Fay, a justice of peace, Okellie, and Sir Charles Coote, see Notestein, *D'Ewes*, 509.

96. Lady Mary Hibbots, widow of Sir Thomas Hibbots, had married Lord Viscount Nettersfield. For an account of the problems with the settlement of her estate and the petition preferred by Thomas Hibbots to the Earl of Strafford, see Rushworth, *Hist. Collections*, VIII, 221–227.

97. Following the account of Lady Hibbot's case in the diary, and separated from it by a line, is the following entry: *253,000 due to both armies 6 April.*

98. *C.J.*, II, 108–109. The notes inserted here from f. 129 were written upside down at the end of the diary.

99. Strafford's petition is not printed in full in the *C.J.*, II, 109 or in Notestein, *D'Ewes*, 515.

100. The petition against Thomas Lane, M.P. for Wycombe, submitted by Wm. Widmere (Widucere) concerned among other things his "profanation of the sabboath by sportes and games". Notestein, *D'Ewes*, 513; *C.J.*, II, 108. The petition was read earlier in the day than this diarist indicates.

101. The saving is not printed in Notestein, *D'Ewes*, 515–517, but is included in Whitelocke's committee report 16 March, *C.J.*, II, 105–106.

102. For Hyde's report from the committee to draw up heads for a conference on the matter of the King's army, etc., see *C.J.*, II, 109–110; also, Notestein, *D'Ewes*, 516–518.

103. See Drake, 22 March and nn. 108–110.

104. The matter concerned the first head of the ministers' remonstrance. It had been resolved on 11 March that a bill be drawn to this purpose. See above, 11 March, n. 82. For an account of the afternoon session see Harl. 162, ff. 345–348.

105. *C.J.*, II, 110.

106. See the notes in Drake on the trial proceedings this day (23 March).

107. The conference was agreed to and, according to D'Ewes (Harl. 164), f. 143v, Sir Walter Earle and Mr. Reynolds were appointed managers. See Harl. 164, 351v–353.

108. Pierrepont's report is given in full in the *C.J.*, II, 111.

109. D'Ewes (Harl. 164), f. 143v, reports that: *we resolved to go presently and the messengers being again called in the Speaker told them our resolution, and so we went.*

The Earl of Bristol spoke first and told us the Lords would join with us to have the new Irish army disbanded, the papists disarmed and removed from court. That they had joined before us if we had called upon them, and that they would send to the King speedily to know when they might attend him; and that in respect of the urgent necessity of the kingdom they are willing to join with us in matter of money or anything else.

The Earl of Holland said there was a letter sent from about forty commanders of the King's army to the Earl of Northumberland, Lord General, and he gave it the Lord Paget to read.

The letter was dated at York, March 20, 1640, and the effect of it was: That the House of

Commons had suspected their abilities and numbers, but they hoped that we should know by their valor shortly their number. That they were forced for want of due payment to live upon the poor people in Yorkshire. That the time of the year now grew on for action and they were ready to hazard themselves to regain their honors formerly lost. That the Scottish army, under color of enlarging their quarters, was already advanced. That they understood that there was a commission of oyer and terminer to come down to examine the abuses of the army, which was a dishonor to them to have judges come and determine matters of soldiers which they [the judges] understood not. So they desired money to be sent to them promising that in themselves there should be neither courage nor resolution wanting.

Then the Earl of Holland showed that these commanders who had subscribed this letter had great jealousy by reason of their former dishonor received at Newborne and of those judges that were to be sent amongst them; besides, they had long wanted to pay and, therefore, we might pardon them though they wrote in too high a strain and wished we might use all means to get money to satisfy all their wants and take away all their jealousies.

After our return to the House and some agitations of little moment we appointed to meet again tomorrow at two of the clock in the afternoon. The report of this conference was made the following day (24 March) in the Lower House and is included in Moore, ff. 91–93, but not in the C.J. On the preparations for the conference, see L.J., IV, 196. For the letter, see Cal. S.P. Dom., 1640–1641, pp. 507–508.

110. On the conference, see above note.
111. C.J., II, 112; Harl. 162, f. 357.
112. For the first and second Articles see above, p. 181. D'Ewes (Harl. 164) does not include an account of proceedings at the trial this day and the notes in Drake, 24 March, are fragmentary. Moore's account for 24 March is lengthy (Harl. 476), ff. 87–89.
113. For the Articles, see above, p. 181; and see Drake, 25 March. For D'Ewes's account, see Harl. 162, ff. 357v–358.
114. C.J., II, 112; Harl. 162, f. 359.
115. See above, 16 March, n. 92.
116. The heads were drawn up by a committee and reported to the Lower House by Sir John Culpepper. C.J., II, 112; Harl. 162, ff. 359–361.
117. See Drake, 25 March, n. 129.
118. See Drake, 26 March; Harl. 162, ff. 362–363v; Harl. 476, ff. 96–97. For the afternoon session see, Harl. 162, ff. 364–365; Harl. 164, f.145.
119. See Drake, 27 March.
120. Moore (Harl. 476), ff. 106v–107, records that: Then Mr. Glynne began with repetition of what was proved against him. . . .we intend to proceed to the vi article for putting the Lord Mountnorris forth of 220 l. per annum by a bare paper petition. And whereas my Lord of Strafford does pretend it was in the Chancery, we conceive their was no such thing. Then we produced Mr. Little to prove the decree, who said it was, and then read it.

Then we produced the Lord Mountnorris for a witness, who said that he was in possession from May 1620 till August 1639, and that he was put forth of possession by virtue of that decree.

Mr. Annesley said that his father [L. Mountnorris] was put forth of the possession by virtue of that order, and that his father had been long in possession. And he also said that there was a petition to the Lord of Strafford and other commissioners that he might proceed according to law, and it was declared that he could not proceed.

Then we demanded that Strafford might presently answer. Then he desired a little time, which being granted after a while he began as follows: May it please your Lordships, we are *now entering into the second week for the trial of my life, and I doubt not but in time, by God's assistance, to give your Honors and the honorable House of Commons such content that I may leave off all sorts of government and retire to my own home, which I have long desired, but could rather have wished I might, like a full grown and ripe fruit, have fallen from the tree, and not to be pulled down, root and branch.*

Then the Earl, going on impertinently, we called for justice to hold him to the point. Then he said, my Lords, I must confess it being an arrow from that quiver it does penetrate my heart, though not with guilt, and I am sorry that I shall be so unfortunate to be accused by those amongst whom I have spent so much of my time; and I am like to be hard set to, for my eloquence is but small, though their learning be great, and I doubt not but to make it appear that I have done nothing contrary to the instructions and proclamations and to the practice of former deputies.

121. After Strafford's remarks the trial proceeded this day with examinations of Henry Dillon, Mr. Slingesby, Sir Adam Loftus, Lord Dillon, William, Earl of Cork, Lord Ranelagh, the Earl of Bath, William Breteridge, and the case of Lord Baltinglass was read. Moore (Harl. 476), ff. 107–110; L.J., IV, 200–201.

122. The Upper House this day ordered the preparation of a commission under the Great Seal of members of both Houses to procure testimony from James Usher, Archbishop of Armagh and Lord Primate of Ireland. L.J., IV, 201.

123. Concerning Lady Hibbotts's case, see L.J., IV, 202. The most detailed diary account of this day's proceedings is that of Moore (Harl. 476), ff. 111–116. See also Harl. 162, f. 375. For the afternoon session see, Harl. 162, ff. 377–379; Harl. 164, f. 146.

124. Apparently this diarist left parliament on 31 March to be with his dying mother. For the proceedings on some of the days he was absent (5, 7, 10, 12 April) see the account in Drake. Moore's record of the trial during the days 31 March – 13 April (Harl. 476), ff. 117–179) is very thorough, although he recorded little of the business of the House during the same period. D'Ewes (Harl. 164, ff. 147–170) for these dates is not as detailed concerning the trial but his account of proceedings in the House for the same days is more complete than that of Moore; D'Ewes's account (Harl. 163, ff. 9–163) includes the proceedings from 6–13 April.

125. Mr. Rigby delivered the report but the vote on Mr. Prynne's case was ordered postponed. C.J., IV, 120. A fragmentary account of the report is included in Moore (Harl. 476), f. 178, and no account is given in D'Ewes. Further debate and the vote occurred on 20 April. C.J., II, 123–124; Moore (Harl. 478), ff. 10–11; D'Ewes (Harl. 164), f. 180. See also Cobbett, Parl. Hist., II, 762–763.

126. See Drake, 14 April and n. 174.

127. The diarist is again absent. Drake has no entries in his notes for this period of 15–23 April. Moore's account of 15 April is included in Harl. 476 (ff. 180–184) and his account of 16–23 April is in Harl. 478 (ff. 1–7). D'Ewes, Harl. 164, covers the days 15–21 April (ff. 171–182), and Harl. 163 covers the entire period 15–23 April (ff. 47–92).

128. Following Hyde's report three resolutions were made concerning the Court at York, C.J., II, 127. D'Ewes (Harl. 163), ff. 97–98, and Moore (Harl. 477), ff. 7–8, give the report itself.

129. C.J., II, 127.

130. C.J., II, 128. Moore (Harl. 477), f. 10, records that: *Then falling into debate concerning the Scots' demands Mr. Jervoise Holles made an invective speech against the Scots, for which he was interrupted. The words were, he compared the Scots to Jacob's worst part, which was to supplant his brother of his birthright. And that compared the Scots to Nahash, who put*

forth the right eyes, and so put ignomy upon us, and that he was troubled at the dishonorable propositions of the scots, and that we do [not] only meet them the half way but embrace them. These words were ill taken by the House and so he withdrew; and after a long debate he was called forth of the Committee Chamber by the Serjeant being resolved per question that he must come to the bar, and suspended from this House during this session of parliament. And according to the order Mr. Holles was called and brought to the bar, and there kneeled, but the mace in grace was not in the Serjeant's hand but upon the table, the Serjeant standing by him at the bar. This speech is misdated in Rushworth, *Hist. Collections*, IV, pp. 168–169, and is included there with the proceedings of 4 Feb.

131. For the fuller title of the bill concerning John James, see *C.J.*, II, 128. According to Moore (Harl. 477), f. 10, *The cause was for stabbing Peter Heywood with a rusty dagger when he was employed by warrant from this House for the returning the names of all popish recusants within his precincts.*

132. See *C.J.*, II, 129. The bill of attainder has been carried to the Upper House on 21 April but not first read there until 26 April, see Drake, n. 174.

133. *C.J.*, II, 129.

134. I find no resolution on fines and penalties in this day's proceedings.

135. The diary has no entries for 29 and 30 April; either the diarist was away again or simply took no notes for these days.

136. *C.J.*, II, 131. According to D'Ewes (Harl. 163), f. 121, *It was long disputed whether this bill should be sent up alone or some others sent up with it. The Speaker was very desirous to have sent up other bills with it, and he had read the titles of two that had been sent down from the Lords to us and passed here also. But at last it was overruled that this bill only and another, entitled An act for the suppressing and destroying of all Turkish, Moorish, and other pirates, should be sent up to the Lords presently. Mr. Arthur Goodwin carried them up and divers went [with] him. I was not present but understood he delivered the said bills to Sir John Bankes, Lord Chief Justice of the Common Pleas, at the bar, who still supplied the place of the Lord Littleton, Lord Keeper of the Great Seal of England, who had been long sick.*

137. In his report on Browne, Anderson included the information that Brook, Winter, Weston, Ploydel "and two others", according to Moore (Harl. 477), f. 25, were responsible for the cutting of timber. See Drake, n. 176 and also S.P. 16/479:82.

138. The diarist is absent again and consequently fails to take the Protestation. See Drake, for proceedings on 3, 4, and 5 May.

139. According to D'Ewes (Harl. 163), f. 139, on 6 May *The Clerk read the names of all those who had not yet made the Protestation, some of which were in the country, some with leave, some without leave, and some being sick both in the town and country.* Unfortunately neither Moore nor D'Ewes include the names. Concerning the complete list of all who took the protestation, see Drake, 3 May, n. 185. See also below, n. 165.

140. Following a conference with the Commons the Upper House this day passed a resolution (resolved on in the Lower House on 5 May, *C.J.*, II, 135) concerning the rumor of invasion which stated "that whosoever has counseled, assisted, or joined or shall counsel, assist or join to bring in any foreign forces into this kingdom, but by leave of the King and advice of parliament, shall be accounted an enemy to the King and kingdom". *L.J.*, IV, 237–238; S.P. 16/480:16. Regarding the E. of Essex, see *L.J.*, IV, 241.

However, the Upper House spent most of its time this day on passing the bill of attainder against the E. of Strafford. Warner, f. 64v, relates *That the judges, upon all these former votes of the Lords in point of fact, shall declare whether Strafford deserve punishment for High Treason by law. The judges (8 in number) withdraw and soon return with an unanimous affirmation delivered by Chief Justice Bramston. . . .whereupon the bill read and Strafford by bill presently voted guilty. L[ord] have mercy on him and on us all.* According to a letter from Sir Henry Vane to Sir Thomas Roe "many who had appeared much for him absented themselves; yet there were 60 present, whereof 51 voted for the bill and 9 against it. . .". S.P. 16/480:20.

141. According to D'Ewes (Harl. 163), f. 154, on Saturday, 8 May, *About four of the clock divers peers and many members of the House of Commons attended the King at Whitehall. Sir John Bankes, Lord Chief Justice of the Common Pleas, spoke in the name of both the Houses (in [the] absence of the Lord Littleton, Lord Keeper of the Great Seal, being still sick) and moved the King that the bill of attainder of the Earl of Strafford and another bill having passed the said Houses, and there being great necessity in respect of the distractions and dangers of the present time, that his Majesty would be pleased speedily to give his royal assent to both the same bills. . . . The King, looking very sadly, said that he would take time to consider and give us an answer on Monday next at ten of the clock.* See also L.J., IV, 242.

142. See Drake, 11 May.

143. The diary has red stains on the page for this day. Although D'Ewes makes no reference to Strafford's execution Moore (Harl. 478), ff. 66a–67, contains the following account:

> *The Earl of Strafford before he went out of the Tower, the Lord Primate spent the former day, and that morning, in pious endeavors to fit him for death.*
>
> *At first he complained that though he sought God, he could not find such answer of comfort as he desired; yet considered how much God had taken him off from all trust in the arm of flesh, and hedged him out from all wordly helps, for though till within few days, he suspected no message of death, yet God by decrees, had mouldered away the several props of this hope, leaving him no comfort but only by seeking him, first his strength in the House of Commons failed him, then Mr. Percy's fleeing reflected a jealousy upon him and deprived him of the use of his friendship. Then the protestation (at once) took the votes of all the catholic Lords from him. Then the tumults in the City no little distracted the rest.*
>
> *After some prayer in private (to himself) he acknowledged such dilectation of heart by the sense of God's love to him in Christ, that it comforted him to his death, he was retarded an hour in the morning by an error in his indentures, meanwhile he fell asleep, and waking said, 'Well, I shall be quickened anon', then he entreated the Lord Primate to desire the bishop of Canterbury that he would look out of his window at his execution, that he might take his last leave of him, which the bishop did accordingly.*
>
> *Upon the scaffold he was interrupted by two several accidents which made him desire that he might be heard quietly, then he desired the sheriff that after execution his body might be peaceably convoyed away. . . .*

144. L.J., IV, 247.

145. Again the diarist is absent or has ceased taking notes for almost a two week period. For proceedings on 22 May, see Drake.

146. C.J., II, 158–159. An account of Taylor's case is printed in Cobbett, *Parl. Hist.*, II, 815–816. On 10 June Taylor requested the House to pardon him. According to D'Ewes (Harl. 163), f. 305, the Speaker said that Taylor was a barrister, his father had recently died and he (Taylor) had five brothers and sisters to take care of. The House agreed to consider the situation and ordered Taylor to appear at nine the following morning. He did not make an appearance until 10 June (C.J., II, 172) when he was ordered to be brought in again on 12 June (*Ibid.*, 173) and that day was discharged from further imprisonment.

147. C.J., II, 159: Cobbett, Parl. Hist., II, 814–815.

148. Again the diarist is absent; for proceedings on 1, 2, 3, and 4 June, see Drake.

149. Debate on the matter of the new canons had begun on 14 Dec. and continued on the following day when the resolutions concerning the clergy were passed *nullo contradicente*. Notestein, *D'Ewes*, 146–157. Debate of the illegality of the canons took place on 16 Dec., *Ibid.*, 162–163. Maynard's speech at the conference on 7 June sums up the arguments presented in Dec., see D'Ewes (Harl. 163), ff. 280–284. See also C.J., II, 170; L.J., IV, 268.

150. D'Ewes (Harl. 163), f. 286, reports that: *It was then debated whether we should have a fortnight's cessation longer or not, to begin from the 14th day of this instant June. Some were against it but others showed without this all hope of pacification was taken away and the two armies must come to fight or plunder the countries. So at last we all agreed to a fortnight's cessation, and that we should confer about it with the Lords.* See also C.J., II, 170.

151. C.J., II, 171.

152. I.e., repeal of a branch of 1 Eliz. I, c. 1, concerning commissioners for causes ecclesiastical.

153. Digby's remark was precipitated by the report this day of Colonel Goring's examination concerning a plot within the army. See Drake, 5 May. Apparently Goring had taken an oath at Whitehall to maintain secrecy concerning the army and therefore was not free to answer all of the parliament's questions. Lord Digby claimed that the oath Goring had taken was itself unlawful and therefore Goring should not have felt bound by it. Commissary Willmott reiterated the charge of perjury initiated by Digby. D'Ewes, (Harl. 163), ff. 299v–300, concluded his account of this day's proceedings with the following description: *before any question was put [to] the Lord Digby, having twice offered to withdraw and been both times stopped by divers crying in a tumultuous manner, contrary to the orders of the House, 'No, No', did twice again take his place, whereupon some stood up to hinder such as would have stopped him, and things were very likely to have come to some uproar, confusion, and bickering among ourselves but at the last both the said Lord Digby and Mr. Willmott did withdraw into the Committee Chamber; and then a long dispute or debate followed touching their censure, which was prosecuted with so much heat and animosity on both sides as the Speaker could scarce direct who should speak. We sitting so long that it began to grow dark whereupon the Houses did at last rise in confusion without having determined anything touching the said Lord Digby or Mr. Willmott, but left them together in the Committee Chamber.* A "narrative" of the plot is printed in Cobbett, Parl. Hist., II, 819–822.

154. C.J., II, 171, An act to prevent the danger that may happen by popish recusants.

155. Price and Widdrington were sent to the Tower for their offense. Concerning the case see Drake, 9 June, n. 210.

156. The ladder was used to get to the gallery seats. D'Ewes (Harl. 163), f. 305v, records that: "*Mr. John Digby, younger brother of the said Lord Digby, came into the House and going up upon the ladder that stands at the door of the House, by which the members thereof usually go up to those seats which are over the same door under the gallery, he sat still upon the said ladder. Whereupon the Speaker called out to him and desired him to take his place and not to sit upon the ladder as if he were going to [a] hanging, at which many of the House laughed. But Mr. King, a common lawyer, said he thought that in this the Speaker had transgressed his duty in using so disgraceful a speech to so noble a gentleman. But the Speaker stood up and solemnly protested that he had no intent to disgrace that noble gentleman but only according as his duty was to call everyman to his place he admonished*

him to leave that seat which he thought unfit for any man to sit in. Divers spake to this matter and at last Mr. King was commanded to withdraw into the Committee Chamber which he did and then, after some debate, we agreed that he should be called down again and that standing in his place he should acknowledge his error in having used such language to the Speaker.

157. I.e., of the bill of Episcopacy. C.J., II, 173.

158. C.J., II, 173, Commissary Willmott, Captain Ashburnham, and Captain Pollard were committed prisoners under suspicion of High Treason on 14 June. C.J., II, 175.

159. C.J., II, 173 and see above, p. 82. On 28 June (C.J., II, 190) Savile was ordered to receive a discharge from further imprisonment.

160. See Drake, n. 212. Extracts of the letter are included by D'Ewes (Harl. 163), f. 314, as well as an account of the examinations of Willmott, Ashburnham, and Pollard (ff. 314–317).

161. D'Ewes (Harl. 163), f. 317v, notes that: *It was then disputed whether a cause should be expressed or not in the Speaker's warrant; some showed that it had been accounted an high offense against law in the Council Table to send men without a cause expressed in the warrant. . . . But it was at last ordered that they should be sent to the three prisons before mentioned and that it should be expressed in the warrant that it was for the suspicion of High Treason.*

162. The Price-Widdrington business came up earlier in the day than this diarist has indicated. According to D'Ewes (Harl. 163), f. 310v, their petition *was for this present rejected and they left still in custody*. Their exclusion from the House was exacerbated by the remark of Sir Robert Harley who *showed that one of them in the Tower whose name he concealed (but it was Sir William Widdrington) had spoken dangerous words. Sir Walter Earle seconded him and he desired he might relate the words, whereupon Sir Robert Harley stood up again and showed that one of the two gentlemen now in the Tower of London had said, in the hearing of one Mr. Ashe, [Edward Ashe, M.P. for Heytesbury], a member of this House, that whosoever in this House should call the Scottish men brethren should be called to the bar. The said Mr. Ashe was not then present, and there was nothing more done in that matter.* Neither Moore nor Peyton report on this business. The C.J. (II, 175) reports that Price and Widdrington were this day discharged from their imprisonment and restored to the liberties of the House.

163. This diarist has included a list of rates at the end of his diary (ff. 111–114v) which are printed below, pp. 65–67. The list is also printed in C.J., II, 179–180 and Cobbett, *Parl. Hist.*, II, 842–843. See also Rawl. 1099, ff. 74v–77.

164. C.J., II, 181, An act against the enjoying of pluralities of benefice, and non-residency. According to Cobbett (*Parl. Hist.*, II, 843) this act provided "that whosoever had two livings, should, before the 21st of Sept. next, resign one of them: and that if any clergyman should be absent, at one time, 60 days from his living, he should, *ipso facto*, forfeit it.

165. Father Phillipps had written a letter on 16 May which had been intercepted and was in John Pym's possession. The letter, which stated that the protestation of parliament (presumably that of 3 May) was like the Scottish covenant but somewhat worse, was being used as evidence against Phillipps. D'Ewes (Harl. 163), f. 347v. The letter is printed in Rushworth, *Hist. Collections*, IV, 257–258.

166. Concerning Phillipps see C.J., II, 188–189 and Rushworth, *Hist. Collections*, IV, 301–303.

167. Herbert Morley of Glynde, Sussex, sat for Lewes 1640–1653. Keeler, *L.P.*

168. See above, n. 159.

169. C.J., II, 195.

170. See above, n. 163.
171. 20 *l.*, C.J., II, 179.
172. These are notes from Sir John Hotham's reports from the committee for the King's army. The bracketed words have been supplied from the C.J., II, 177–178.

APPENDIX A

Undated Material

[f. 3] [Blank] aforesaid that every person of what degree soever he be which now has and possesses by virtue of any license, commendam, qualification, or dispensation 2 or more benefices or ecclesiastical promotions with cure of souls shall, before the 1 Feb. 1641, resign, avoid, and yield up all the said benefices and ecclesiastical promotions aforesaid (except one at the elections of the person so resigning) into the hands of the ordinary of the diocese where such benefices or ecclesiastical promotions shall be respectively situated, and in case of refusal or neglect all to be void as if the incumbent were dead.

Any act, law, statute, ordinary, provisions, license, faculty, commendam, dispensation, qualification, toleration, perpetual union or any other thing, use, or matter whatsoever to the contrary in any wise notwithstanding, and that from and after the 1 Feb. 1641 all licenses, faculties, commendams, dispensations, tolerations, contrary to the true intent and meaning of this act shall be utterly void and non effect.[1]

[f. 128] Q[uestion], English Proceedings. Q[uestion] now, when the Marshalsea was erected.

760,000 *l.* in 13 years clear

115,000 *l.* interest defalcations

45,000 *l.* currency

[128v] 185,000 *l.* good in stock of our 6 subsidies.

He hoped to see whole herds of red deer feeding in their fields. Q[uestion]: What become of the poor. Ans[wer]: We must have a new press and send them to a new plantation. 2. How each advised.

> Heaven twinkling fires
> While from their glorious seat
> Their influence gives life and heat
> But Oh how few there are though danger in the act is far
> Will come to catch a falling star.

> I fall, I fall,
> Whom shall I call.

[f. 127v] 31 *H*. 8 a commission of oyer and terminer granted to the Bp. of Llandaff. This continued till 1 *Jacob.* then renewed with relation to instructions but none came.

7 *Jacob.* renewed and the trial by legal men and by the laws and customs of England left out. 14 and 16 *Jacobi* and then came instructions and the same clauses left out.

4 *Car.*, relation to instructions and the commission renewed again. 5 *Car.*, the instructions came and the commission renewed. 8 *Car.*, renewed again and great additions to the instructions. [f. 127] 13 *Car.*, renewed again and 58 instructions to try clandestine marriages and perjury, to set up a court of Chancery, to disobey *habeas corpus*, and prohibitions.[2]

[f. 127] 1,286 *l.* per annum it cost the King, and he loses all the fines.[3]

[f. 126v] 29 *H*. 8 the Commons rebelled, it was because they were oppressed by the great men, and they propounded this article that none beyond Trent should be served with a privy seal or a [blank] unless it concern their allegiance to the King; and upon this the court was erected about 31 *H.* 8.

2 subsidies and 4 fifteens given about 31 *H.* 8 and one reason was because he had erected this court by which the common people may have justice at home.[4]

NOTES

1. A draft of an act against pluralities of benefice. See the Anonymous diary (Yale Uncat. 226), n. 164.
2. This speech may be part of the debates of 10 and 11 March on ecclesiastical matters.
3. I am unable to determine to what this figure refers.
4. I have been unable to date this speech.

INDEX

The odd sequence of numbers following each index entry reflects the fact that the notes are at the end of each section rather than at the foot of each page.

The numbers following each index entry are first, the page of text on which the entry is mentioned, second, as the case may be for corresponding notes, the page number and, within parentheses, the note number.

The numbers included in parentheses but not preceded by 'n' show the number of times an entry is mentioned on the stated page.

148 TWO DIARIES OF THE LONG PARLIAMENT

Hanchett, Edward, Usher of the Court of Wards, privilege of, 83, 128(n17)

Harby, Sir Job, 13, 55 (n51, 52)

Harley, Sir Robert, M.P.,140(n162); messenger to Lords, 85

Harrison, John, 23, 58(n98)

Harrison, Sir John, 13, 55(n55)

Haslewood, Francis, 56(n65)

Henrietta Maria, Queen of England, 20, 21, 57(n87), 22, 59(n108), 50, 123; Articles of Marriage (1625), 21, 57(nn87, 88), 127(n1), jointure read, 87; message to Commons, 82, 127(n10); servants of, 20, 57(nn 84, 86), 21

Herbert, Mr., 5

Herbert, Philip, Earl of Pembroke and Montgomery, Lord Chamberlain of the Household, 129–130(n34), 123

Herbert, Sir Henry, M.P., 18, 57(n77)

Heydon, Sir John, Lieutenant of the Ordnance, 17, 57(n76), 24, 59(n101)

Heyman, Sir Peter, M.P., xvii

Heywood, Peter, 116, 137(n131)

Hibbots, Lady Mary, 109, 134(n96), 136(n123), 114

Hibbots, Sir Thomas, 109, 134(n96)

Holland, Benedict, 117, 137(n137)

Holland, Earl of, see Rich, Henry

Holland, Sir John, M.P., requests leave, xviii

Holles, Denzil, M.P., committee of seven, 69–70(n194), concerning Strafford, 25; notes of, 60(n109), suit against Cooper, 3, 52(n16), 84, 128(n24); reports by: 46, 70(n201), 72(n212)

Holles, Denzil or Gervase, M.P., speeches by:
8 Mar, 56(n69)
10 Mar, 105
16 Mar, 21
7 Jn, 48

Holles, Gervase, M.P., suspended, 116, 136(n130) speeches by:
undated, 75, 77(n9)
26 April, 116

Holles, John, Earl of Clare, 36

Hotham, Sir John, M.P., 82, 121; report by: 141 (n172) speeches by:
17 Feb, 6
15 Mar, 20
10 Feb, 84

Howard, Charles, Viscount Andover,

Howard, Thomas, M.P., 116, 137(n131)

Howard, Thomas, Earl of Arundel and Surrey, Earl Marshal, Lord Steward at Strafford trial, 25, 59(nn 108, 109), 60(n110), 36; and Marshal's court, 88, 131(n46)

Howard, Thomas, Earl of Berkshire, 97

Hunt, Robert, M.P., requests leave, xviii

Hyde, Edward, M.P., excuses himself, 127(n2); in chair, 6, 59(105), and Scottish paper, 12; reports by: 53(n33), 88, 111, 134(n102), 136(n128); speeches; 2 Jn, 47; 9 Jn, 71(n210)

Idolatry, etc., bill against, 82, 128(n12)

Ignatius, St., 44

Ingram, Sir Arthur, M.P., Strafford trial, 25, 110

Iron pots, etc., Monopoly of, 22–23

Jacob (Biblical), 116, 137(n130)

Jacob, Sir John, 13, 55(n52), 14, 55(n56)

James I, King of England, 30

James, John, 137(n131)

Jehu (Biblical), 29, 61(n127)

Jermyn, Henry, Master of Her Majesty's Horse, charged with treason, 45, 70(n197)

Jermyn, Sir Thomas, Comptroller of the Household, M.P., Strafford trial, 25, 110; speech; 8 Mar, 16

Jerome, St., 100

Jones, Roger, Viscount of Ranelagh, Strafford trial, 29, 61(n128), 32, 63(nn143, 144, 146), 136(n121)

Kennedy, Robert, 28, 61(n125)

Kildare, Earl of, see Fitzgerald, George

Kilmallock, Viscount, see Sarsfield, Dominick

Kilvert, Mr., 5

King, Richard, M.P., 121, 139(n156)

Kinge, Sir Robert, Muster Master General of Ireland, 33, 35

Kirton, Edward, M.P., speech; 3 Feb, 127(n6)

Lambe, Sir John, Dean of Arches, etc., 65(n168)

Lane, Thomas, M.P., petition against, 111, 134(n100)

Langdale, Eden, petition of, 128(n15)

Laud, William, Archbishop of Canterbury, 43, 96, 97; Articles against, 99–100, 132(n62); report on, 9, 54(n39); speech; 26 Feb, 100

Leicester, Earl of, see Sydney, Robert, 11

Lenthal, William, Speaker of the House of Commons, M.P., explains William Taylor, 138(n146); and Herbert-Wilde business, 18; to attend Strafford trial, 110; speech to King, 87; report by: 67(n177), 83

Letter, to the Commons (5 May), 43, 69(n193)

Letter, to Earl of Northumberland, 72(n212), 134(n109), 122

Lewis, Sir William, Bt., M.P., committee of seven, 69–70(n194)

Lilburne, John, 42, 68(n187)

Lindsey, Earl of, see Bertie, Robert

Lisle, John, M.P., committee of seven, 69–70(n194); report from Lords, 46

Littleton, Sir Edward, Baron Littleton of Munslow, Lord Keeper, concerning Strafford, 90; Order to, 83; sick, 137(n136), 138(n141); on triennial bill, 6, 87; and in parliament 1628, xvi

Loftus, Adam, Viscount Loftus of Ely, late Lord Chancellor of Ireland, 92, 136(n121)

London loan, 4, 53(n26), 7, 33, 63(n150), 37, 47, 74(76n1), 84, 112, 134(n108), 113

London petition, 2, 3, 84, 128(n21)